Routledge Studies in Human Resource Development
Edited by Monica Lee
Lancaster University

HRD theory is changing rapidly. Recent advances in theory and practice, in how we conceive of organizations and of the world of knowledge, have led to the need to reinterpret the field. This series aims to reflect and foster the development of HRD as an emergent discipline. Encompassing a range of different international, organizational, methodological and theoretical perspectives, the series promotes theoretical controversy and reflective practice.

1. Policy matters
Flexible learning and organizational change
Edited by Viktor Jakupec and Robin Usher

2. Science fiction and organization
Edited by Warren Smith, Matthew Higgins, Martin Parker and Geoff Lightfoot

3. HRD and learning organisations in Europe
Challenges for professionals
Edited by Saskia Tjepkema, Jim Stewart, Sally Sambrook, Martin Mulder, Hilde ter Horst and Jaap Scheerens

4. Interpreting the maternal organisation
Edited by Heather Höpfl and Monika Kostera

5. Work process knowledge
Nicholas Boreham, Renan Samurçay, and Martin Fischer

Also available from Routledge:
Action research in organisations
Jean McNiff, accompanied by Jack Whitehead

Understanding human resource development
A research-based approach
Edited by Jim Stewart, Jim McGoldrick and Sandra Watson

Work Process Knowledge

Organizational change is affecting many workplaces, with major implications for management, trades unions and the design of vocational education and training. Among the major changes are the introduction of new technology, the replacement of rigid demarcations by more flexible forms of work organization and a relentless intensification of work itself.

Work Process Knowledge brings together the findings of twenty-four leading researchers on the demands these changes are making on the competence of the workforce. Based on a new set of investigations in a wide range of manufacturing and service industries, they identify the kinds of knowledge and skill required to work effectively in the post-Taylorist organization.

'Work process knowledge' is defined as an understanding of the labour process and the production process in the organization as a whole. Knowledge of this kind is needed by employees of flexible organizations to enable them to deal with new situations and work across boundaries. Work process knowledge is also crucial wherever communication and information technologies are introduced to make better use of knowledge assets.

Raising fundamental issues for industrial policy, science and technology policy, vocational education and training policy and the day-to-day management of the post-Taylorist organization, this book will be of essential interest to academics and professionals working in the fields of industrial economics, management, human resource development and industrial training.

Nicholas Boreham is Professor of Education and Employment in the Institute of Education, University of Stirling, Scotland, and was previously Professor of Education in the University of Manchester, England. He has researched and published widely in the field of occupational competence, work-related knowledge and vocational training, with particular reference to decision-making and learning in health care and industrial process control.

Renan Samurçay was chargée de recherche at the CNRS research unit on Cognition et Activités Finalisées at the Université Paris VIII at Saint-Denis, France, until her death in December 2001. She completed an extensive programme of research into the cognitive processes of operators in complex dynamic environments such as blast furnaces and nuclear power plants.

Martin Fischer is Head of the Department of Information Technology and Competence at the Institut Technik und Bildung, Universität of Bremen, Germany. His current research and teaching focuses on the relationship between changing work requirements and the acquisition of work-related knowledge and skills in education and training.

Work Process Knowledge

Edited by Nicholas Boreham,
Renan Samurçay and Martin Fischer

London and New York

To the memory of Renan Samurçay

First published 2002 by Routledge
11 New Fetter Lane, London EC4P 4EE

Simultaneously published in the USA and Canada
by Routledge
29 West 35th Street, New York, NY 10001

Routledge is an imprint of the Taylor & Francis Group

Typeset in Baskerville by Wearset Ltd, Boldon, Tyne and Wear
Printed and bound in Great Britain by MPG Books Ltd, Bodmin

British Library Cataloguing in Publication Data
A catalogue record for this book is available from the British Library

Library of Congress Cataloging in Publication Data
A catalog record for this book has been requested

ISBN 0-415-27929-1

Contents

Figures

Tables

Contributors

Mariana Gaio Alves
Ciências da Educação
Faculdade de Ciências e
Tecnologia
Universidade Nova de Lisboa
Monte de Caparica
Portugal

Patricia Antolin-Glenn
Laboratoire Cognition et Activités
Finalisées
CNRS-Université
Paris VIII
Saint-Denis
France

Nicholas Boreham
Institute of Education
University of Stirling
Stirling
Scotland
United Kingdom

Maria Caprile
Fundació CIREM
Barcelona
Catalunya
Spain

Stella Duvenci-Langa
Laboratoire Cognition et Activités
Finalisées
CNRS-Université
Paris VIII
Saint-Denis
France

Martin Fischer
Institut Technik und Bildung
Universität Bremen
Bremen
Germany

Geert van Hootegem
Department of Sociology
Katholieke Universiteit Leuven
Leuven
Belgium

Rik Huys
Hoger Instituut de Arbeid
Katholieke Universiteit Leuven
Leuven
Belgium

Karsten Krüger
Fundació CIREM
Barcelona
Catalunya
Spain

Wilfried Kruse
Sozialforschungstelle Dortmund
Dortmund
Germany

Norma Lammont
University of Manchester Institute
of Science and Technology
Manchester
England
United Kingdom

Michele Mariani
Multimedia Communication
Laboratory
Department of Communication
Science
University of Siena
Siena
Italy

Leena Norros
VTT Industrial Systems
Espoo
Finland

Maaria Nuutinen
VTT Industrial Systems
Espoo
Finland

Maria Teresa Oliveira
Ciências da Educação
Faculdade de Ciências e
Tecnologia
Universidade Nova de Lisboa
Monte de Caparica
Portugal

Ana Luisa Oliveira Pires
Ciências da Educação
Faculdade de Ciências e
Tecnologia
Universidade Nova de Lisboa
Monte de Caparica
Portugal

Marielle Plat
Laboratoire Cognition et Activités
Finalisées
CNRS-Université
Paris VIII
Saint-Denis
France

Pierre Rabardel
Laboratoire Cognition et Activités
Finalisées
CNRS-Université
Paris VIII
Saint-Denis
France

Lauge Baungaard Rasmussen
Department of Manufacturing
Engineering and Management
Technical University of Denmark
Lyngby
Copenhagen
Denmark

Felix Rauner
Institut Technik und Bildung
Universität Bremen
Bremen
Germany

Peter Röben
Institut Technik und Bildung
Universität Bremen
Bremen
Germany

Janine Rogalski
Laboratoire Cognition et Activités
Finalisées
CNRS-Université
Paris VIII
Saint-Denis
France

Renan Samurçay
formerly Laboratoire Cognition et
Activités Finalisées
CNRS-Université
Paris VIII
Saint-Denis
France

Christine Vidal-Gomel
Laboratoire Cognition et Activités
Finalisées
CNRS-Université
Paris VIII
Saint-Denis
France

1 Work process knowledge in technological and organizational development

Nicholas Boreham

This book developed out of the work of a ten-country network sponsored by the European Commission within its Framework IV Targeted Socio-Economic Research Programme. All the participants were carrying out research into organizational change and the introduction of new technology into workplaces. We came together to compare our findings, methodologies and theoretical assumptions, focusing in particular on the kinds of knowledge required by workers in the new industrial landscape that is emerging in European and other advanced industrial countries.

New ways of organizing work

It has become a truism to assert that we are living through a time of transformation in the way goods are produced and services are delivered. The liberalization of world trade has exposed companies to the rigours of international competition, creating serious challenges for long-established industries in the more advanced economies of Europe and the USA. The response has often been to reorganize businesses along more flexible lines and to introduce new technology in order to improve productivity. Similar changes have also been taking place in the public services; with service users demanding higher standards and governments demanding cost savings, this sector too has come under pressure to change the way it organizes its work.

A policy document which has influenced the political debate on the nature of work in Europe is the optimistic but flawed Green Paper, *Partnership for a New Organization of Work*. This calls for 'new forms of the organization of work ... based on high skill, high trust and high quality' (European Communities 1997: 1). The Green Paper is significant because its message has been taken up by European politicians and has been written into national trade and industry policies. Its central argument is that the production systems that have dominated European industry for the past 100 years are now becoming obsolete, especially the method of scientific management associated with the name of Frederick Taylor and the system of mass production associated with the name of Henry Ford.

The essential characteristic of these systems is that work is planned in 'the office' by managers and highly qualified technical staff, while the production operations themselves are carried out in 'the works' by employees with relatively poor qualifications. There is a strict division of labour, vertically between grades of staff and horizontally between departments. The bulk of the workforce performs narrow, routinized tasks under the supervision of foremen and supervisors, following procedures laid down by management. The Green Paper argues that although this might have been appropriate for mass production by a relatively uneducated workforce, modern conditions – such as the need for more flexible responses to the challenges of global competition, rising levels of education in the workforce and expectations of a better quality of working life – require a different approach. The case was argued in detail at the Essen meeting of the European Council in 1994, which ended by declaring the need for 'a more flexible organization of work in a way which fulfils both the wishes of employees and the requirements of competition' (European Communities 1997: 3).

For most of the 1990s, industrial sociologists and economists in both Europe and the USA have observed an uneven change in work organization in this general direction. In many sectors, bureaucratic work systems have been replaced by more flexible systems of continuous improvement. The new industrial philosophy is expressed in an extensive literature that includes Appelbaum and Batt's (1994) *The New American Workplace* and Kern and Schumann's (1984) *The End of the Division of Labour?* While there is no single recipe, most of the new ways of organizing work are characterized by:

- abolishing the Taylorist top-down command-and-control structure (passing instructions from 'the office' to 'the works') and adopting more participative approaches to decision-making;
- delayering, especially removing supervisory grades and collapsing traditional hierarchies of skilled and semi-skilled workers into much flatter structures;
- replacing a rigid departmental structure by work units that integrate operations previously carried out in different departments (such as preparation of materials, machining and quality checking);
- organizing work in teams, and delegating significant degrees of autonomy to them (although truly self-managing teams are rare);
- replacing a multiplicity of narrowly defined technical trades by multi-skilled employees willing to work across traditional demarcations in the interests of meeting the demands of the customer;
- replacing narrow qualifications with broader ones, and increasing budgets for continuous learning in the workplace, including 'soft skills' such as listening and collaboration;
- engaging employees in the continual improvement of the work

process through quality assurance and dialogue between different work units, and in general encouraging staff at all levels to share their knowledge with colleagues throughout the whole organization.

Hand-in-hand with the move towards more flexible forms of work organization has come a widespread introduction of information and communication technologies (ICTs). The appearance of computers in offices and factories, the coming of the Internet and e-business developments, such as intranets, extranets and new genres of software, have impacted on most people's jobs, either directly or indirectly. One advantage is that they dramatically reduce the cost of storing and processing information. More significantly, however, they permit rapid communication between remote sites, and when used to control flexible manufacturing systems, they enable new products to be made without the need for costly new capital equipment. Many see ICTs as the key to making business more competitive. One way in which this may happen is 'informatization', a term coined by Zuboff (1988) to refer to the process whereby data generated by computerized systems can make the work process more transparent, creating opportunities to co-ordinate and control business operations.

It would be a mistake to assume, as the Green Paper clearly does, that the introduction of new technology and the replacement of bureaucracies by more flexible kinds of organization is the royal road to increased competitiveness and a higher quality of working life. Researchers have been quick to point out that many companies have achieved economic success by Taylorist and Fordist principles. In some parts of the manufacturing sector, standardized mass production remains the most competitive approach. This point is elaborated by Huys and van Hootegem in Chapter 14, where they report the results of sector-wide surveys of work methods in the Belgian automobile, machine-tool and chemical industries. The data they have collected indicate that the transformation of work in these key industries has been very gradual. For example, the volume automobile industry has experimented with many alternatives to the single driven belt, but in the end has always gone back to this production method. Similar findings have been reported in the service sector, where traditional forms of work organization are achieving competitive advantage, and in the new information industries there has been a burgeoning of 'electronic treadmills' run on lines reminiscent of the worst factory conditions of the nineteenth century. Rasmussen in Chapter 6 describes how competitive pressure on industrial designers has resulted in the replacement of collegial work systems with neo-Taylorism. Equally, many of the promises of ICT have yet to be fulfilled. The real potential of ICT lies in improving business processes by increasing the internal connectivity of the organization. However, innumerable research studies have revealed that ICT may not be used in this way. It appears that many companies are using the new technology to automate existing tasks, making out-of-date business processes run faster, rather than remodelling themselves around the new business processes made possible with ICT.

The central role of knowledge in the new ways of working

Despite these reservations, it is clear that significant numbers of private enterprises and public agencies have attempted to improve their performance by adopting more flexible organizational structures and by introducing new ways of working based on ICT. It is on these organizations that the present book focuses. The key assumption underlying many of the new ways of organizing work is that knowledge is an organization's main resource. Some knowledge is imported from the environment (such as market intelligence, skills learned by sending staff on external courses and the expertise brought in by new recruits), and some is created in the workplace itself – not only by formal R&D, but by learning from day-to-day experience in the ways described by Nonaka and Takeuchi (1995) in their book *The Knowledge Creating Company*. In fact, companies operating according to the new production concepts described by researchers such as Appelbaum and Batt (1994) differ crucially from those in the Taylorist/Fordist industrial system in expecting employees to create knowledge in the workplace and share it with their colleagues. For this reason, policy makers, managers, human resource development (HRD) specialists and employees facing transformations of the kind described, need to develop a clear understanding of the kinds of knowledge needed to work in organizations that have introduced information technology and more flexible ways of working.

The argument of the present volume can be outlined quite simply. When work is designed on the principles of Frederick Taylor and Henry Ford, shop floor employees need very little underpinning knowledge to perform their narrow jobs. Not only has the work been simplified to a routine, but the hierarchical command-and-control system ensures that any necessary co-ordination of functions is carried out by supervisors and managers higher up the organizational chart. In contrast, companies which have introduced more flexible systems of continuous improvement, or which make use of ICT to link different work units into networks, require their employees to have a much broader understanding of the work process. In addition to understanding how their own immediate work role is changing, they need to understand the work process in the organization as a whole. When organizational charts flatten, when supervisory grades are removed and middle management delegates more autonomy to work teams, the latter need to understand how other departments organize their work if they are to achieve the desired flexibility. When occupational demarcations disappear and employees are expected to work across traditional boundaries, they too need to understand the work process of the whole organization. In order to realize the competitive advantage offered by linking work units into networks through ICT and moving information laterally, employees need to understand the nature of operations in every part of the network. When different professions providing a public service seek better collaboration in the interests of continuity of care, they need to understand the mysteries of each other's professions and how the service is organized at the system level. In the scheme of things envisaged by the advocates of functional flexibility and high connectivity, one worker needs to know as much as several workers knew in the past, which means having a much wider knowledge.

The chapters in this volume are based on field studies of the kind of knowledge needed to support new kinds of flexible, ICT-based work. Some analyse the ways of knowing needed in these transformed work situations, developing new theoretical models to explain them. Others address issues of practical concern to HRD professionals, such as how to facilitate a broad understanding of the overall work process, or how to integrate work-based learning with classroom instruction, or the industrial relations issues that arise when companies encourage knowledge creation and sharing across the whole organization. In producing their chapters, the contributors have drawn on a rich body of data from empirical investigations in many European countries in a wide range of industrial sectors. The countries represented include the UK, Italy, Finland, Germany, France, Denmark, Portugal, Belgium and Spain. The sectors investigated include process, assembly and small batch manufacturing, material services, information services and human services. Most of the chapters are based on in-depth investigations of specific workplaces undergoing or contemplating transformations of the kinds described above, but some survey whole sectors. Most of the chapters focus on the new ways of knowing required by changes in the nature of work, but some explore the limits of change by investigating the factors hindering innovation. Taken collectively, the chapters reflect the diversity of the different industrial cultures in Europe, different national systems of innovation, and different European intellectual traditions for defining occupational competence and work-related knowledge.

Work process knowledge

The idea that the employee of a flexible organization needs to understand the work process in the company as a whole must have occurred to many people in the past, and indeed isolated references to 'process knowledge' can be found in the vocational education literature of the 1930s. However, a term for describing knowledge of this kind does not appear to have crystallized in the HRD literature until Wilfried Kruse (1986) coined the term *Arbeitsprozeßwissen*, which translates directly into English as 'work process knowledge'. The development of this concept in the context of one of Kruse's research projects is described below. There is an advantage in using a single term to refer to such a complex phenomenon as the knowledge needed to work flexibly and in contexts where ICT is used to facilitate networking and lateral communication. The disadvantage is that the term might become a mere label, or even suggest that knowledge of this kind exists as a kind of Platonic Form independently of the activity we call 'work'. Adapting the idea of Ludwig Wittgenstein, 'work process knowledge' should be treated as a family of concepts which are closely connected to each other by a number of dyadic resemblances, as well as by a common element or defining characteristic that runs through the whole family. With this caution in mind, an attempt will now be made to characterize work process knowledge in order to orientate the reader to the studies that follow.

As already mentioned, the term was coined by Wilfried Kruse, and he did so in the context of a series of projects carried out for the *Fundació Centre d'Iniciatives i Recerques Europees a la Mediterrània* in Barcelona (CIREM). This organization was funded by the European Commission to promote economic development in the Mediterranean region; among many other things it began a project to improve the performance of a group of hotels on the island of Mallorca. The hotel group wished to attract a more up-market clientele, but they realized that they could do so only if they developed the distinctive ambience of the high-class hotel – the apparently effortless delivery of a personalized service to each individual guest. In an attempt to bring about the desired step-change in quality, a CIREM project entitled 'continuous quality improvement' was launched. Its guiding philosophy was the Japanese quality-circle methodology in which staff are encouraged to identify problems standing in the way of higher levels of performance. Following standard practice, staff from different departments of the hotels met to analyse the root causes of problems that prevented them from achieving better performance. This led quickly to the realization that a problem that manifested itself in one department of the hotel (for example, at the reception desk) might have been caused by events in a second department (for example, the restaurant) and might have repercussions in a third (such as the accounts office).

Spurred by insights such as these, the hotel employees soon gained an awareness of the interdependency of the different departments of the hotel, the job content of staff working in other departments and how they were all interlinked. When they achieved this awareness, they had acquired *Arbeitsprozeßwissen*. Kruse (1986) originally defined the term in that context as labour process knowledge, meaning:

• an expanded understanding of work roles in parts of the organization other than the employee's own;

- an awareness of the interdependency of the activities in different departments, including characteristics of the system as a whole, such as the flow of work through the organization, both upstream and downstream of the worker's own station; and
- participation in a workplace culture which provides a service to colleagues in support of a high quality of service to the actual customer.

Following Kruse's pioneering work, other German researchers applied the concept of *Arbeitsprozeßwissen* to new fields of employment, where its meaning became extended from knowledge of the labour process in the organization as a whole, to that *plus* knowledge of the overall production process. An example of how the concept was extended in this way can be found in studies of mechanical engineering by Fischer (1995) and Fischer *et al.* (1995). In the companies investigated, the labour process was structured by a rigid division of labour imposed by the German system of vocational training, which trains the workforce into 360 specialized skilled trades. However, the modernization of German manufacturing, especially an emphasis on the introduction of new technology and more flexible work teams, made it increasingly difficult to design work around a compartmentalized knowledge base. As the move towards more flexible work gained momentum, it was realized that employees required a broader understanding of both the production process and the labour process in the organization as a whole.

At much the same time, a research network, Cognitive Approaches to Dynamic Environment Supervision, sponsored by the French national research organization CNRS, was investigating the knowledge requirements of new kinds of complex, computer-driven manufacturing systems. One of the outcomes of this project was the recognition that, in order to carry out preventive maintenance on these systems, employees needed 'a broadening of the conventional knowledge base'. In most maintenance training, the knowledge base had hitherto been conceived in terms of the causes of specific faults, together with strategies for narrowing the search process. Now, as maintenance personnel were being integrated into production units, and the systems themselves were becoming more complex, the need was identified for training them to think in terms of 'whole systems interacting with their environments' (Boreham 1995: 103). The need for work process knowledge in this context derives from the fact that the introduction of new technology broadens work roles: for example, when an employee makes the transition from manual worker to controller of an automatic process, he or she usually assumes responsibility for a range of operations which were previously allocated to different employees. The business advantage of computerized systems is that they can run many operations in parallel and integrate activities previously carried out by different departments, and this makes it essential for operators to understand how the whole production system is organized.

Epistemological considerations

In addition to investigating the knowledge requirements of new kinds of work empirically, many of the chapters in this book develop new ways of theorizing this knowledge. In the many meetings the authors held before writing their final drafts, attempts were made to come to terms with the diverse intellectual traditions from which they were approaching their common task. This was not easy, given the differences in how Latin, German, Scandinavian and Anglo-American scholars conceptualize key terms such as 'competence', 'experience' and 'knowledge' itself, and the different paradigms of research into work that are followed in different countries. The reader should remember, for instance, that the French word 'competence' means something broader than the English word competence, and that Russian psychology has exerted a stronger influence on the Finns than on the British. Nevertheless, most of the contributors subscribe to the same three epistemological assumptions.

The first assumption is that that the object of their investigations, work process knowledge, is that knowledge which is useful for work, whether for coping with the demands of functional flexibility, supervising complex computer-controlled engineering systems or operating as one node in a distributed decision-making system. The concern here is not with knowledge in general, which includes much that does not play a part in practical activity. Employers and trainees frequently complain that vocational courses teach too much inert theory, and industrial psychologists have generally agreed with them (Duncan 1981; Patrick *et al.* 1986; Morris and Rouse 1985). The focus in the present volume is on ways of knowing that are integral aspects of work activity, and thus essential to support skilled work in flexible and informated workplaces.

The second assumption, which at first sight seems to conflict with the first, is that work process knowledge should not be confused with what ordinary folk call 'know-how', or what cognitive scientists call 'procedural knowledge'. These terms usually refer to practical knowledge picked up from unmediated experience. But as the following chapters make clear, work process knowledge includes more than this. Most importantly – and this is the original contribution of the present book to industrial epistemology – it includes a dimension of theoretical understanding. Inert theoretical knowledge is integrated with experiential know-how in the course of solving problems at work, and this generates what we call work process knowledge.

The construction of work process knowledge often arises out of efforts to resolve contradictions between what the theory predicts will happen (or what standard operating procedures are telling the workers to do) and the reality that confronts them. Samurçay and Vidal-Gomel (Chapter 11), Fischer and Röben (Chapter 4) and Oliveira, Pires and Alves (Chapter 8) all stress this point. For example, Fischer and Röben explain how, in order to carry out their duties, laboratory assistants in chemical laboratories need theoretical knowledge relating to the various analytical tests that are available, which they integrate with personal experience of how the individual test instruments in the laboratory function in order to devise the procedure which is most appropriate for each new situation. It is not sufficient to talk of theoretical principles being applied, as detailed observation carried out by these researchers shows that the knowledge which guides action in these contexts is constructed out of both kinds of intellectual resource in the process of problem-solving. The process is a dialectical one, resolving the contradiction between theory and practice by constructing a synthesis which then becomes work process knowledge. Similarly, in their study of electrical maintenance work in Paris, Samurçay and Vidal-Gomel note that, although safety procedures are specified for carrying out electrical installations and repairs, skilled operatives use their discretion with regard to the extent to which it is necessary to observe them in any given situation. This is because the electricians frequently encounter non-standard installations which cannot be dealt with by following official maintenance manuals. In-depth studies of the cognitive processes involved show that they rely on their ability to construct a model of the unexpected situation which confronts them, and that these mental models include both standard electrical theory and phenomena that can only be known by direct personal experience. Thus the electricians' work process knowledge is constructed by the electricians themselves, by resolving contradictions between lived experience and the theoretical principles and procedures of electrical maintenance. An important implication for HRD is that intermediate-level employees need sound theoretical knowledge as well as practical experience, and ways of making sense of non-standard situations using both these resources; the implications of this for the design of vocational education and training are taken up by Fischer and Rauner in Chapter 12.

The importance of acknowledging that work process knowledge must be constructed in the process of work by resolving problems follows from the nature of work in many post-Taylorist workplaces. Work in the ideal Taylorist factory is reduced to routine, and if a problem is encountered the foreman or supervisor is called in to solve it. But in the delayered organization where workers have to deal with new tasks and engage in continual improvement, the central activity becomes problem-solving. A good way of explaining why work is often organized in teams is Weick's (1995) observation that in dynamic and unpredictable work environments, workers need a social structure for creating shared meanings in order to make the situation more intelligible and controllable. 'Shared sense making' is a very good way of describing the essence of work process knowledge in the kind of transformed workplaces referred to above. Arguably, it is the only way of dealing with the kinds of problem thrown at the workforce by the kind of flexible organization which delegates decision-making to multi-disciplinary teams, expects them to communicate laterally and respond quickly to external demands.

The third epistemological assumption shared by many of the contributors is that much work process knowledge is held collectively as well as individually – as part of the culture of the workplace. Fischer and Nakakoji (1997) argue that much of our knowledge comes from the collective memory of communities of practice and from the artifacts and technology within them. Many contributors to the present book endorse this view. Part of what it means to possess work process knowledge is to participate in the norms of collaborative work implied by the post-Taylorist organization. The studies by Mariani (Chapter 2), Fischer (Chapter 9), Lammont and Boreham (Chapter 7) and Rogalski, Plat and Antolin-Glen (Chapter 10) all emphasize this. Members of a community create and share knowledge in the practice of their work, and record their individual perceptions in the structures that constitute their culture. Lammont and Boreham in their study of a debt collection agency describe how the 'narrative' – a series of entries typed into a computer database by debt-collectors – serves as a collective memory and guides individuals in the selection of appropriate courses of action. Rogalski, Plat and Antolin-Glen describe the social interactions through which trainee crews in the glass cockpit of a modern aircraft share knowledge by making announcements and call-outs. In an evaluation of training, they are critical of the fact that this interaction is given comparatively little attention in trainers' assessments of crew performance. Mariani describes the social formation of work-teams in an Italian chemical company, an innovative research-led organization in which the free exchange of knowledge is a vital part of the work, and where the knowledge base is as collective as it is individual. These chapters suggest that a significant part of work process knowledge is contained in the interactions between the members of the group, as well as inside the heads of the employees.

The theory of work process knowledge developed in this book is very different from the concept of work-related knowledge used by many investigators in the field of cognitive ergonomics. The latter have usually represented knowledge as a mental model of the technical system the worker is operating (whether this be a machine-tool, an oil refinery, an anaesthetic machine, a cargo ship or an air traffic control system). The new idea which the concept of work process knowledge introduces is that workers need to understand not just the technical system they are operating, but the work process in which they themselves are participating – and creating – by way of operating that system. And this involves re-conceptualizing the worker as a member of a much broader system, where knowledge is partly owned by the individual worker and partly by the organization.

Implications for human resource development

Several chapters discuss the kinds of intervention needed to develop work process knowledge in a workforce. One critical factor that emerges is the way in which the workplace is managed, especially how roles are allocated. In this connection, Oliveira, Pires and Alves (Chapter 8) point out that language is a tool which enables workers to construct knowledge in the workplace, and stress that language use tends to reflect organizational culture. In the Taylorist organization, talking on the job is regarded as a waste of time and a misdemeanour, but to make the post-Taylorist organization function successfully, employees must engage in the free exchange of ideas and information. Huys and van Hootegem (Chapter 14) argue against the creation of specifically 'high skill' and 'low skill' jobs, each of which have disadvantages for their incumbents by creating a polarization of jobs with good opportunities for learning and jobs which offer their occupants no opportunities for participating in the construction of knowledge in the workplace.

This leads directly to the idea that the development of work process knowledge depends on the removal, or at least the blurring, of boundaries between different occupational groups. However, in many workplaces a strong division of labour persists, and is underpinned by status group conflict or a paternalistic culture. Two contributions (Boreham in Chapter 13 and Krüger, Kruse and Caprile in Chapter 15) examine the political barriers to the introduction of more organic working practices, revealing conditions under which knowledge of the work process is not freely shared.

Several chapters draw attention to the boundaries arising from the spatio-temporal arrangement of places of work. Many of these boundaries have been created by new technology. In their studies of various informated work situations, Rogalski, Plat and Antolin-Glen (Chapter 10), Norros and Nuutinen (Chapter 3) and Lammont and Boreham (Chapter 7) all describe how this requires employees to manipulate diverse packets of information, generated at different times in the work process. For example, telephone debt-collectors working with automatic direct diallers must bear in mind that they have only 3 minutes to manage simultaneously their interactions with the computer system and their negotiations with debtors. Glass-cockpit trainers and air traffic controllers must juggle diverse sets of mental representations. Fischer and Röben (Chapter 4) make the point that the work of the chemist and the laboratory assistant in the highly instrumented laboratory are separated by both time and space. Chemists decide the objectives of an analysis, laboratory assistants carry out the investigation and the results are then evaluated by the chemists. The work of each party is carried out in a separate physical and temporal space, but both must understand the work as a whole in order to appreciate the interrelationship between goals, tasks and outcomes.

While many of the contributors view knowledge as a cultural

phenomenon, preferring not to refer to internal mental processes, others make a considerable use of the concept of internal representation. This reflects the extent to which work process knowledge in an organic organization exists on several levels, the individual, the work group and the organization. Norros and Nuutinen (Chapter 3) and Samurçay and Vidal-Gomel (Chapter 11) both describe mental representations or shared mental models of the work-task. Norros and Nuutinen report that the individual's perception of the 'core task' is crucial in the promotion of hazard avoidance. Rogalski, Plat and Antolin-Glen (Chapter 10) illustrate how trainers must not only formulate mental representations of the task of piloting an aircraft, but must also be keenly aware of the representations formed by the trainee crews whom they supervise in the glass cockpit. The way in which workers represent the work process is critical, because many of the new work situations investigated are characterized by work intensification and information overload. The topic of information overload in informated work is investigated by Lammont and Boreham (Chapter 7), Rogalski, Plat and Antolin-Glen (Chapter 10) and Norros and Nuutinen (Chapter 3). Lammont and Boreham describe how one of the essential skills of experienced debt-collectors is their ability to 'get the picture' – to integrate disparate sources of information into a cognitive whole, in order to be able to deal decisively over the telephone with debtors. Rogalski, Plat and Antolin-Glen describe the tense and complex training session of the glass cockpit where trainees, surrounded by instruments, must learn how to interact with the automatic guidance system and with their co-pilots. At the same time, their trainers have the even more complex task of juggling several mental representations and simultaneously managing the dynamic situation.

The concerns of trainers are addressed by several contributors who investigate new approaches to participative work redesign and knowledge management. These include ways of facilitating the sharing of knowledge across occupational demarcations (Boreham, Chapter 13) and the focused use of apprenticeships to stimulate two-way dialogues between new and experienced employees (Mariani, Chapter 2). Attention is drawn to the difficulties implicit in the role of the workplace teacher or mentor in aiding the construction of work process knowledge. Overall, the work reported in this volume demonstrates three general principles that must be observed by any employer who views employees' knowledge as one of their major assets.

Leverage employee knowledge.   Several of the studies point to the need to ensure that knowledge is documented, stored in organizational memory and shared. This is the rationale for the novel use of apprenticeships described by Mariani (Chapter 2). In general, the chapters interpret workplace training as socialization, rather than narrow skill development. Samurçay and Vidal-Gomel (Chapter 11) and Rogalski, Plat and Antolin-

Glen (Chapter 10) illustrate situations where the development of indi-vidual competences are not sufficient to deal with hazardous tasks. Trainees must also learn to function as part of a team, and to develop collective competences.

Provide opportunities for reflection.   According to Polanyi (1958), people in a learning situation do not customarily stand back and watch themselves learning in a reflexive manner. Once a skill has been acquired, they tend to forget the details of the process by which they learned it and regard the acquisition of skill as a seamless process. Chapter 2 by Mariani demon-strates methods of encouraging worker reflectivity.

Deal with the sources of job dissatisfaction in the knowledge-creating organization. In much of the literature on knowledge work, an image is presented of enjoyable and liberating knowledge creation and sharing. Perhaps one of the most significant themes in the present book is that, while work process knowledge is presented as a resource for the flexible firm, it is also acknowledged as contested territory and the subject of ultimately retrogressive conflicts. Rasmussen (Chapter 6) presents a vignette of the deterioration of conviviality and craftsman-like co-working in Danish draughtsmanship due to the adoption of CAD systems. Boreham (Chapter 13) describes how knowledge is used to create the identities of different occupational groups, and how knowledge sharing might be perceived as a threat to group interests; and Krüger, Kruse and Caprile in Chapter 15 describe how lack of trust has undermined attempts to modernize Spanish industry.

The policy context

This chapter began by drawing attention to the challenges the European Union is experiencing due to globalization. At the level of individual firms, these are experienced as intense competition in product markets. At the levels of both the European Commission and national govern-ments, a spectrum of policies has been introduced to assist individuals, companies, regions and member states respond effectively to them. The policies include R&D policy, technology policy, infrastructure policy and vocational education and training policy. In general, these are aimed at the twin goals of promoting competitiveness in international markets and maintaining social cohesion. A theme which runs through all these policy debates is the importance of improving the skills and knowledge of the workforce. In part, this reflects a return to human capital theory, the doc-trine that the knowledge and skills of a firm's employees are among its most important assets. National systems of education and training are now charged with the task of generating human capital and placing it on the labour market. Emphasis is increasingly being placed on developing the ability to work effectively in teams, to communicate with others both inside and outside the company, to willingly assume responsibility, to be quality-conscious and to provide good customer care. In these debates, however, little attention has been given to the knowledge needed to underpin such traits. If employees are to work effectively in flexible and informated environments, they need to understand the overall work process with which they are dealing. The present book, based on empirical studies in a range of economic sectors in many European countries, offers some suggestions about how to address this task, and begins the important task of building theories to explain the ways of knowing that will increasingly be expected of the workforces in advanced industrial countries in the twenty-first century.

2 Work process knowledge in a chemical company

Michele Mariani

A growing number of researchers in the field of industrial sociology, organizational development and related disciplines perceive a need for organizational theories and models that break from the tradition of scientific management (Taylor 1947). In large measure, this is due to the rapid pace of product innovation, the widespread diffusion of ICTs and the growth of sectors other than manufacturing. Among the new theoretical approaches are those representing organizations as organic systems (Burns 1963), sense-making environments (Weick 1995), learning organizations (Nonaka and Takeuchi 1995) and knowledge networks (Conklin 1996; Davenport *et al.* 1998). Locating itself within this field, the European research network WHOLE (Boreham and Lammont 2001) focused its activity on the concept of work process knowledge as a key construct for explaining success in the highly competitive marketplace of today.

> The concept of work process knowledge was developed to define the knowledge that workers, whether hotel employees, machinists or laboratory assistants, need in order to cope with more organic and knowledge-creating working environments. Developing work process knowledge helped them to adjust to more flexible processes.
>
> (Boreham 1998: 3)

In essence, work process knowledge:

- in opposition to the well-known Taylorist principle of selecting and training 'round people for round holes', implies an expanded understanding of work roles in the whole organization;
- identifies the complex of different knowledge and skills necessary to be active participants within modern organizations, in contrast to the notion of abstract knowledge provided by formal education;
- implies an awareness of the interdependency of the activities in different departments, including characteristics of the system as a whole;
- is conceived as being continuously produced in the workplace (Kruse 1986; Boreham and Lammont 2001).

Clearly, there is a need for research to substantiate the claim that work process knowledge is an essential resource on which flexible organizations depend. This chapter will attempt to provide such substantiation by reporting an in-depth investigation of a major Italian chemical company that focuses on innovation. This case has been selected because it represents a flexible company that is succeeding in the present-day competitive business environment, among other things conducting continuous experimentation and research into its own work organization. Some of the findings reported in this chapter come from previous studies that have analysed the company's innovations in work organization (Bordogna 1989; Fasulo 1990; Carbognin 1997; Catino and Fasulo 1998). Other data come from the analysis of internal documents (Foschi 1995; Gandini *et al.* 1999) and from interviews and observations on the site carried out by the author in the context of the EU TSER Thematic Network WHOLE.

The site

The site is one of the locations of a leading chemical company which operates on a global scale and has branches in fourteen different countries. It has been in existence for more than 40 years and employs about 1,000 people. Its mission is both the manufacture of chemical products and research into new substances in the field of plastics. The site has three main divisions: production plants, pilot plants and laboratories. As the names imply, manufacturing is the responsibility of the production plants, while research and development take place in the laboratories and pilot plants.

The product

The market for plastic products is very competitive, and given the high price of the basic component (oil) the profit margin is very small. This makes plastic production a risky business, especially for western countries which have high labour costs. Profit margins, on the other hand, are much higher for companies which develop innovative production processes, especially new catalysts. Catalysts are one of the key components of plastic production. The special properties of plastics, such as softness, hardness and resistance to temperature, are due to the type of catalyst that is used. New catalysts make it possible to create products with enhanced qualities (e.g. more transparent and resistant plastic mineral water bottles).

The competitive advantage

In the competitive context of the modern chemicals industry, time to market has been acknowledged as a crucial element in success (Reich 1991). The research and technology side of the site has achieved a high degree of success, mainly because of its ability to achieve an extremely short time to market for its innovations. '...[To] create innovation in extremely brief times, making the most of all the best opportunities, is to get a jump start on the competition' (Galli 1998: 96). When the site was established, the majority of the 800 workers were employed in production, with only 200 working in laboratories and pilot plants. Around the mid-1970s, the chemical industry in Italy went through a deep slump. In the region where the site is located, employment fell from 4,000 to below 1,500. While employment in the site's production area followed the trend, falling from 800 to 200, the research and development side grew continuously from the initial 200 to 800, with a turnover which has increased by a factor of five in the last 5 years. Two main principles underpin this success: the joint development of products, technologies and processes and the belief that innovation is a process of trial and error.

Joint development of products, technologies and processes

Over the years, the site has become particularly effective in integrating two activities, the invention of new catalysts and experiments with new technological solutions. The joint operation of products, technologies and processes is claimed by Govoni (1998) as one of the main reasons for the site's success. The installations that achieve this are the pilot plants, which reproduce on a smaller scale the complete processes of catalyst production. Experiments for finding new chemical formulations are run in the pilots so that once the new catalyst has been found, the technology to produce it becomes immediately available too. Investigations run in the pilot plants result in the development of new production processes, the development of new products, formulae for new catalysts, optimization of plant production efficiency and new ideas for product research and development. Moreover, inventions can be immediately tested on a scale which both permits the production of materials for application testing, and provides enough data for scale-up to industrial production (Catino and Fasulo 1998: 100).

Innovation as a process of trial-and-error

For about three decades, the site management has been convinced that innovation and especially the invention of new products are a function of the number of tests and experiments that are run. Research processes, in contrast to production processes, have very uncertain outcomes and it can be very difficult to make a rational selection of trials. On the other hand, it is relatively easy to design the trials themselves.

> When the R&D project is planned, managers of the different customer areas and researchers are asked their 'wish list' of activities. They

always say that they need a research centre that is three times bigger. But when the R&D starts, we find that the eighty per cent of the new ideas originate from everyday activities on the basis of local insights.

(Excerpt from an interview with the person responsible for Planning and Control)

Such an approach has interesting parallels with the concepts of 'bounded rationality' (Simon 1981) and 'situated cognition': '. . . the circumstances of our actions are never fully anticipated and are continuously changing around us. As a consequence our actions, while systematic, are never planned in the strong sense [. . .] Rather, plans are best viewed as *weak resources for what is primarily ad hoc activity*' (Suchman 1987).

Successful R&D depends critically on two preconditions: the capacity to perform a large number of experiments and the capacity to rapidly modify or adjust production programmes so that, whenever a line of research produces promising results, processes in the plant focus on producing the chemical in question. Acting on these assumptions, at the beginning of the 1970s both the pilot plants and the laboratories started to operate on a 24-hour cycle, in order to maximize the rate of experimentation. The importance accorded to increasing the rate of experimentation is also demonstrated by changes in attitudes towards confidentiality. Between 10 and 15 years ago, all the site installations were covered by steel shields so that it was impossible to observe and copy the technical process that was being tested. Now these have been removed on the grounds that they slowed down the whole process and the pragmatic observation that 'if we are first, it doesn't matter who copies us' (excerpt from an interview with the employee responsible for Planning and Control). Simple as the principle is, the more experiments carried out, the greater the chances of making a new discovery. Following this philosophy, on the basis of a very small increase in personnel, activity in the pilot plants was increased from one experiment per month at the beginning of the 1980s to the present rate of two per week. Thanks to the introduction of a continuous work cycle, the output of the laboratories was increased from two or three tests per day to 20 to 25 per day.

The dynamics of work process knowledge in teams

The objective of running as many experiments as possible and rapidly modifying the R&D plans and the plants themselves has created the need for flexible employees with broader competencies that integrate a wider range of skills. At the individual level, of course, there is a limit to how far multi-skilling can be taken. But if work is organized in teams it then becomes possible to bring a far wider range of skills into the same operational unit. Within teams, individual knowledge and competencies fuse to create an integrated and polyvalent human resource.

Working in teams

Teamwork has been used most intensively in the pilot plants. As stated above, the work of these plants consists mainly of running investigations to discover new products and develop new production technologies. This work is managed by two types of team, one performing on a technical level and one on an operational level. The technical teams are responsible for setting up and modifying the programme in each pilot plant. They consist of three people with different responsibilities:

- a process engineer responsible for designing the test which is to be run. This role was created in the mid 1980s;
- a technologist responsible for the technology needed to perform the test. This role was created in 1990. Its rationale is that, to modify/adjust activities as a function of progressively emerging findings, it is critical that the technological configuration of the scaled-down chemical installations can be altered very rapidly. While the time required by the investigation itself is fixed, the time needed for installation set up can be shortened as a function of team efficiency;
- a plant manager who takes responsibility for the overall functioning of the plant, a role that dates back to the early 1970s.

The operational team consists of from three to eight people. To cover a 24-hour work schedule, each pilot plant is run by three operational teams working in shifts. Personnel levels are determined by the optimal combination of the needs of the developing R&D programmes and the need for the effective and reliable management of the installations. The latter can operate with a different number of people in each team (and different work schedules) as a function of the number of reactions (and investigations) that are running. There are three main roles in these teams:

- a process driver, who continuously monitors the process from a control room, the main task being to keep the process in equilibrium by varying the ingredients of the chemical reaction based on information displayed on the control panel;
- an external operator, who checks and adjusts the physical parts of the plant;
- a shift leader, who co-ordinates the team's activity on the basis of targets set by the plant manager.

Members of the operational team rotate between roles. For example, it is quite common for a process driver to revert to the role of external operator when circumstances require. A kind of rotation exists for technical employees too. Before a new employee, such as an area technologist, becomes fully operational, he or she is asked to work for a period in the operational teams as an ordinary team member. This eliminates the

familiar problem of engineers and researchers who are very knowledge-
able theoretically, but whose knowledge of plant structure and organization is almost nil.

Within both teams, therefore, everybody comes to know everybody
else's job and to compensate each other's lack of experience. '[Within
teams] information circulates among people: everybody needs to know
everything; there should be no "grey areas" where only a few know how to
operate' (Catino and Fasulo 1998: 140). In this way, the different phases
of the work process become well known to all members of the team,
making it possible to develop a common language that allows a tight
coupling of activities.

> A team shifts the workload among its members to achieve balance in
> situations characterized by high workload, time pressure and high
> risk. Task reallocation assumes that the team members have become
> familiar with a range of tasks beyond their immediate responsibilities.
> In this sense, there is a degree of overlap in the task of team members
> which serves as a redundancy function.
>
> (Kontogiannis 1999: 19)

Learning in teams

The fact that teams are privileged places for knowledge creation and knowledge sharing is demonstrated by the central role that they play in the
training of novices. Following the trend in other countries, in the last few
years companies in Italy have increasingly been able to employ personnel
on short-term contracts. The chemical sector is now aiming to get 25 per
cent of its total workforce on such contracts. The research site is one of the
first companies to have taken advantage of the new flexibility policies,
having 10 per cent of its personnel on one-year contracts. The use of temporary workers gives the company the advantage of external flexibility, and
from the beginning this was perceived as a way of strengthening R&D programmes by enabling them to quickly vary the number of experiments and
lines of research being pursued. However, to exploit the new opportunity
effectively, the company needed to solve a crucial problem. Becoming an
effective chemical plant operator requires 2 to 3 years' experience, and it is
impossible for employees on one-year contracts to develop sufficient skill to
become useful employees. This difficulty is overcome by giving temporary
workers specially designed, less responsible work roles within programmes
run by teams of experienced employees. By bringing in temporary workers
to discharge these roles, it becomes possible to move an experienced
worker out of each team to create a new group to conduct R&D on a new
process. However, the problem of reducing the time needed before
novices can become active participants in the work process still remains,
and this has been solved by establishing a structured course of learning on

the job that lasts between 3 and 5 months. This consists of two main phases: 1 month of formal teaching, and from 2 to 4 months of work experience in the division where they will be employed for a year. The practice of using temporary workers started in 1996 and at the moment is in its ninth cycle. In total, more than 200 employees have participated in this scheme. After selection, the one-month period of formal teaching is given by experienced technicians working in the centre. Novices are selected on the basis of psychometric tests, an interview and their educational record. The minimum entry requirement is completion of the Italian middle school certificate. Over the nine intakes, the number of university graduates has continuously increased, rising from 10 per cent in the first cycle to more than 20 per cent in the most recent ones. Having experts to teach their work to novices can be regarded as very positive *per se*. It represents a step back to the tradition of apprenticeship that has been undermined by industrial change. It also

> ... increases our professionalism. For example, if we did not have to teach some of our plant schemes to newcomers, we would not look at those schemes for four-to-five months. In this way, we have got to continuously refresh our knowledge in order to be able to transmit it.
>
> (Excerpt from an interview with a skilled worker)

The morning is devoted to classes on theoretical subjects, the applications of which are observed in the afternoon during guided tours on the site. Regardless of the units in which they will be employed for their one-year contract, during the first month the novices are taught about all the work processes in all the divisions. At the end of the month they are assigned to a specific division for between 2 and 4 months, depending on its complexity. During this period, the novices deepen their knowledge of a specific work process by directly observing how the experienced workers operate. As part of the learning experience, novices are given a basic knowledge of a model of the overall functioning of the site, and great reliance is placed on the capacity of the work teams to serve as learning environments. Teams, in fact, become 'training contexts, setting an example for activities performed and the professional behaviour and orientation required ... The novice learns how the organization operates on the basis of cooperation and self-organization' (Catino and Fasulo 1998: 139). At the end of this phase, the novices are given a 'certificate of competence'. The whole experience (training plus contract) is in the process of being recognized by credits that can be used in further education, thus realizing the concept of a vocational curriculum that integrates academic study with real-world experience. The certificate is based on writing a short thesis covering the following topics:

• short description of process main phases;
• main characteristics of raw materials and final products;

- flow sheet of the work process;
- plant management;
- accident prevention and safety procedures;
- activities performed by the student and comments on the experience.

A content analysis of the short theses written by the novices was carried out to establish what was being learned. The analysis found that three types of competence were being acquired: technical, conceptual and social. Comparisons between the different divisions showed that different contexts led to the acquisition of different competencies. Social competencies were emphasized more in laboratories and pilot plants than in the production plants.

After successful completion of this period, a contract is issued for 12 months' employment. During the year, the novice works as a full team member, albeit in the simplified role referred to above. A maximum of one novice is added to each team. It was found that effective training and team management called for heterogeneous and flexible work groups, which mix different levels of experience and types of skill. In this way, 'the exchange of knowledge is strongly enforced, given that there is the need to bring the less experienced member to autonomy in the shortest time' (excerpt from an interview with a skilled worker). When the contract is over, the temporary worker goes on a list from which future permanent workers are hired. However, as the site management decided not to increase the overall number of workers and there is a young age distribution, only a small number has been taken on permanently in the last few years.

Participation

The research site has been described as '. . . an organizational system very flexible in its way of functioning but definitely fixed in the rules and places for co-decision and participation' (Carbognin 1997: 10). Besides teams, participation mechanisms are regarded as essential to create opportunities for both exchanging knowledge and producing new knowledge. The system of organizational participation is particularly effective and consists of six different types of meetings, summarized in Table 2.1.

At the macro level there are joint committees, company bargaining meetings and union meetings. Joint committees are constituted to solve problems that concern the site as a whole. Company bargaining involves the top managers on the site and union representatives, and is the place where new performance requirements are introduced and manpower levels are decided. Finally, union meetings take place at all the levels of the organization (teams, areas and divisions) and involve both workers and union representatives. At a lower level, work, operative and technical meetings take place with more frequency. The function of these meetings

Table 2.1 Six types of formal mechanisms for participation

Type of meetings	Participants
work meeting	workers from teams/areas/divisions
operative meeting	leaders of teams/areas/divisions and technical staff concerned with the problem
technical meeting	union delegates and technical staff
joint committee	union delegates and technical staff
company bargaining	union delegates and senior managers
union assembly	union members and delegates

is to verify, modify and adjust, within the agreed framework of working practice, the labour process for new R&D programmes at the team, area and divisional level. In particular, 'Technical meetings are essential to clarify the design of the programmes and reciprocal commitments ... to locate in a global vision the variability and the interdependence of the different work processes' (Foschi 1995: 23). In general, participation mechanisms are

> ... an instrument for information exchange on the responsibilities of the different work groups for integrating and involving themselves in the research programme ... they ensure that information circulates more rapidly ... it is in these meetings that updates are given on the work schedules, on the technical innovations to be achieved and on the work organization.
>
> (Excerpt from a Union–Corporate agreement dated 1995)

Conclusion

In recent years, knowledge has been identified by both researcher and practitioner communities as a company's most important asset, being a major factor in competitive success (Drucker 1997, Conklin 1996). However, knowledge is difficult to create, capture and share. Solutions to the problems of knowledge management have been mainly technologically oriented, especially through the development of software systems. However, information systems can deal to only a limited extent with the dynamic and socially constructed nature of knowledge. As Davenport *et al.* (1998) put it: 'Knowledge often resists engineering ... knowledge is created invisibly in the human brain, and only the right organizational climate can persuade people to create, reveal, share and use it.' When talking about knowledge management, 'the real issues aren't technical' (O'Dell and Grayson 1998: 265). In the case reported in this chapter, the company's strategy of running scientific research and the development of production technology in tandem, and its view of scientific innovation as a process of trial and error, resulted in a need to integrate the different work processes and redesign the organization to be as flexible as possible. In particular, to provide the conditions for the speedy modification of plants and R&D plans in order to exploit opportunities for innovation, it was essential for

> ... everybody [to have] a knowledge of the overall work process. It should never be allowed to happen that an individual cannot interpret a certain output because he or she does not know what happened at a previous stage in the process.
>
> (Excerpt from an interview with the employee responsible for Planning and Control)

The team structures and participation mechanisms described above have been found to be effective ways of ensuring that the company's reservoir of work process knowledge is continually generated, updated, shared and used in this highly successful business.

3 The concept of the core task and the analysis of working practices

Leena Norros and Maaria Nuutinen

The anticipated change from an information to a learning society calls for more than an increase in formal education – it also demands a better understanding of learning in the workplace (Pantzar 1997). There are many ways of conceptualizing learning, and whichever we choose will direct our research and development activity down a different pathway (Heiskanen 1999). As Launis and Engeström (1999) have pointed out, the traditional concept of a hierarchy of professions and skills is becoming less relevant to present-day circumstances, and needs to be replaced. The concept of work process knowledge, on the other hand, is a way of representing the kind of expertise needed under modern working conditions. Studies of work process knowledge are related to both pedagogically oriented research on expertise and ergonomically oriented research on work activity. By exploring the concept of work process knowledge in greater depth, we can facilitate interaction between these two research traditions and integrate the relevant contributions of both into a more powerful account of the abilities many employees need today.

The concept of work process knowledge emerged within the vocational education community. It emphasizes that in work we need knowledge of a kind that can be constructed only within the work process itself, and that this type of knowledge is not always explicit or even explicable. This way of conceptualizing work-related knowledge has its roots in sociological and psychological theories which see human action as practice (see Fischer, Chapter 9 in this volume). They draw on an epistemic position in which knowledge is not restricted to declarative concepts and to conscious behaviour (e.g. Dewey 1929/1999; Merleau-Ponty 1962; Polanyi 1958). One can even go so far as to say that originally, knowledge was not what a person could say but what he or she could do. However, while emphasizing the importance of skill, it is also necessary to recognize that, particularly in modern kinds of work, the precondition for efficient learning in the workplace is the ability to use theoretical and conceptual knowledge as a means of organizing actions and perceiving the work process. Implicit in the concept of work process knowledge is the key notion that understanding work involves understanding how individual or group actions are connected to the work process as a whole. This aspect of the concept links it with the concept of community of practice (Lave and Wenger 1991; Wenger 1998) and Engeström's (1987) theory of expansive learning. The former approach stems from the ethnomethodological tradition of work analysis, the latter from the cultural–historical theory of activity.

The research experience of the present authors has been mainly in the analysis of process operators' actions in controlling open systems in dynamic, complex and uncertain industrial environments. Due to the critical functional features of the processes in these domains, the most effective way of controlling them requires the ability to act on distal and often partly obscured cues of target object performance, and the readiness to act promptly in unexpected problem situations. This assumes a capacity for judgement based on skill and knowledge, the general characteristics of expertise (Schön 1983). Also needed is confidence in one's own (or in the team's) capacity to cope with the situation. It is likely that similar changes in the profile of abilities needed by employees are occurring in domains other than process control. The coming of the information society and the increase of knowledge-intensive work bring with them a dissolution of the boundaries of time and place, and increase the extent to which the agent, the object of his or her work and interactions with other workers are mediated. Studies of the work carried out by process controllers can provide insights to these more general changes in working life and into the nature of expertise. But if we are to generalize from the case of process control, we need first to represent it as a generic problem of human conduct. In fact, it has been the goal of the present authors to use our studies of process control work as a way of developing such a generic theory of human action in dynamic, complex and uncertain environments. The strategy has been to focus on work activities through analyses of everyday practices and on the basis of this, to seek generalizations about human action and expertise. The methodology developed for this purpose is called core task analysis (CTA). In this chapter, we present it both as a practical way of identifying work process knowledge in particular work situations, and as an operational definition of this way of knowing.

Theoretical underpinnings of a naturalistic study of action

The authors' studies approach work from the perspective of a situated action that is conceived as human–environment interaction. We try to adopt and formulate a vocabulary that describes the forms and reveals the mechanisms of the mutual determination of the human being and his or her environment. Such an ecological or naturalistic perspective on human conduct has its philosophical origins in attempts to overcome the Cartesian dualisms between the human being and the environment, mind and body, cognition and emotion. The cultural historical theory of activity developed by Vygotski (1978), Leontiev (1978) and Luria (1976) on one hand, and the American pragmatist tradition represented by Peirce (1903/1998) and Dewey (1929/1999) on the other, are two major methodological approaches to human action that make determined attempts to overcome these dualisms. In both schools of thought, the notion of practice is seen as a bridge between the dichotomies that also characterize many theories and conceptions of modern psychology.

Coping with uncertainty as an epistemic key feature of action

The problem of the empirical analysis of occupational expertise is to find a valid psychological vocabulary to describe action as a human–environment interaction. The major deficiency in the dominant cognitivist approach in psychology is the underlying methodological division between the subject and his or her environment, and the related conceptualization of cognition as a process internal to the subject. On this view, the world is represented internally as knowledge held in the subject's mind. Cognitive action is reduced to internal operations on this representation, and the adequacy of cognition becomes the extent to which the internal model corresponds to the objective world. The complexity of the connections between the elements in the environment makes adequate representation difficult, and for this reason it is seen as the major challenge which cognitive capacity has to overcome. Action is the implementation and verification of what has been processed internally, not something that determines how the world is perceived. This way of thinking is typical of cognitive ergonomic analyses of process control, where the chief aspect of the environment on which research concentrates is the complexity of the connections between elements (Cellier *et al.* 1997).

From the perspective of the process of human–environment interaction emphasized in the pragmatist and cultural–historical traditions, human cognition is understood in a much more active and apparently subjective way. Cognitive processes are seen as being determined both by the existing possibilities in the world, and by the personal position of the actor within the context of on-going activity. Through actions taken in a social context, the world becomes shared and meaningful. The adequacy of acting and thinking is related both to survival and to the possibilities of action that are created by previous actions. The environment is interpreted in terms of its significance for one's activity, and not only in terms of its structural complexity. The subjectivity of perceiving and acting is not seen as a source of error but instead as a necessary condition for constituting the world as the object of action and knowledge (Megill 1997; Klemola and Norros 2000). This approach seems to offer a more realistic basis for understanding what people actually do in their daily working activities.

In making sense of the environment, people face the fundamental uncertainty of the world. As the significant features of the object of a process are distal, people reason about the process on the basis of signs that refer to the object. Consequently, they do not achieve verified knowledge of the fundamental laws of the process. Instead, they develop understanding of the process behaviour and an ability to make judgements about it. According to John Dewey (1929/1999) it is this kind of reasoning that provides people with the possibility of anticipating phenomena. It also allows the environment to be steered if so intended. Such reasoning is conceived by Peirce (Collected Papers 1931–58) as abductive, and relates particularly to the discovery of the possibilities in a situation. Abductive hypotheses mediate continuously between the state of doubt and the state of belief in situations that are never exactly repeatable (Boreham *et al.* 1996). Consequently, the actors are obliged to construct knowledge of the process of the world in action. This makes it essential to analyse psychological operations in the control of the environment from an epistemic point of view. Thus, in addition to asking what are the constraints and possibilities of controlling processes in the environment, we should ask what are the constraints and possibilities of knowing the processes for the purpose of controlling them (Klemola and Norros 1997). In short, human control of the world is inseparable from the activity of creating knowledge, and in the context of many modern working environments, such knowledge is best understood as work process knowledge.

Emotions as a key feature of coping with uncertainty

Polanyi (1958, 1983) uses the term 'tacit knowledge' to refer to the formation of patterns of cues that signify features of the environment that are relevant for action. Because these cues are not within focal attention during action, but rather in a peripheral position, the resulting knowledge is tacit – implicit but operative. This is attributable to the comprehension of the meaning of the cues in the context of the whole. Polanyi (1958, 1983) emphasizes the fundamental involvement of the actor in constructing objects of action by his use of the concept of 'personal knowledge'. He emphasizes the personal participation of the knower in all acts of understanding and claims that this fact does not make understanding subjective, but personal. Personal knowing is the act of comprehending the world in a way that should have general validity. It also includes the notion of being committed to the conviction that there is something to be discovered. This draws attention to the close relationship between the epistemic and energetic dimensions of acting. Polanyi writes:

> The tracing of personal knowledge to its roots in the subsidiary awareness of our body as merged in our focal awareness of external objects, reveals not only the logical structure of personal knowledge but also its dynamic sources.
>
> (Polanyi 1958: 60)

These ideas of Polanyi regarding the formation and nature of personal knowledge have clear connections to the thoughts of Dewey and Bourdieu, who also emphasize the pre-reflective nature of understanding operational relationships with the environment (Dewey 1938; Bourdieu 1990). These authors use the term 'habit' to indicate the learned sensitivity of the organism towards the environment.

Current theories of emotion such as Parrot and Harré (1996) approach human–environment interaction from a different perspective and tradition. However, they illustrate the role of emotions as subsidiary cues indicating the success or otherwise of one's actions. The functions of emotions arc primarily to give information about and regulate one's actions (Laird and Apostoleris 1996; Oatley 1992, 1996). Emotions are a part of the solution to the organism's problem of the organization of information, acting as it does with limited resources in an incompletely known world. According to Oatley and Johnson-Laird's communicative emotion theory, emotions signal the likelihood of achieving a goal or a plan. They make it possible to concentrate, to configure mental resources and make ready certain kinds of action. A positive emotion connected with the achievement of sub-goals signals encouragement to the self to continue the current action. When the possibility of attaining a goal decreases, a negative emotion interrupts the course of action (Oatley 1992, 1996). This makes it possible to adapt to the unexpected.

The core task analysis methodology

The core task concept

To understand expertise, it is necessary to view work activities from both an operative perspective and a perspective that combines its constructive, knowledge-creating and learning aspects. The naturalistic methodology that we have developed and called core task analysis is an attempt to meet this methodical requirement. By 'core task' we mean the result-critical content of a particular work activity on which the achievement of the goal of the work depends. Core task analysis is a tool which workers can use to reflect on this aspect of the working practices in their organizations, and facilitate the development of new ones. It can thus be a crucial resource for developing work process knowledge in organizations such as the chemical company described by Mariani in Chapter 2.

There are two main reasons why workers need to continually reflect on and improve their working practices. The first relates to the difficulty most people experience in identifying the essential functional demands of their work, and maintaining a focus on them even when their critical role is not apparent. The technological and organizational developments taking place in many industries today make it difficult to maintain such an orientation towards the goal of work activity, as they generally mediate work processes and outcomes. For example, in organizations where very high reliability needs to be maintained for safety reasons, such as nuclear power plant, transportation systems or medical work, mediating processes are often designed-in to create defences against errors and disturbances. In these circumstances, functionally critical demands are not necessarily evident at each stage of the work process and efficiency demands may make them even less salient. It thus becomes more difficult to construct personal meaning out of the work situation, and harder to see the results of one's own actions. The second reason for encouraging workers to reflect on the core task is that the activity systems within which the core tasks are performed are historically constructed entities in a process of evolution. It thus becomes necessary to continuously re-evaluate and re-define the content of work and the nature of the core task. The import-ance of this can be seen by considering the role the worker's identity plays in his or her competence. According to Lave (1991; Lave and Wenger 1991) the development of identity is inseparable from the development of knowledge and skills – it provides motivation, structure and meaning as the individual's position within the community develops into that of master. But many of the changes that are taking place in the contempor-ary working environment are destroying this identity (Zuboff 1988). Changes in the organization of the work, demands for continuous learn-ing and other changes that increase the unpredictability of work can threaten the worker's identity, moving him or her to the position of a beginner.

Our concept of core task analysis is more comprehensive than the tradi-tional concept of task analysis found in the human factors literature. In an extensive review of different task analysis techniques Kirwan and Ainsworth define task analysis as follows:

> Task analysis can be defined as the study of what an operator (or team of operators) is required to do, in terms of actions and/or cognitive processes, to achieve the system goal. Task analysis method can also document the information and control facilities used to carry out the task.

> (Kirwan and Ainsworth 1992: 1)

According to the above definition, 'task' refers to the requirements for a particular kind of work within a particular division of responsibilities between individual actors, not to the worker's actual performance, nor to the actions of a larger community of people as a community. In a preface to a special section on task analysis, Hoffman and Woods (2000) discuss the distinction between 'task' and 'action' and show that the term 'task analysis' is used in both senses. They suggest that instead of arguing about the concept, it would be more fruitful to accept a diversity of approaches to task analysis because they share the common object of the 'cognitive systems in context'; the existence of a variety of methods provides an opportunity for dialogue and learning.

We agree with this constructive suggestion. However, we also see the conceptual differentiation between 'task' and 'action' as fruitful. This distinction is useful for investigating the role of actions in the development of practices, and has often been made before. For example, Hacker (1998) and Leplat (1991) define the *prescribed* and the *effective* task as the objective and subjective aspects of the task, or alternatively as its organizational and individual aspects. The distinction is also made in the classical work by Hackman (1969), who emphasizes that to understand a task requires analysing the actions needed to perform it. In this sense, the subjective is prior to the objective and the objective should not be understood as a pre-given ideal reference for action, a point stressed by Theureau (1996) in his phenomenologically oriented analyses of actions. Rogalski (1995) also refers to the distinction between the subjective and objective in task analysis, and defines a further dimension, the structural aspect of the task. According to her, three structural components must be included in the analysis: the goal of the task, the criteria for achieving the goal and finally the resources that enable and the constraints that hinder its achievement.

In our concept of core task, we make a deliberate conceptual distinction between task requirements and task performance. Moreover, because we take the cultural–historical theory of activity as our starting point, we insist that the concept should not be restricted to individual actions, but that action should be interpreted in a wider perspective of a societal activity that is carried out co-operatively by a number of actors.

The object-orientedness of activity is one of the corner stones of the cultural–historical theory of activity (Leontiev 1978). The object is the part of the environment that may become an actual source of the fulfilment of human needs, and therefore forms the societal motivation for activity (Leontiev 1978). Another theoretical contribution by Leontiev (1973) is that human activity becomes hierarchically structured through the historical division of labour. During the formation of this hierarchical structure, the object of activity retains its capacity to motivate action, but its orienting function is transformed. The goals of individuals and groups at different levels in the hierarchy now assume this orienting role. And because activity exists only through actions (Leontiev 1978), a dynamically important relationship between the object and the goal emerges. According to Leontiev, the relationship between the societal object-related motive for the activity and the situated goals constitutes the personal sense of action. This relationship is thus the key factor in energizing personal action, and extremely important for the understanding of the construction of situated actions. The problem is how in practice the researcher can study personal sense and its constructive role in work. In our earlier work we used the concept of orientation to indicate the person's subjective relationship to his or her work. Orientation is the subjective framing of the object of activity (Norros 1995) and it was assumed to regulate actual performance. Usually, we determined this by interviewing people about their work, but we also studied orientation in action with the help of a disturbance orientation model (Norros 1996).

During the later development of the CTA methodology, however, the pragmatist notion of habit was gradually developed as the means of approaching the process of societally formed meaning and the personal sense that is embedded in situatively constrained operations (Peirce 1903/1998; Dewey 1901/1991). Consequently, an empirical research method that focuses on the identification of semiotic structures of behaviour in particular working situations was developed for the study of the construction and content of actions. In our ongoing work we attempt to develop further the emotional–energetic aspect of the core task concept. Nuutinen (2000) suggests that the concept of expert identity includes the emotional–energetic aspects intertwined both with work performance and development of expertise in work. Expert identity is defined as consisting of three components: meaningfulness – the sense of the importance of a person's own work; professional self-confidence; and a sense of control.

These three components are interrelated and affect each other. Meaningfulness refers to the person's feeling of the general and personal importance of her or his profession or work. The self-confidence of an expert is the feeling of possessing skills, knowledge and experience, by which he or she believes it is possible to assume responsibility. Confidence also enables co-operation, making effective co-operation possible because the person does not feel in so much danger when he or she co-operates with others. The sense of control means situational control of one's actions and the emotions awoken by reaching goals. A positive emotion (exercising control) energizes actions and focuses it on target. A negative emotion (losing control) interrupts action and makes it possible to re-direct action, but it can also paralyse action if the sense of control is totally lost. Then the person can try to find the sense of control with another goal, for example 'saving face', and the action is directed to the new goal.

The role of the emotions in the control of one's action is emphasized in the communicative emotion theory by Oatley (1992, 1996). According to this theory, emotions regulate one's behaviour when the consequences of the behaviour are not perceived. The components of expert identity suggested above are quite similar to those identified by Antonovsky (1988, 1993a, 1993b) in his well-known concept of sense of coherence (SOC).

The model of analysis

In the analysis of the core task, we use empirical material including interviews and observations of the actors' behaviour in natural or simulated normal situations. Accident investigation data can also be used as material, as can various kinds of documents. A model of core task analysis is depicted in Figure 3.1.

Figure 3.1 describes the inferential steps that are necessary when analysing the content of situated actions in a particular work domain. The two-way arrows in the model indicate the iterative nature of the conceptualization during which the definitions of the constraints and possibilities on the one hand, and the criteria for the core task on the other, are defined from data using a grounded theory approach (Charmaz 1995). The illustration of the analysis as a three-dimensional model represents the idea of linking particular expressions of the task in different empirical situations to the functions that in a formative sense define them (Vicente 1999). Thus the modelling of the task performance and the corresponding perception–action cycles necessarily refer to particular situations, whereas the critical functions and the psychological core task demands relate to the task in a generic sense. The functional–formative context conveys the meaning of the particular actions. In the following, we briefly describe the analytical steps and give examples of our analysis of the activity of piloting a ship, based on a study of marine navigation in a natural

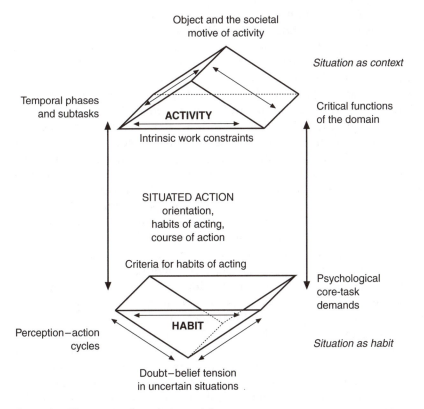

Figure 3.1 The core task analysis model

setting (Norros *et al.* 1998) and on an investigation of ten marine piloting accidents in Finland. Several case reports have already been published of the investigation (AIB 2001) and a further comprehensive report has been published (Nuutinen and Norros 2001).

In the core task analysis, we take an ecological point of view while perceiving the actions as determined both through the environment and through the actor. Thus, action must be contextualized in the analysis in two ways: situation as the context and situation as habit (Klemola and Norros 2000). Both aspects are necessary in a core task analysis.

Situation as context

First, there is a need to model the domain to determine the situated possibilities and constraints of the action under investigation. This part of the analysis is depicted in the upper part of the model in Figure 3.1. The activity–systemic theory of Engeström (1987) and the functionally oriented formative analysis of work domains by Vicente (1999; Rasmussen 1986) provide the concepts for this part of the analysis. According to the activity–systemic approach, we first define the object of activity, which provides affordances (Gibson 1979) for human action, the historically evolving contexts of activity. Engeström's (1987) model is based on Vygotski's (1978) observation that activity consists of relations that have an instrumental tool- or sign-mediated structure. In this model, an activity system has three original elements, the individual actor, the collective and the environment as the possible object of activity. The relationship between the individual and the environment becomes mediated through tools and signs, the relationship between an individual actor and the collective through rules, and the relationship between the collective and the object through the division of labour. The activity–system thus forms an extremely complex system within which there appear tensions and pressure for change. Such tensions also exist between neighbouring activity systems, as Engeström has shown (Engeström 1987, 1999). This activity–systemic and historical aspect is not directly expressed in the model of Figure 3.1, but should be taken as included in the upper corner of the pyramid that represents the object of activity. Thus, for example in our studies on marine navigation, the object of piloting was comprehended first in a generic form as accurate navigation and steering of the ship in an area of the sea where knowledge and experience of local conditions are necessary for safe and economical ship operation.

According to our core task model, the object should also be decomposed from a process-centred point of view. This takes place in two respects that are represented in the upper part of Figure 3.1. These are the decomposition of the sequential phases of the task on the one hand, and the decomposition of result-critical functions of the domain on the other. The functions provide a generic formative aspect to the task and express the functional significance of different tasks that may be decomposed to fulfil specific goals. The need to model tasks in particular situations creates the third dimension. During a number of studies, we have developed practical modelling techniques for the analysis of the features of the work domain and the work situation (Hukki and Norros 1993; Hukki and Norros 1998; Holmberg *et al.* 1999). These models can be characterized as representing a functional constraint oriented analysis of situations and resemble those proposed by both Rasmussen (1986) and Vicente (1999).

The piloting task can be seen as special case and a combination of the more generic tasks of navigation in which the crucial goal is to keep the vessel on course and to steer it to its destination. In order to achieve this in the narrow and complex areas of sea around ports, it is also necessary to know where it is safe for the ship to sail. Piloting is thus a task for navigators who are acquainted with local waters. In the next step of analysis, we decomposed piloting into three phases: preparation, building a team and co-operative navigation and steering. The phases are interdependent, as becomes evident when the phases are set in relation to the functionally significant features that give meaning to the tasks they include. They are divided into navigational and co-operative features. For example, there are several critical features of co-operation. One of the most significant is transparency of performance – allowing the bridge crew and the pilot to perceive what is going on. This can be subdivided into the transparency of the goal, the transparency of the interaction and the transparency of the tools. A chart showing the planned route makes the goal transparent, a helmsman repeating directions to change course makes interaction more transparent and clear displays on automatic equipment make the tools more transparent. Thus in the team-building phase, the transparency of the activity puts constraints on the division of labour and the use of the available navigation equipment. Unfortunately, in these studies it was not possible to carry out orientation interviews that would have provided information about the subjects' own framing of the object of activity, and the intrinsic constraints they placed on their activity.

Situation as habit

In our core task analysis, action is contextualized also from the point of view of the subjective dispositions to act in it. We are interested in analysing how the actors take into account the possibilities and the constraints of the situation in their action. To analyse this, we apply the pragmatist idea that the situation can be understood as the sensitivity of the person to the situational possibilities and constraints and his or her readiness to act in it (Peirce 1903/1998; Bourdieu 1990). Thus the situation is conceived as habit. The inferences we make are depicted in the lower part of the model in Figure 3.1.

According to the model, the behavioural criteria which define habits of action are alternative ways of taking into account the constraints and possibilities of the situation. They can be identified as perception–action cycles of human–environment interaction, and evaluated against the psychological demands placed on the activity. These demands are conceptualized by the analyst as psychological task-related expressions of the logic according to which individuals themselves take into account the critical functions of the activity. These different logics reflect the above mentioned internal dynamism of the habit (doubt–belief mediated through abductive reasoning) when a person is interacting with the environment. The components of the expert identity concept are used in the core task analysis to interpret the meaning of critical functions in respect of psychological core task demands and criteria for habits of acting.

In the study of piloting, the habit-centred analysis provides a basis for the analysis and evaluation of the empirical observations of the course of action taken during the voyage. The perception–action cycles are conceived as operations that describe the use of the material resources and the consideration of situational demands. In piloting, the central material resources are maps, plans and other information about the route; information about the progress of the voyage; communications; and professional concepts. The tool-using interactions are connected with relevant psychological core task demands and interpreted as meaning structures (habits) which express the actors' accounts of the functional constraints. Psychological core task demands that refer particularly to the co-operative aspects of the task include:

- active constructing and maintenance of an *ad-hoc* team;
- formation and maintenance of a shared interpretation of the situation;
- communication of intentions; and
- exercising control of performance through monitoring action.

The situational resource-related criteria for ways of navigating express these (and other) psychological evaluation categories to greater or lesser extent. The criteria are drawn from the empirical material on which the analysis is carried out. As a result of the analysis the ways of piloting could be defined in navigational and co-operative respects. These results were used to explain actual courses of action (see the centre of Figure 3.1).

Our studies of normal piloting and accidents indicate that the problems in piloting actions arise from two major causes. First, there are difficulties in making use of the available navigation technology within the frame of traditional piloting practices. The technology, if implemented properly, increases the accuracy of navigation on the constricted routes that have small safety margins for large ships, but its use conflicts with established ways of doing the job. Second, effective piloting depends on co-operation, a skill not emphasized in traditional models of piloting practice. In fact, communication and the use of collaborative tools may be interpreted as indications of lack of expertise. The contextual analysis of action provides an empirical description of the critical content of the work in question, what we call the core task. This includes the actions that constitute the work, the habits of action and how the habits of action are realized in particular courses of action. Finally, it reveals what consequences the particular features of the habits of acting have on the development of expertise.

Conclusion

Core task analysis and the concept of expertise

Core task analysis methodology is a promising tool for clarifying the nature of expertise and how competencies develop through practice. The strength of the model is its suitability for the empirical analysis of everyday working situations. In the past, it has been difficult to bridge the gap between knowledge and skill in studies of expertise (Lehtinen and Palonen 1997). Schön (1988) called the dominant conception of practice the model of technical rationality, which represents knowledge as specialized, scientific and standardized and superior to practical know-how. This conception of expertise still exerts some influence today. However, in recent studies of expertise, attention has been given to the social and contextual nature of expert knowledge (Eteläpelto 1997). In this connection, the interplay between knowledge and skill offers an explanation of how people manage novel or problem situations. Expert thinking has been found to be characterized by metacognitive processes postulated as necessary for acting in such situations (e.g. Chi *et al.* 1988; Cannon-Bowers and Bell 1997; Klein 1993). The major components of expert knowledge are defined as practical, formal and metacognitive knowledge (Bereiter and Scardamalia 1993). What distinguishes metacognitive knowledge from the other two forms is that it is always related to the person's own action and its control. The specific role of metacognitive knowledge is to integrate and filter the use of practical and formal knowledge about the object, which would explain people's ability to cope with situational constraints (Bereiter and Scardamalia 1993).

With the habit-centred analysis of situated actions that is included in the core task analysis methodology we attempt to identify the interplay of operative and epistemic intentions in the course of action in the normal working situation. The instrumental interactions of an actor with his or her environment are interpreted as habits, and they express a more or less complete realization of the unity of operating and knowing, and routine and reflexivity in action. Our empirical results of analyses of actions in several process control domains indicate a distinction between interpretative and reactive habits of acting among experts. This distinction is related with observed differences in the epistemic attitude towards the object of activity. The interpretative habit of acting, that seems to facilitate a constructive practice, is connected with the acknowledgement of the contingencies in the object and an intention therefore to create knowledge through engaging oneself attentively with the particular object (Klemola and Norros 2001).

The contribution of core task analysis to understanding organizational and work processes

Due to the distributed nature of many modern work processes and the highly specialized knowledge needed to cope with them, supervisory control is normally focused on separate functions, each of which relates mainly to one of the main objectives of organizations: safety, quality and effectiveness. Neither the management, nor the authorities that in many cases control the activities of industrial or other organizations, are in direct contact with the requirements of the ongoing production process itself. Thus achieving production goals has to be verified in a mediated, indirect manner. The control measures are also more or less indirect (Reiman and Norros 2002). In this situation, it seems rational from the point of view of management to create different kinds of standard measure to guide and control the practices of the production personnel. The increase in reliability can be seen as a result of the very standardization of practices. This 'reliability through standardization' philosophy has its roots in the epistemology of technical rationality and it is reflected in the concrete methods used in organizations, such as automation of functions or the proceduralization of work performance.

There is a need to analyse whether and in what sense the standardization-oriented reliability strategy contradicts with the two major functionally necessary qualifications that we have found to be important features of expertise in process control and in modern knowledge intensive work in general. First, as indicated by Mariani in Chapter 2, the uncertainties and complexities of the work processes call for expertise that is characterized by judgement and ability to meet situational demands. This is incompatible with reliability-through-standardization thinking, and the contradiction is related to Perrow's (1984) distinction between the need for centralized control and distributed decision-making in complex and tightly-coupled systems. Second, the major component of expertise is personal. Expertise is inseparable from the active, intentional subject. The reliability-through-standardization strategy clearly jeopardizes this principle as it explicitly requires a decrease in the dependence of the outcome on the person. As a result, this reliability strategy and its practical methods may convey to workers a message that neither their practical skills nor their personal efforts are valued in the organization. This psychological effect may be one of the significant sources of unreliability in the modern knowledge-intensive organization.

In recent years, ensuring the effective creation and distribution of knowledge has become a major managerial concern in many organizations. This indicates a preference for an alternative survival strategy that acknowledges the intelligence and creativeness of human actors in maintaining high reliability and quality. This strategy may be called a strategy of adaptation and development and it aims at finding ways to cope with the contingencies typical in the knowledge-intensive organization as an open system. In this context, the concept of work process knowledge may be interpreted as a means of making tangible what knowledge is as an organizational phenomenon. We have described core task analysis methodology as one possible tool for defining work process knowledge in a contextualized way in a particular organization or work domain. Beyond its capability to specify the core task in a particular domain through modelling and analysis of actual performance, it has a further advantage. In coherence with the concept of work process knowledge, it adopts an epistemological position that emphasizes the unity of knowing and acting. Knowledge is conceived as constructed through personal instrumental practice in a social community. Practice is the means to make sense in an uncertain world. For these reasons, we believe that core task analysis methodology provides organizations with an effective tool for articulating and developing the work process knowledge that is embedded in the communities of practice which constitute each organization, and which expresses itself in the everyday work of the employees.

4 The work process knowledge of chemical laboratory assistants

Martin Fischer and Peter Röben

This chapter presents two case studies which reveal how work process knowledge is embedded in the historically established division of labour in chemical laboratories, and how it is constructed from experience as well as from scientific knowledge. Although laboratory assistants' work consists mainly of following the instructions of the laboratory scientists, detailed study of the work in this context reveals that the assistants create knowledge about the work process. We theorize this way of knowing as knowledge about the aim of the work, its object, the form of the object and working procedures for achieving the desired aim.

Growth of the modern chemical laboratory

The origins of chemical technology lie in the inorganic chemicals industry which emerged in the eighteenth century, due to the rapidly growing demand for textiles and the discovery that chemical substances such as sulphuric acid and soda could be used for manufacturing and colouring textiles (Strube 1989). The procedures developed by chemists to produce inorganic elements – as, for example, the Leblanc process (1791) for the production of soda, which was transformed into the first mass production of chemicals by James Musprat in 1813 – was fundamental in the further development of the process industry. The work processes required for these procedures were simple transporting and charging actions, performed under the most unfavourable conditions. The first examples of skilled work in chemistry are not found in this production context but in the chemical laboratory. The job of the laboratory assistant evolved from the assistants or helpers who were initially given tasks such as stirring solutions and cleaning glasses. The rapid development of colour chemistry, followed by the growth of pharmaceutical chemistry, created large industrial laboratories which differed fundamentally from the scientific laboratories by then common in universities. In these industrial laboratories, the emphasis was not on ingenuity with test tubes and retorts, but on the systematic and exhaustive search for new variations of already discovered compounds. All these new variations were thoroughly tested for properties that could be used commercially. Standardized procedures and methods were developed in order to make this search as effective as possible. These routine procedures did not have to be carried out by chemists, so special staff were employed for this role – laboratory assistants. They existed long before the first recognized occupational profiles for them were developed in the 1930s and 1940s in Switzerland, and in the 1950s in Germany (Mohler 1970; Schmauderer 1973).

Later in the century, technological developments, such as the introduction of electronic and mechanical instruments, made this work unnecessary, and a new division of labour between the laboratory assistant and chemist gradually emerged. The new role of the laboratory assistant has been created by developments in the chemical industry; these have led to a new kind of laboratory work which can be carried out by assistants without the direct supervision of chemists. Recent investigations of the work of laboratory assistants demonstrate that they possess a specific kind of work process knowledge (Kruse 1986; Fischer 1996, 2000) which is quite different from academic knowledge of chemistry (Fischer and Röben 1997). In the following sections, we will analyse work in chemical laboratories in large companies and in smaller independent laboratories, in order to clarify the nature of this knowledge.

The investigation

As part of a research project entitled 'computer-aided and experience-guided learning in chemical work' (Röben, Siebeck and Storz 1998), nine sessions of participant observation (each of one day's duration), 26 qualitative interviews and three workshops were arranged to investigate the social shaping of work and technology. The project focused on the introduction of two technical laboratory information systems into the two laboratories that participated in the project (A and B). This was evaluated for a period of about 2 years. In addition to the laboratories participating in the project, two other laboratories (C and D) were included in the investigation.

- Laboratory A is the analytical laboratory of a pharmaceutical company with around 1,800 employees at the site and 48 employees in this laboratory.
- Laboratory B is an independent environmental laboratory with around 15 employees.
- Laboratory C is the central laboratory of a large chemical industry group (with about 200 employees in the laboratory).
- Laboratory D is the quality assurance laboratory (around 200 employees) of a world-wide pharmaceutical company of medium size (around 5,000 employees).

Work in an analytical laboratory in the pharmaceutical industry

Our first case study is the analytic laboratory of a large pharmaceutical concern (Röben, Siebeck and Storz 1998). Here the work is similar to what was described in the previous section: variations are introduced in existing substances by a synthetic chemist, and these are subjected to standardized tests to determine their chemical properties. The analytic laboratory is involved in both the development of new medicines to the laboratory standard and the translation of the chemical reaction from the laboratory standard to the production standard. It provides the following services:

1   To the synthetic chemist: the analytic laboratory is responsible for determining the structure, purity and content of the substances produced by synthetic chemists.
2   To the pharmacologist: the laboratory develops the first procedure for ascertaining the identity, purity and content of the screening substances.
3   To the production department: the laboratory offers advice with regard to possible ways of synthesizing the substance. Protocols for determining the identity, purity and contents of the by-products of this synthesis are worked out.
4   To galenics: all galenist examinations, stability tests in particular, are carried out in the laboratory.

Laboratory organization

The fundamental principle of the organization of a chemical laboratory is the established division of labour between the chemist and the laboratory assistant. Traditionally, the latter is considered the former's helper. In the companies we surveyed, this was the way the roles were perceived, although some changes were on their way. The employees of the laboratory work in teams mostly made up of one chemist and several laboratory assistants. Every team has access to one or more analytical procedures. The number of people working in a team depends on the amount of work needed for the analytical methods used, and also on the complexity of these methods (which sometimes create great demands on the capacity of the teams).

The work of the chemists in the laboratory

Chemists alone possess scientific knowledge regarding the structures, reactions and properties of chemical substances. They and other scientists (for example, pharmacists) usually hold two basic functions in the laboratory. One is acting as heads of the laboratory, i.e. they are in charge of a team which usually consists of two to five laboratory employees, and the other is

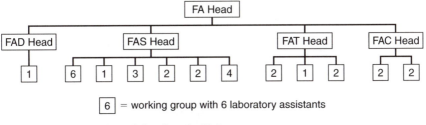

6 = working group with 6 laboratory assistants

Figure 4.1 Organization of the chemical laboratory

Note
FA: Department of research in analytical chemistry. D: Documentation.
S: clarification of structure. T: process technology. C: chromatography.

taking charge of projects (see Figure 4.1). In the latter role, they have to decide what is to be measured, in what form and with which methods. These decisions often result from discussions with other chemists.

The work process of laboratory assistants

The work of the laboratory assistant in an analytical laboratory is generally focused on determining the quality and the quantity of substances (Ciommer 1996). The most important outcomes of the laboratory assistant's work are measurements, in contrast with other kinds of work where measurements are a means to an end (see Figure 4.2).

For the chemical laboratory assistant, documenting the measurement is usually the end of his or her task, whereupon he or she turns to the next analysis. Although, at first glance, the work of the laboratory assistant seems incomplete, this is due to the division of labour which in this well-developed form can be found only in the chemical laboratory. If we look at the stages of fulfilling an order in an analytical service laboratory, we can see the work of the laboratory assistant in the context of the work of the chemist (Figure 4.3). The 'incompleteness' of the laboratory assistant's work is due to the fact that the scientist in the laboratory – usually a chemist – decides which methods of analysis are to be used before the laboratory assistant starts work. The bare figure, the pure measurement, only achieves meaning through the chemist's work.

A chemical analysis in its entirety goes through the stages of taking samples, preparing samples, analysis and evaluation. The work of those in jobs like the laboratory assistant consists mainly of the preparation of

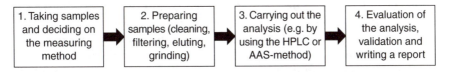

Figure 4.2 Schematic representation of the stages in the measuring process

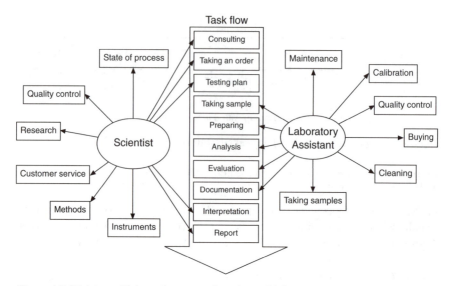

Figure 4.3 Division of labour between chemist and laboratory assistant

samples and then the process of taking measurements. The academic staff in the laboratory (the chemists and the pharmacists) are occupied with planning and carrying out analyses as well as evaluating and controlling the results for validity.

The work of the non-academic laboratory staff in preparing the samples is of course critical to the quality of the measurement. The actual measuring is done automatically by computer-controlled instruments. When they were first introduced, these instruments made it seem as if the job could be done by semi-skilled assistants. However, this is a misapprehension: while the analysis is performed on a sample, the results are not supposed to speak for the sample itself but for the population from which the sample is taken. If, for example, the water from a lake is tested to ascertain whether it is safe to swim, the samples must be representative of the whole lake. Quite apart from the way the samples are drawn, the representativeness of the sample must not be compromised by any treatment carried out before measuring. Meeting these conditions requires working closely to the instructions – but also being aware of the context of the analysis.

The procedure for a given analysis might specify, for example, that the sample should be crushed with a pestle and mortar, dissolved in a solution and then filtered. The procedures frequently do not say anything about the method of filtering, although it is by no means a trivial issue which filter is used. Especially with tests for minute traces of a substance, choosing the wrong filter can lead to useless results, as the dissolving of parts of the filter in the solution influences the results. Thus in order to follow instructions successfully, laboratory assistants need a kind of knowledge which can be called 'context awareness' (*Zusammenhangswahrnehmung*) (Fleig and Schneider 1995: 8) or 'context comprehension' (*Zusammenhangsverständnis*) (see Laur-Ernst *et al.* 1990: 14). This knowledge connects the requirements of the task with the company-specific conditions under which the task is to be carried out. Inevitably, such knowledge is acquired from the experience gained by working in a specific laboratory. Thus a laboratory employee knows 'his' or 'her' ultrasonic baths, and also knows that (for instance) the 5 minutes referred to in an instruction for ultrasonic baths might require 8 minutes with his or her particular device. Consider the following statement by an employee:

> In everyday work, I think it is better if everyone works with his own equipment. Then one knows immediately whether or not the result is a true one – someone else cannot make this judgment so quickly. For example, someone else might think that water titration would just take a certain time on my equipment, but I know that when a Karl-Fischer-titration has exceeded a certain time, then the process has not gone right. One gets a feeling for this. And no one can have this feeling, if he or she carries out the procedure only once in a while. I do water titration every day.

Experiential knowledge of this kind is often founded on lack of success in previous attempts to take measurements. It is paradoxical that if a measurement procedure is always carried out without error the opportunity to learn from experience is limited (Wehner 1993: 53). The experience of failure forces laboratory assistants to think out their actions and prompts them to reflect on them. The increased cost of having to repeat failed measurements has to be balanced against the contribution to the development of individual competence and quality assurance within the organization:

> Another example from UV-spectroscopy: I had made a solution of a substance and noticed it getting cloudy. In these cases you have to work out how to do it right. You have to do that by yourself; only you can think of how to do it better. Usually the substance was (separately) placed in methanol in hydrochloric acid and soda lye and dissolved. But once I had the problem that the solution became cloudy in hydrochloric acid as well as in soda lye (hence a mixture of solvents). Because the otherwise pure soda lye and the otherwise pure hydrochloric acid contained an element of methanol it stayed clear. To think of something like that you have to have experience. In that case I learned that from my colleague.

In the next part of the chapter, two typical examples are described to illustrate how work process knowledge grows out of practice. Both cases also show the extent to which knowledge accumulated by experience and scientific knowledge are integrated in the construction of work process knowledge.

Experience and scientific knowledge in thin-layer chromatography

The first example is thin-layer chromatography. Figure 4.4 shows the principles of this technique. A substance sent through to the laboratory for examination is separated as in Figure 4.4B, and a quantitative evaluation is carried out. Although this can be done automatically, setting up the machine can take so much time that automatic methods are used only if a more precise measurement is needed than can be achieved by the naked eye. Despite the obvious advantages of automation, thin-layer chromatography can be performed routinely by human operators, provided that full instructions are given and the right mobile liquid is supplied. With practice, the skill is automatized, freeing the conscious mind for other activities such as scheduling work loads. However, thin-layer chromatography becomes more demanding for a newly synthesized substance, because in this case, it is unusual to know in advance which is the optimal mobile liquid for separating the sample. Tests have to be carried out to find out which combination best divides the mixture to be examined, and it may well take several weeks before the optimal mobile liquid is found.

The work process knowledge of the laboratory assistant is a combination of theoretical and experiential knowledge. The experiential compo-

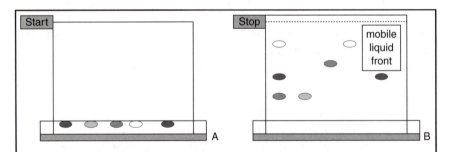

A substance to be examined is applied to a silica gel plate (stationary phase) (first patch down left in A). For comparison, four reference substances are applied (the four patches to its right). The plate is put in a mobile liquid bath. The mobile liquid (mobile phase) carries the applied substances, and depending on the substances different dynamic equilibria are obtained which cause the different substances to pass the separation distance at different speeds. Staying behind the mobile liquid front is called 'retention' (see B). The chromatograph to be evaluated (B) allows the conclusion that some of the reference substances (the first, the third and the fourth patch right of the substance examined) are contained in the examined substance. The intensity of the colouring and the size of a patch can be used for quantitative evaluation.

Figure 4.4 The principle of thin-layer chromatography

nent can be illustrated by the fact that the laboratory assistant learns from carrying out many experiments that there is a relationship between the 'tail courses' which appear on patches of the substance under test and the way the substances divide. This purely contingent knowledge is used to narrow down the search for the right mobile. The accumulation of these experiences over many years leads to a unique memory for tail course forms similar to what has been observed in other workers, for example workers who deal with materials such as steel and china clay (Rubinstein 1973: 92).

An example of the laboratory assistant's use of scientific knowledge is when the solution is systematically varied on the basis of the polarities of its components, in particular the size of the dipole moment of the substance. In this way, experiential knowledge (the form of the tail courses of different solvents) may be combined with scientific knowledge (about the polarity of substances) to support a decision about how to carry out the measurement. (Figure 4.5 shows an example of a thin-layer chromatograph.)

It is important to appreciate how the laboratory assistant uses this scientific knowledge. The knowledge of dipole moment used by the laboratory assistant is that the more polar a solvent, the more successfully can

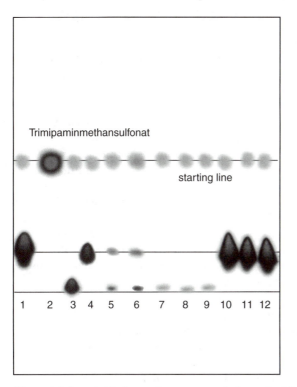

Figure 4.5 A real thin-layer chromatograph from the laboratory

a polar substance be dissolved in it. Rarely does a laboratory assistant make use of knowledge about the structure of the substance to be dissolved. For this reason, laboratory assistants generally refer to substances using the numbers assigned to them within the company, as they are easier to use than the long chemical names. The chemist, on the other hand, always makes use of his or her knowledge of the structure of the substance. For him or her, the numbers assigned within the company are only 'house numbers'. The properties of a particular substance the chemist discovers in the course of his or her work on that substance is related to general chemical structures. The laboratory assistant's thinking, on the other hand, remains embedded in a practical schema such as 'substance A reacts like substance B, therefore I can use what I know about A in dealing with B'. The laboratory assistant does not give the reason for the similarity in terms of the chemical structure of the two substances. The judgement based on experience can be right, but there is no scientific justification for it.

Experience and scientific knowledge in atom absorption spectroscopy

The second example concerns the work of a laboratory assistant in charge of atom absorption spectroscopy. This is a relatively costly technique for detecting metals in quantities as small as 1 nanogram ($1\,ng = 0.000\,000\,001\,g$). The measuring procedure is basically the same as for other spectroscopic procedures. A source of light sends a wavelength typical of a certain metal. This light crosses a test chamber in which the sample is vapourized at temperatures between 850 and 900°C. On its way through the test chamber, the light is absorbed and then measured. The extent of absorption of light by the sample gives the concentration of the test substance. Newly built instruments for atom absorption spectroscopy are controlled by a computer program. The values for temperatures, wavelengths, light power, etc. are entered into a graphical user interface and are not adjusted at the device itself. Thus the laboratory assistant does not gain direct experience of the effects of these adjustments, whereas in older instruments the power is adjusted directly at a potentiometer near the lamp case. There are considerable differences in the error detection rates of the different generations of instruments. For example, a simple typing error can cause a completely unexpected reaction from a newer instrument. This kind of problem is difficult to diagnose on the basis of familiarity with the equipment, and so the requirements for abstract thinking are considerably higher than with the old instruments.

In an interview, the laboratory assistant in charge of atom absorption spectroscopy expressed a preference for the old instrument because it could measure arsenic in different valences, which she claimed the new instrument could not do. This was done by selecting a temperature which allowed the two arsenic modifications to be detected at different times. In fact, this was possible with the new instrument too, but the layout of the graphical user interface did not make this clear and the laboratory assistant was not aware of it.

The computerization of laboratories has created a new range of ways in which laboratory assistants interact with measuring instruments. The older instruments were more suitable for learning from experience, due to the tight coupling of the controls and the effects on the instrument. This also made it easier to diagnose errors. However, with modern computerized measuring instruments, the relationship between adjustments of the graphical user interface and changes in the instrument is less tightly coupled, and demands an increased ability to think in the abstract. In the laboratory studied, the introduction of computers was stressful for the laboratory assistant concerned. This was due to the business environment in which the laboratory was operating, providing analytical services in a highly competitive field where laboratories compete on the basis of price and willingness to deliver results quickly if requested by the customer (Röben 1997). Having invested a lot of money in the new instrumentation, the laboratory wished to intensify the work. While the laboratory assistant was one of the most experienced employees, she was not experienced with computers and tried to come to terms with her anxiety by exploring the relationships between the adjustments she made on the graphical user interface and the behaviour of the instrument. This pragmatic way of making sense of the work situation – What does the instrument do when I adjust it like this? – is central to the construction of work process knowledge. It is a way of overcoming the dissonance between theoretical knowledge and practical activity (Schumann *et al.* 1994).

Conclusion

The example of the laboratory assistant mastering the technique of thin-layer chromatography shows how the work process requires both scientific and practical knowledge. Knowledge about the dipole moment of the solvent does not come from personal experience but from the science of chemistry. The laboratory assistant makes a pragmatic reconceptualization of this knowledge in the light of her knowledge of both the effects of varying the different polar components of the mobile liquid and the form of the tail courses. Both of the latter are derived from practical experience. This integration of scientific understanding and practical know-how into what we call work process knowledge is pragmatic in the sense that it is done to guide the activity of separating the substance under test (compare the similar way in which the work process knowledge of electrical maintenance technicians is constructed, described by Samurçay and Vidal in Chapter 11).

An important implication is that if a laboratory assistant lacks the relevant scientific understanding, it is not possible to develop adequate work process knowledge. This is very clear in the second example. In the course of her working life, the laboratory assistant has not only acquired practical experiences but also a *method of learning* by experience. An important element of this method is analysing the phenomena she observes in the laboratory. When provided with an unfamiliar tool (the computer-controlled measuring instrument) she can no longer rely on this way of acquiring the experiential component of work process knowledge, experiences anxiety and tries to find a new way of generating the practical knowledge she needs.

If work process knowledge is defined as a construction out of scientific and practical knowledge, the problem arises of explaining how such different ways of knowing can be integrated into a unitary cognitive process. Earlier definitions of work process knowledge do not enlighten us on this point, as they represent it as a separate category of knowledge defined by its content, i.e. understanding both the labour process and the production process. However, theoretical models of the work process have been extant since the ancient Greeks, and are just as valid when applied to modern work processes. Aristotle's work is relevant to the point under discussion and will now be briefly introduced.

The four aspects of the work process according to Aristotle are the *causa finalis* (the aim of the work process towards which all other aspects are oriented), the *causa materialis* (the work object, the material worked on), the *causa formalis* (the form embossed on the material) and the *causa efficiens* (the working procedure, the tool). For Aristotle, the most important aspect is the *causa finalis*, i.e. the ultimate target at which the whole work process is aimed (Figure 4.6; Aristotle 1982). In a modern workplace characterized by a Tayloristic division of labour, this probably appears unreal. Whose job description in such a workplace (other than the senior managers') specifies the ultimate aim of their activity? While Aristotle is thinking of the sculptor who carves a figure out of marble and who is aware of the finished sculpture as the ultimate aim of his or her work,

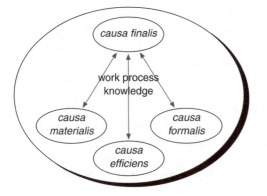

Figure 4.6 The four aspects of the work process according to Aristotle

much modern industrial work is characterized by the fact that the target of the production process lies beyond the scope of individual responsibilities. However, at a time when industry is adopting the principles of flexible production and total quality management, it is important for all employees to be aware of ultimate goals. Take, for example, the laboratory assistant's work. The immediate aim might be to isolate chemical substances for testing, but this is in pursuit of a more ultimate aim such as checking the water quality of a lake for health reasons. During all steps of the work process, the laboratory assistant has to keep this overall aim in mind in order to ensure high quality.

According to Aristotle, the *causa finalis* organizes all other components of the work process in order to ensure that the overall aim is met. It is the most important in that it guides the others, although they are also important for the success of the work process. For Aristotle, the *causa formalis* is the form which the sculptor has in mind before he or she makes the first cut with the chisel, but in modern industry it may be a technical drawing or a business plan. In the case of the chemical laboratory assistant, it is the specification for the analysis or the synthesis that is required. Although this drawing or specification is often made by someone other than the skilled worker who uses it, the worker will have to learn and understand it before he or she uses it in the work process. The *causa formalis* or specification given to the chemical laboratory assistant has to be converted into concrete actions, and during this conversion, both theoretical knowledge and practical knowledge gained from experience are integrated in the process we call the construction of work process knowledge.

The *causa materialis* in the broadest sense includes the objects which are needed to carry out the work process and which are altered within the course of work. In Aristotle's example of the sculptor, this would be the marble of which the sculpture is made. In modern work processes the *causa materialis* could be raw steel, for example. The classification is of course relative to the situation under consideration; raw steel is the *causa finalis* of the work process at the open-hearth furnace, and marble is the *causa finalis* for the quarry worker while at the same time it is the *causa materialis* for the sculptor. In the case of the chemical laboratory assistant, substances are separated by chemical reactions and these are supplied by nature. The fourth element in the work process, the *causa efficiens*, is the energy brought to the work process and which is therefore responsible for its dynamics. While for Aristotle's sculptor this is muscle power, in chemical laboratories various computer-controlled instruments and auxiliary substances such as solvents are used. While knowledge of the material and its relationship with the tool are of great importance in the sculptor's work, careful handling of instruments and substances without neglecting safety regulations is a major requirement of the laboratory assistant's work.

On the basis of this model, we suggest that work process knowledge includes the elements of the work process, i.e. the aim of work, the material or object of work, the work procedure, and the form embossed on the object.

This schema enables us to relate experiential and scientific knowledge (Figure 4.7). Using the four-way classification of the different aspects of the content of work process knowledge, we can enquire whether each was gained from practical experience or from scientific study (see also Kruse, Krüger and Caprile in Chapter 15). Of course, the Aristotelian model has to be expanded and adapted to fit modern work situations. The model itself allows detailed insight into relevant aspects of work process knowledge as far as concrete actions for work purposes are concerned. Today, and in contrast to the example used by Aristotle, these actions have to be integrated into a framework of co-operation and a division of labour, and these actions have to be interpreted within the economic goals being pursued by modern capitalist societies.

At the beginning of this chapter, we suggested that work process knowledge has several facets. It includes on the one hand knowledge of the aspects of the direct work process as actually performed by the worker. On the other hand, this usually takes place in a company. Thus the work process of the individual worker is not only aimed at a concrete product but also at contributing to the economic framework of profitable production and services. In other words, every work process is also part of an economic process. In recent years, many sectors have undergone a process of delegating more responsibility for business success to the workers themselves. In some cases, ordinary workers now perform tasks previously reserved for managers. But there remains a basic difference between work process knowledge and the knowledge of managers. Those who have acquired work process knowledge know the demands of the work process by direct experience – production procedures, specifications and work out-

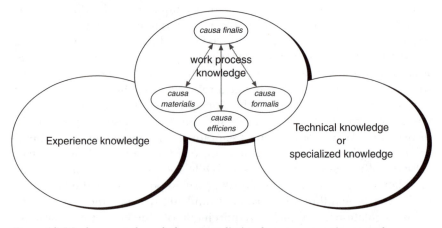

Figure 4.7 Work process knowledge as mediation between experience and technical or specialized knowledge

comes – and not only how these elements are depicted theoretically. Such knowledge is often tacit. Hence, the significance of work process knowledge is that it is a way of knowing that relates the concrete and individual experience of work on the one hand with the rules and objectives of the overall labour process within the life of the company on the other. It is a way of understanding one's own direct responsibilities in relation to the company's overall organization. It includes the elements of the individual work process described by Aristotle as well as knowledge of how to embed one's own work within the work process of the company as a whole.

In this chapter, we have mainly discussed the relation between subject and object inherent in the working practices of laboratory assistants. This relation is included in a wider activity system as described by Engeström (1987) and Engeström and Cole (1997: 304). As Figure 4.8 shows, this contains elements such as social rules, community and a division of labour as well as mediating artifacts. We suggest that work process knowledge refers to all the aspects of an activity system. Both case studies presented in this chapter concentrated on the upper part of the pyramid suggested by Engeström (Figure 4.8).[1]

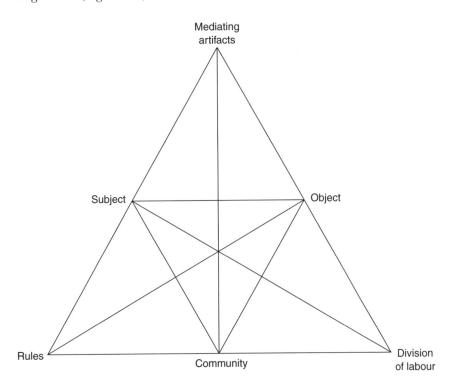

Figure 4.8 Elements of an activity system according to Engeström (1987)

Source: © 1987 Yrjö Engeström, *Learning by Expanding*, p. 178. Reprinted here with permission.

What kind of conclusions for the organization of vocational education and training can be drawn from these case studies? In order to become competent an individual needs to acquire work process knowledge in terms of the elements of work postulated by Aristotle. This implies that learning should be organized in the form of 'learning and working tasks' through which these elements of the work process can by explored by the individual learner. This is not usually the case in vocational education and training, as these elements have often been separated from each other by the practices of both technical colleges and companies, which tend to reproduce a Taylorist division of labour (see Rabardel and Duvenci-Langa, Chapter 5). The new European occupational profile of car mechatronics and its innovatory curriculum can be seen as an attempt to put these elements together again. It is structured according to the overall work process, allowing the learner to explore these elements from the very beginning (see the account of this curriculum by Fischer and Rauner in Chapter 12).

Note

1 The aim of a current research project on organizational learning in the European chemical industry to explore the subject–object relationship within a wide activity system (Fischer and Röben 2001, 2002).

5 Technological change and the construction of competence

Pierre Rabardel and Stella Duvenci-Langa

As Chapter 4 demonstrates, although formal training is important, there are many kinds of competence that are acquired only through experience (Rogalski 1995; Samurçay 1995; Leplat 1997; Fischer and Stuber 1998). Consequently, the study of the forms, modalities and mechanisms of the development of vocational competence in and through work is a central concern for research in this field. One of the characteristics of this development is that it takes place over periods measured in months or years, another that it is strongly contextualized by the situations the learners encounter in the workplace. The research presented in this chapter investigates both of these characteristics. Context dependence is analysed from two perspectives. First, we focus on a situation of technological change in which an operator converts from a manual machine-tool to a digital machine-tool (CNC) (for further discussion of this transition, see Böhle *et al.* 1994; Jeantet and Tiger 1998; Rabardel *et al.* 1988). Second, given that the dynamics of the work process continue to evolve after the worker transfers to the digital machine-tool, we compare the two parallel processes of the development of the work process and the development of competence. The second characteristic, the long period of time over which competence develops, is studied by collecting data for more than a year. This enables us to monitor the cumulative construction of competence in considerable detail.

In the first part of this chapter, we will present the assumptions that underlie the training that the operators received before the change to a new type of machine. These underestimate the role of experience (Malsh 1987), an assumption questioned by some researchers (Adler 1992; Osaki 1992; Rabardel 1995) as well as by the present data. We then present an analysis of the development of tasks related to the change from one machine to another, before analysing the twin dynamics of change in competencies and change in the work process (Engeström 1991; Kuuti 1995). We will then expand on our results by constructing a general analytical model – 'People at Work' – which among other things is intended to give insight into the nature of work process knowledge. Finally, we will conclude by discussing three points: the temporal dimensions of the dynamics of competence, the mechanisms by which competence is acquired and transferred, and the interaction between dynamics of competencies and the dynamics of work processes.

Training in CNC machine-tools: which competencies for which job?

One operator skilled in the handling of a manual machine-tool (MMT) was chosen to begin using the new digital machine-tool (CNC). To prepare for the change from one machine to the other, management set up a training programme based on the acquisition of declarative and procedural knowledge for the use of digital commands. This training was in two stages, one week of training with the supplier and one week in a vocational training centre for adults. The week's training with the supplier aimed to provide general familiarization with the new system and the procedures for its use. This training consisted in essence of taking the trainee through the user's manual detailing the digital controls. It was the operator's first encounter with the new system. However, he was not given the opportunity to use the machine for actual jobs, or even to observe them, for the machine was non-operational at the time of training. The operator described the training as a 'guided tour' of the machine.

A few weeks after the CNC machine was installed in the workshop, the management sent the operator on a course at a vocational training centre. This was largely remedial, as he was considered to have a low level of education. The training consisted of theoretical and general knowledge on the functioning of the digital commands, illustrated by very few practical applications. The training situation was very different from the work situation in terms of the materials used: in training, the operator worked on metal units, whereas in the factory he worked on grindstones with special characteristics. The configuration of the machine, the interactive mode and the machining tools were all completely different. According to the operator, the work situation and the training situation had nothing in common. Consequently, we can state the assumptions underlying the company's ways of retraining the operator for the CNC machine as follows.

- The operator is considered to have a 'low level of education' and this can be compensated for by the acquisition of general and 'theoretical' knowledge on the machine and its modalities of use.
- Moving from one machine to the other is seen as discontinuous. It is viewed as a dichotomy in which either completely new competencies are required for the CNC machine, or the old competencies can be used to operate the new machine.
- The digital nature of the new machine is seen as the heart of the problem. The work process under the new conditions, the specific nature of the work objects and the units to be produced, the mater-

ials, tools, etc. are considered irrelevant and are eliminated from the training process. As a result, the operator can establish few connections between his own work situation and the training situations.

Differences between turning with a traditional machine-tool and turning with a digital machine-tool

Performing a manual task can be described as closed loop behaviour. The operator's action on the machine is simultaneous to his awareness of the effects of this action, allowing him or her to gain information on the state of turning in real time and to continuously regulate his or her action. This process is known as regulation by retroaction. Turning with a CNC machine is characterized by the existence of an open loop. The operator's action on the machine (programming) precedes his or her awareness of the effects of this action (i.e. it takes place before the machine goes to work on the material). This does not allow the operator to gain feedback in real time. He or she must anticipate the intermediary states of turning when acting on the machine at the beginning of the cycle. This type of regulation is known as proaction. Changing from one machine type to the other thus implies, at least in principle, a move from retroactive behaviour to proactive behaviour, and changes in corresponding competencies. We will see that these changes develop over long periods and are much more complex than an initial analysis of the task leads us to believe. We now turn to examine the twin dynamics of competence development and changes in the work process.

The twin evolutionary dynamics of competence and work processes

The crucial feature of the situation under investigation is that we are dealing with two types of dynamics: the dynamics of the operator's progressively increasing ability to operate the machine and his or her discovery of new ways of completing the work, and on the other hand, the dynamics of the changing context which includes the machine, the tasks and the organization of the work in general. These twin dynamics develop over long periods. Our observations were carried out over more than a year and allowed us to identify several phases in the introduction and use of the machine after digitalization: an initiation phase followed by a phase of constructing new competencies. Throughout these two phases, the machines themselves also undergo major changes. The twin dynamics were observed in each phase. We will now examine the nature of each phase in detail.

Phase one: the first 3 months of initiation to the CNC

During this first phase, the operator encounters digital commands for the first time in a real situation. The operator and the project team as a whole have limited knowledge of the real operational characteristics of the new system and they endeavour to find out more. Referring to the instructions manual is not enough. The operator mobilizes his competencies from turning with a traditional machine to resolve problems that arise during the use of a CNC machine. Confronting these previous competencies with the new system leads to a transformation of the machine as well as a change in the operator's activity and competencies.

An example of the reinvestment of competencies is the act of reducing the occurrence of chips by changing the tool position. In the first months, the grindstones were often chipped and preventing this proved difficult. Chips may result from interaction between the tool and the unit. Turning a unit on a machine-tool is based on the principle of a cutting surface (the knife) rubbing against the unit to be transformed (in this case, the grindstone). The knife strikes the unit and removes matter to give it the required shape. The position of the tool is one of the factors that determines how it is cut. The grindstone is made of an abrasive substance that varies enormously in terms of the nature of the material, its dimensions and its form. The grindstones reach the machine-tool as a series of identical units of varying numbers (from one unit to over a hundred). On a manual machine, to position the knife with an appropriate cutting angle, the operator uses his knowledge of the material to be treated (density of grain and hardness), the operations to be carried out (shapes of grindstone), the tool (state of wear and tear) and his leeway (instructions). He knows that a knife leaning over horizontally and on a sharp vertical angle (a large cutting angle) gives a fast, strong cut. This position is unsuited to soft grindstones with a coarse grain, which could easily be chipped. It is more suited to a hard grindstone with a fine grain requiring slow speeds and minor setting adjustments. However, in this position, the tool wears down quickly and bends out of shape.

In this situation with a CNC, the addition of a digital commands director eliminates the crank and allows the automation of tool movements with higher turning speeds. The knife remains the same, but its position is fixed to allow automatic control of wear and tear. In the new situation, in principle, the operator should not change the position of the tool. Nevertheless, when he observed the poor quality of the grindstones produced in these conditions, the operator tried to adjust the position of the tool as he had done on the manual machine. He believed that the (programmed) turning speed was too high, and as such incompatible with the fixed cutting angle. After perceiving the reason for the chips, he decided to change the position of the tool. This attempt failed due to technical constraints – on the CNC machine, the position of the knife cannot be changed because of the set course of the sensor. In this way, the operator realized that the position of the CNC machine-tool and the course of its sensor are fixed. The failure of his attempt to change the position of the tool led him to question other elements in the technical system (the high rotation speed of the mandrel, the direction in which it turns, etc.).

The process observed can be described as the reinvestment of competencies relevant to the traditional machine-tool. It constitutes one of the ways the operator was learning by experience, even if, in this particular case, the attempt was not met with success. However, it is precisely the analysis of this failure which allowed him to learn certain key features of the new machine.

The operator's actions in the workplace during this 3-month phase were constructed around the logic underlying the old system and aimed to provide solutions to malfunctions and incidents which occurred. Decisions were made to modify the system to adapt it to the reality of the problems encountered. In the second phase, treating unresolved problems led to a questioning of the programmes that controlled the turning. A management decision to allocate this job to the procedures department meant training the foreman and the procedures operators in the programming of the machine-tool.

Phase two: constructing new competencies and modifying programs

Training the foreman and two procedures operators in programming allowed all three to review all the existing programs in the CNC machine. In technical terms, this second stage focuses on the functionality of these improved systems and better knowledge of the properties of the technical system. We will illustrate the twin dynamics at work in this stage, first with the managing of turning speeds where the operator transfers retroactive control methods from the manual to the CNC machine, and second with an incorrect use of programs where the operator functions proactively.

Managing turning speeds

One of the operator's important tasks when turning with the manual machine-tool is managing the turning speeds in a mediated relation to the object of his activity. In this relation, he manipulates the different cranks in 'sighted conduct'. To do this, the operator makes use of his knowledge of the material to be treated, of the tool, of the operations to be realized and of the way the machine functions. He knows, for example:

- that a hard grindstone needs to be turned slowly, whereas a soft grindstone can tolerate high-speed cuts;
- that a boring action requires slow speeds but deep boring (in thick grindstones) necessitates fast, strong movements to the bottom to obtain a perfectly cylindrical hole;
- that for a shaping operation, i.e. when turning the edges of the grindstone, the speed must be slow at the beginning and at the end of the movement;
- that a very slow rotation speed in the opposite direction to that used for turning allows him to sharpen the knife on the unit.

Working manually allows the operator to build a representation of the situation based on signals generated by tool-unit interaction (such as vibrations, the nature of the shavings and noise) and to act on them directly. The operator can anticipate incidents and increase or decrease speed in line with his perception of a given situation. As a result, the turning speed is not constant. The operator modifies it in line with different variables in the retroactive regulation circuit in real time. With the CNC machine, however, the tool's movements are automatic and controlled by a commands director. The role of the operator consists of entering the parameters into pre-existing programs which manage speeds automatically. This requires him to anticipate all the turning conditions when programming. The operator's relation to the object of the activity (turning the unit) occurs in deferred time. He interacts with the system in a symbolic mode and the regulation results from prediction, which can be described as proactive behaviour. The operator anticipates incidents based on his appraisal of the future situation.

In the study of this particular operator, we found that in order to manage turning speeds on the CNC machine, he made use of his previous knowledge of the product, the tools and the operations, as well as his new knowledge of the programs. Thus when chips occurred, he looked for the cause of the problem in the programmed speeds. The visual and aural information gathered during turning also enriched the construction of this representation. To resolve the problem, he used the programs in an incorrect manner, relying on previous competencies. For example, he provided incorrect information on the nature of the material to be used so as to obtain the cutting speeds that he deemed appropriate, even though they were different from those contained in the programs.

Another strategy for managing turning speeds in real time was the systematic manipulation of the potentiometer, a command designed for occasional use in the event of an incident. Turning this command, graded in percentages, allowed the operator to modify the speed from 0 to 120 per cent. In this action, we can identify a return to sighted behaviour in real time, which typifies the ways of operating a manually controlled machine based on a retroactive circuit.

In this phase, then, we found that the operator diagnosed the origin of the chips on the basis of his previous knowledge. He then performed whatever actions were possible using the new technical system. This required him to adapt his cognitive structures to the new procedures. Understanding the cause of chips depends on previous knowledge and experience of turning grindstones, and the operator knew that speed is one of the parameters he needed to act upon.

Operating with the CNC machine obviously required new knowledge of how the machine functioned. Mastering the new system required the operator to develop new competencies that had little or no connection with his previous competencies. Based on his experience (constructed progressively around his knowledge of the technical system and a good mastery of the various hazards encountered in carrying out his task), he elaborated new action modalities, which helped him carry out operations that theoretically were not possible with the programs that were available. We illustrate this process of constructing new competencies with a second example, in which the turning programs are broken down so as to create operations that are available in the original codes.

The partial use and coupling of programs: 'new' competencies

The programs available in the CNC machine allow the operator to make twelve different forms. Each program is illustrated by a drawing, which depicts the form to be made geometrically and specifies the parameters to be entered. The operator enters the turning parameters after consulting the production sheet and measuring the gross dimensions of the grindstone to be made.

We observed a situation in which an operator was required to make a symmetrical form which did not exist in that state in the CNC programs. The grindstone required had a complex groove form on both sides. The operator chose a program that matched the required form on only one side. He began the program, using only the part that was useful. After obtaining the required form on the first side, he turned the grindstone to carry out the operation on the second side. He entered the real thickness as the gross thickness, changing the data already entered, and started the cycle. In this way, he obtained the same form on the second side. Throughout the operations, he wrote down the thickness values entered (gross and finished) each time, so he would not make a mistake on the following grindstones.

This example demonstrates the acquisition of a new skill, breaking down a program by schematically representing the intermediary states in the turning process. With the manual machine-tool, these states were managed by his own hand through continuous regulation. With the old system, he worked by sight, running the machine in time with the information the work situation threw back at him. He kept measuring until he obtained the final shape and size. The intermediary states of the grindstone gave rise to the continuous regulation of his action on the unit in a retroactive mode. With the CNC machine, however, there is a geometric model on which the operator can base his representation of the final state of the grindstone. He can also use the geometric model to represent the intermediary state, i.e. in this case, the state after turning only one side, after the automatic interruption of the cycle. However, the geometric model is not enough to inform him about the intermediary state because it does not give real dimensions.

Characteristics of competence evolution

Following these examples, we will now outline the dynamics of the development of competence in this context. These will be analysed on two levels:

- on a global level, with the move from retroactive activity to proactive activity;
- on a developmental level, in relation to the problems encountered in the new work situation.

The transition from retroactive to proactive behaviour

We will present two aspects of the overall development of competencies: development of anticipation, and transposition of modalities of retroactive regulation into the new situation.

Development of anticipation

In proactive regulation, the operator works by anticipating the turning conditions in a program with parameters. In retroactive regulation, however, he works with successive approximations. Retroaction requires the continuous gathering of information during turning. The operator's actions depend on the information gathered. In this case, anticipation consists of organizing the action using schemes that allow this anticipation. Although proaction requires anticipation of the (machine's) actions, information on the actions undertaken is gathered later. The operator anticipates the future situation without knowing the indicators that will be provided by the turning situation.

The proactive nature of the activity requires competencies on the CNC machine which concern:

- relations between the information entered in the programs and the machine's functioning, knowledge of the turning programs and the digital command functions;
- tool–unit interaction, which is different from that of the manual machine-tool. Previous knowledge, schemes and representations concerning this interaction are efficient but must be adapted to the preset high speeds of the tools, the higher rotation speeds of mandrels and to the tool's fixed position;
- managing the turning tools in new conditions; previous competencies concerning tool management are still valid because the same tools are used in the CNC machine; however, changes in the means of checking their wear and tear and their quality, as well as changes in their conditions of use, with high turning speeds and a fixed position, require new knowledge, representations and schemas;

- managing the variability and diversity of the grindstones in new conditions. Previous competencies concerning the product are not sufficient here – digital command requires new competencies in programming within parameters and in preparing the mandrel.

Transposing retroactive regulation modalities

We observed the operator trying to get round the demands of proactive regulation and return to the retroactive regulation he used in the old situation. This transposition of regulation modalities from the old situation requires new competencies because the way of obtaining information is different with a CNC machine. On a CNC machine, there is no direct contact of the kind which allows the operator to sense the vibrations caused by the turning. A casing restricts access to visual information. So the operator developed new ways of retroactive regulation. He followed tool movements on a screen, stopped the turning cycle to watch it closely, did blank practice runs or used a deformed grindstone to observe the tool's movements.

The general direction of the development of competencies

We found three types of competence development underlying the use of the CNC machine. This was preceded by a state in which the operator followed instructions on how to use the new machine. He considered the situation completely foreign to him: 'Everything was so different that I didn't even notice the mandrel was turning the wrong way.' This period, which was very short, led to a loss of trust in the knowledge acquired in training, instructions and procedures. The three types of competence development were as follows.

Transferring competencies

Various problems encountered when using the CNC machine required the operator to make use of previous knowledge and competencies. As a technician stated: 'Only someone who has worked on the lathe can find the right solutions to programming problems.' Transferring competencies learned on the manual machine was the operator's preferred way into the new situation. As a result, it occurred more frequently in the early stages of getting to grips with the CNC machine.

Transforming competencies

Searching for solutions to problems helped to improve the operator's knowledge. It allowed him to explore the machine, and understand the limitations of the procedures and instructions used. Interaction with the machine allowed him to construct technical and functional knowledge requiring the adaptation of previous competencies: these are transformed competencies.

Constructing new competencies

Finally, the operator constructed new competencies more specific to proactive problem solving and the nature of the new machine.

The operator applied transferred, transformed and new competencies in different phases of the dynamics of change. However, in the second phase we observed an increase in transformed and new competencies due to improved mastery of the new system and the experience acquired through time spent on the machine. The operator knew the exact rather than the estimated mechanical relationships between the information provided and the execution of a turning job, thus facilitating the process of anticipation.

Towards a general framework for an analysis of the dynamics of the development of work process knowledge

The operator in our study developed skill on the new machine by transferring competencies from previous work with a manual machine, transforming those competencies or constructing entirely new ones. The two driving forces behind this dynamic are production demands and the need to resolve many problems encountered in the transition process. The learning is based on previous competencies, technical knowledge gained in training or on the job from the other members of the team, and experience gained progressively on an individual and collective level. We will now propose a general framework for the systematization of the dynamics of this process of acquiring knowledge and skill in the workplace. This framework, called 'People at Work' (PAW), was originally developed by Samurçay and Rabardel (1995) and here we will illustrate its main features with the results of the study reported above.

People at work

In the following, we will first describe the dimensions of the model (the subject, socialized knowledge, the collective, situations and the context). Then we will focus on determining factors and dynamics of change at play in the evolution and construction of work process knowledge and competence. Finally, we will show how different views of competencies can be constructed depending on the entry points chosen by analysts, and we will look at possible uses for PAW (Figure 5.1).

The model we propose is organized by five main levels:

- the *subject level*, considered to be the most important;

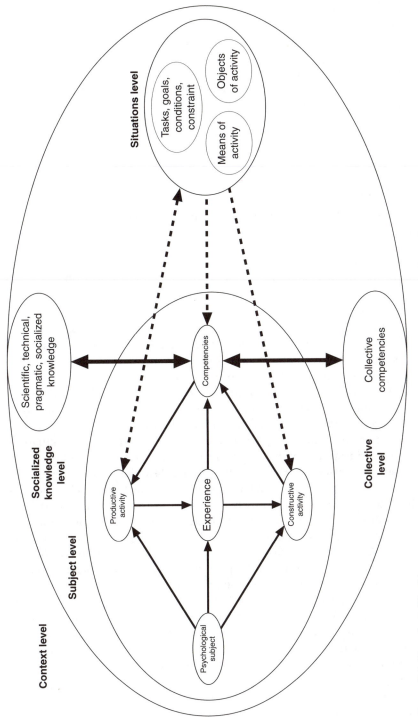

Context level

Situations level

Tasks, goals,
conditions,
constraint

Objects
of activity

Means of
activity

Socialized
knowledge
level

Scientific, technical,
pragmatic, socialized
knowledge

Competencies

Collective
competencies

Subject level

Collective
level

Productive
activity

Experience

Constructive
activity

Psychological
subject

Figure 5.1 'People at Work'

- the *socialized knowledge level,* which generates subjects' competencies and is in turn enriched by them;
- the *collective level,* which in this case only features collective knowledge and competencies, but which could be developed in the same way and to the same extent as the subject;
- the work *situations level,* in which the subjects develop their activity;
- finally, the *context* in which all the other levels exist.

We will now define these different levels in greater detail, starting with the most important.

The subject level

This is a model of the subject adapted to a competence-based approach. Several entities are distinguished.

The psychological subject, i.e. the finalized, intentional actor, the subject of his or her work, who develops several types of activity. In the case discussed, the subject operates the machine-tool. His name is Mehmed. Of course, he works with other subjects but we will restrict ourselves to him in order to clarify the model.

The productive activity (also called work activity or functional activity in the literature). This is finalized activity carried out, oriented and checked by the psychological subject in response to the tasks he or she must accomplish and in accordance with the nature of the situations. This activity has epistemological functions (directed toward understanding the work situations), pragmatic functions (directed at the transformation of work objects and the use of tools) and heuristic functions (directed toward the subject himself). Thus, in a traditional machine-tool situation, Mehmed constantly watches over the different stages of turning. When turning is underway, he does this by looking, listening to the noise of the machine and also by checking vibrations and other informal indicators. When he has finished an activity, he measures how much material has been removed. This is the epistemological dimension of the productive activity. Turning of this same unit involves installing it, fastening it to his machine, adjusting his tools, moving the tools with the mandrels, etc. This is the pragmatic dimension of the productive activity. At the same time, he organizes his work by classifying the grindstones into operational types, by planning the day's turning timetable, and also by ensuring that he alternates the sequence types so his activity does not become monotonous and is not too tiring or dangerous to his health. This is the heuristic dimension of the productive activity. The productive activity is partly determined by the nature of situations, the context within which they occur, etc.

Competencies are the personal resources at the subject's disposal with which he develops his productive activity in line with the tasks and nature of the situations he is confronted with. For an English-speaking audience, it is necessary to stress that they include knowledge as well as a repertoire of behaviours, for here we will use the word 'competence' in its French sense. These competencies are activated as a means of accomplishing work activity. They contribute to production and to the management of the productive activity. In the example of the machine-tool, there are three types of competencies of equal importance:

- those related to the use of the machine and its local characteristics (e.g. knowing the precision of a given mandrel, knowing how to accommodate wear and tear on the machine);
- those related to turning (e.g. the different types of materials the grindstones are made of in relation to turning speeds based on the required precision);
- those related to tactical choices (e.g. the organization of turning operations when a series of identical units must be made).

Competencies concern all dimensions of the activity, particularly relations to others and oneself. The psychological subject determines the properties of competencies that are also partly determined by the nature of the work situations with which they must be functionally appropriate. Competencies enrich constructive activity.

Experience has a double status. On one hand, it is a product of work activity. In carrying out tasks, operations and actions, the subject accumulates information on the situations encountered, the properties of objects, the forms and modalities of his own actions, the conditions and modalities of his work with others, etc. On the other hand, experience can be considered a material in its own right, an object worked upon by constructive activity. Operating invariants, representations, concepts, activity schemes and organizers of different levels, and more generally, competencies, result partly from this elaboration of experience through constructive activity.

Constructive activity is oriented and controlled by the subject who carries it out so as to construct and improve his or her competencies in line with situations and professional fields of action. It is thus also partly determined by the nature of the situations. Competencies have an object status in constructive activity. In the example of changing from a manual to digital machine-tool, the constructive activity occurs within the activities formally concerned with building competencies (the training programme with the supplier and professional training provided at the beginning), as well as in the later development of competencies in the real situation. Thus, Mehmed initially tries to reinvest competencies acquired using the manual machine-tool. To make this possible, these competencies have partly to change. He progressively develops new competencies that allow him to move from retroactive to proactive checking of his productive activity. Constructive activity incorporates external knowledge, but also shapes experience in order to produce competencies.

The socialized knowledge level

The social group level is considered here as one of the generators of competencies. It is at this level that we find norms, trade rules, defensive ideologies as well as formal socialized knowledge. These aspects are socialized in that they are shared by a social group. Furthermore, they are generally explicit and they are related to the work. Socialized knowledge is knowledge as a whole (epistemic or pragmatic) which enriches the construction and evolution of competencies, and which works toward producing work activity and constructive action. In our example, knowledge of the grindstone's 'grain' or of the specific function of a digitally operated machine is socialized knowledge. This knowledge can be of many types: scientific or technical concepts, pragmatic concepts, or even model representations (see Samurçay and Vidal-Gomel, Chapter 11). In return, individual and collective competencies as well as the constructive activity contribute to enriching aspects of this level. The long period required to make the machine fully functional, as opposed to merely operational, also provides an opportunity to construct new and shared knowledge of the nature and way of using the machine.

The collective level

Collective competencies are related to individual competencies in the course of their application. Collective competencies are resources in the management of collective aspects of the work activity and the constructive activity. In our example, the new and different capacities of the digital machine-tool lead to a partial reorganization of work in the factory. The fork-lift truck operator develops new strategies for distributing units, new ways of identifying where the various operators are up to in work on the different series, etc. The foreman, the procedures agents and Mehmed develop new collective work modalities and specific competencies in order to do so. These competencies, linked to the collective nature of work in the new situation, are only one example of collective competencies. The forms and modalities of collective work are diverse: coaction, co-operation, distributed co-operation, etc. As a result, there are many forms of collective competencies. Individual and collective competencies mutually enrich each other in their construction and their evolution.

The situations level

This constitutes a minimal model of finalized activity. Here, we focus on competences in their relation to work situations. Taking into consideration situations where the activity is finalized by training calls for the production of another framework in which the trainer and the situations would intervene, considering it a didactic situation. The model includes:

- the objects of the activity (e.g. managing the turning of a series of grindstones);
- the work tools (commands, cutting tools, programming means, etc.);
- tasks defined in terms of desired outcomes (e.g. shape, dimensions and resistance of grindstones to be made);
- conditions (cutting tool to be used, turning speeds, etc.);
- constraints (minimal production time, turning quality, etc.).

These entities as a whole are placed in a context that contributes to making them meaningful to the subject. They are also indicative of the social grounding of work or activity situations. The work activity is carried out in situations. Situations thus contribute to determining the work activity, but they are also determined by it (hence, the nature of the turning that has to be performed partly determines the operator's behaviour, and what he does transforms the situation for himself as well as others). Situations also contribute to defining the constructive activity, particularly in terms of the contents they act upon (for example, Mehmed will only have the opportunity to develop competencies allowing a proactive control of turning behaviour after the introduction of a digital machine-tool). Situations and competencies are therefore determined reciprocally. Competencies are also functionally equivalent to situations in terms of their treatment in which the subject mobilizes them as resources.

The context

This includes the elements related to work which, even if they have no immediate influence on situations, are nonetheless liable to influence them in their medium to long-term evolution. Examples of this are inter-subjective and inter-professional relations (Clot 1999), the company's security policy, management of human resources and economic stakes.

Multi-determining factors of competencies

- Competencies are resources for work activity. They are produced by constructive activity, which is based, among other things, on experience. Hence, Mehmed will transpose his initial competencies, then develop profoundly new ones, particularly in the surveillance of productive activity.
- Competencies are also determined by external knowledge and collective or social competencies which the subject accesses through the mediation of other workers or artifacts. Formal apprenticeship through training, the documents that he reads as well as professional dialogues with experienced colleagues are examples of determining factors born of external knowledge.
- Competencies depend on the situations encountered and those to be

dealt with. Learning to manage turning proactively requires being confronted with situations where this activity is both possible and functional.

- Competencies also depend on the subject and his or her leanings. The criteria the subject responds to or sets himself always have a personal, even identity related aspect. These criteria could be the quality or beauty of the work carried out, the relation between the work activity and its developments elsewhere in his life, modalities of his relations with others, etc.

Each of these determining relations can be considered as a major point of view or reference in describing or analysing competencies.

Three major competency dynamics

Work activity dynamics

The work activity dynamic is controlled and oriented by the subject. Competencies are positioned in it as *resources*. The productive activity is situated in that it is immersed in situations and their specific evolutions. Its temporality is that of the specific changes in situations and work, i.e. short and medium term.

Constructive activity dynamics

Competencies are positioned as *objects* for constructive activity, which is controlled and oriented by the subject. The constructive activity is also situated, but not in the same way as the work activity. It is connected to invariant aspects of situations and of action. Invariants do not refer to a static or mechanical view of situations or the subject. Hence the variability of the subject's functional state at various times of the day (linked to tiredness, biological rhythms, etc.) is true of all subjects. This variability is thus an invariant. It occurs over the medium or long term, i.e. the period of development and evolution of competencies.

Dynamics of socialized knowledge

This dynamic is mediated by other subjects and artifacts. It is a dynamic of situated cognitive activity in which the relationship between knowledge and situations is one of functional equivalence. It occurs over the medium or long term, i.e. in the time taken to construct, transform and circulate knowledge.

Each of these three dynamics can also be taken as a major point of view for describing or analysing the process of developing, using and circulating competencies and knowledge on individual, collective or social levels.

Some possible uses of the PAW framework

The model can be explored from several entry points, each of which defines, in a sense, a possible point of view or reference. Hence, for example:

- It is possible to take socialized knowledge as a departure point (and as a reference) and to question, for example, the relation between the subject's competencies and socialized knowledge in terms of the way knowledge is incorporated into competencies, the validity of competencies compared with knowledge, the pertinence of knowledge compared with situations, etc.
- Furthermore, if we take situations as a departure point, we can question relations between the work object, tools and tasks, as well as their connections with competencies. We can also look at the conditions in which the characteristics of situations influence both constructive activity and work activity. Other questions could concern the situation models necessary. Which differentiations (levels, types, fields of reality)? Which conceptions?
- Other departure points are also possible on the subject level. Each departure point represents a different perspective. These could focus on work activity, constructive activity or the subject. For example, we can examine the modalities and mechanisms of production and the dynamic evolution in competencies in terms of the subject's constructive activity. We can question the factors that generate and develop competencies; relations between work activity and constructive activity; relations between constructive activity and the subject's leanings and commitments in situations and in his life in general; the way socialized knowledge and work situations contribute to and influence training and the evolution of competencies; the roles played by other actors and the collective in training and the evolution of a subject's competencies; and in return, the contribution of the subject's skill to training and the evolution of collective competencies.
- Finally, the model can serve as an analytical framework in real work situations. We thus attempt to fill in the different blanks and identify the effectively functioning determining factors, just as we did for the work with turning machine-tools.

Conclusions and perspectives: competence evolution in continuity and discontinuity

One of the first conclusions of this research concerns the *temporal dimensions of competence dynamics* in the work situation. The temporal span is unrelated to the length of training and is measured in months, probably years. Clearly, the implications for research are important: identifying the evolution of competencies linked to the subject's constructive activity in a work situation supposes medium or long-term studies. This can be done by longitudinal studies based on subjects followed over long periods, but it is difficult to bring together the required conditions. This can also be done by polling subjects at different stages of competence dynamics. This second solution implicitly supposes that we consider the subjects as being relatively homogeneous at the outset and that competence dynamics are the same from one subject to another. Both assumptions are dubious given what we know about the diversity of competencies and the vicariousness of their evolution modalities.

A second conclusion concerns the mechanisms of skill evolution. *Competencies develop in terms of their connection to previous competencies. This connection can be one of continuity or a complete break.* In our research, management of rotation speed is a good example of connection through continuity. The subject relies on the invariant aspects of the two situations: rotation speed is a variable that influences cutting quality. Operators therefore transpose their competencies in rotation speed management onto the new situation by more or less diverting the potentiometer and the programs themselves from their original functions (the operators choose the program depending on the desired cutting speed rather than the hardness of the grindstone, as intended). The principle of managing the rotation speed remains the same (thus the competencies are connected to previous ones), yet they develop within the modalities of this management because the tools are different.

Moving from retroactive to proactive management of turning is a good example of skill connections through discontinuity. In this case, the management modalities are profoundly different. With the traditional machine, they are based on the results obtained, whereas with the digital machine-tool they are based on anticipation before all action. The two modalities are almost completely unrelated and the nature of the situations they are based on are themselves different. Management by anticipation becomes possible, and no doubt economical, due to the CNC machine's programming potential which allows high repeatability. It is low repeatability combined with easy access to the object during turning that encourages the retroactive management of work with the traditional machine-tool. Finally, we observe that the move from one type of management to the other and the development of 'expert' competencies based on proactive management only occurs fairly late in evolutionary competence dynamics.

Our third and final conclusion concerns the *connection between competence dynamics and situation dynamics*. The 'People at Work' model takes into consideration a double connection between competencies and work situations:

- on one hand, the need for competencies appropriate to situations and the nature of the classes of situations leading to a relatively situations-based determination of competencies;

- on the other hand, a second connection between evolutionary competence dynamics and work situation dynamics, both of which occur over medium or long periods.

Competencies thus appear to be situated in their relations to circumstantial situations and to classes of situations, in their relations to the evolutionary dynamics of situations and more generally, the overall context of the company.

6 Work process knowledge and creativity in industrial design

Lauge Baungaard Rasmussen

Particularly in the field of engineering, studies of design methodology have tended to describe the process of design as a sequence of technical activities based on a strictly rational approach to a clearly defined and purely cognitive problem-solving process. However, these studies do not grasp the essence of creative design. They fail to appreciate that design practice is not just a matter of following procedures but also depends on work process knowledge. During the last three decades, a variety of design studies have produced a slowly growing body of understanding about the design process. Some of these studies rely on observation of designers at work, while others are based on elicitation of expert knowledge and protocol analysis. A few design practitioners have written about their own working methods, but most studies rely on observations and/or interviews. The present chapter is based on all these sources. The intention is to let industrial designers themselves explain how they believe they do their work, and then to add another layer of interpretation. The latter is based on theoretical knowledge about how rational and intuitive ways of working may interact, with a focus on the *creative* aspects of designing. It is generally accepted that design is a creative occupation and that designers themselves are creative people. But what does it mean to be creative? Should we restrict ourselves to the personal aspects of creativity, or should we also include the design context? If we adopt the latter approach, then work process knowledge becomes a crucial requirement for creative design.

Ideal types of design

Design as the leap of insight or visual thought

The French mathematician, Jules Henri Poincaré (1854–1912), divides the creative process into phases in order to explain why the initial investigation of a problem is followed by a period of apparent inactivity. The solution, according to Poincaré, often appears after this period in a sudden and often unexpected manner:

Often when one works at a hard question, nothing good is accom-
plished at the first attack. Then one takes a rest, longer or shorter,
and sits down anew to the work. During the first half-hour, as before,
nothing is found, and then all of a sudden the decisive idea presents
itself to the mind. It might be said that the conscious work has been
more fruitful because it has been interrupted and the rest has given
back to the mind its force and freshness. But it is more probable that
this rest has been filled out with unconscious work and that the result
of this work has afterwards revealed itself.

(Poincaré 1952: 38)

Following Poincaré's idea of different phases in the creative thinking
process, several psychologists attempted to classify the stages of creative
thinking. According to Lawson (1983), for instance, researchers in this
tradition seem to agree on a five-stage process consisting of insight,
preparation, incubation, illumination and verification. The period of *first
insight* involves the recognition that a problem exists. The next phase of
preparation involves much conscious effort to develop a solution. The third
period, *incubation,* involves no apparent effort, but is a period during
which the unconscious is supposed to be actively creating possible solutions. This phase is often terminated by the sudden emergence of an
unexpected idea in the fourth phase, *illumination.* Once the idea has
emerged, a period of conscious *verification* is necessary, when the outline
idea is tested and further developed into operational dimensions. The
leap-of-insight viewpoint focuses on a high level of tolerance of ambigui-
ties, the intuition, and the subconscious processes that may slowly or suddenly create a new idea, pattern or vision. The creative designer must be
able to step behind his or her usual way of thinking and acting to take a
reflective and transforming viewpoint. The leap of insight is a transforma-
tional process by which a complicated problem is changed into a relatively
simple one. However, Gardner (1984) argues that visual image processing
is not merely intuition but a particular kind of *spatial intelligence* that
includes abilities to recognize instances of the same elements and the
transformation of one element to another. Moreover, according to
Gardner, spatial intelligence includes the capacity to produce a graphic
likeness of spatial information, to conjure up mental imagery and then
transform it to another kind of imagery. Although Gardner's model
remains controversial, other researchers have confirmed the presence of
visually oriented thought processes (Shepard and Cooper 1982; Kosslyn
1990; Henderson 1998).

Visual thinking may also be linked to tacit knowledge (Polanyi 1958,
1967; Polanyi and Prosch 1975; Rasmussen *et al.* 1987a, 1987b). Polanyi is
clearly influenced by both gestalt and cognitive psychology. He accepts the
gestalt point of view that we may know a physiognomy by integrating the
awareness of its particulars without being able to identify these particulars.

But he also stresses the cognitive point of view of an active organization of experiences in the mind during the process of recognition:

> I am looking at a gestalt ... as the outcome of an active shaping of experience performed in the pursuit of knowledge. This shaping or integrating I hold to be the great and indispensable tacit power by which all knowledge is discovered and, once discovered, is held to be true.
>
> (Polanyi 1967: 6)

According to Polanyi, all tacit knowledge includes at least three aspects: a functional relation, a phenomenal aspect and a semantic aspect. *The functional relation* means the relation of particulars to a focal target – that is, the particulars or subsidiaries that we are aware of in the act of focusing our attention on something else. Polanyi also terms it *from-to-knowledge* – that is, a knowledge of such particulars as they appear functionally in establishing the object of focal attention (Polanyi and Prosch 1975). *The phenomenal aspect* of tacit knowledge means that the coherence may have new sensory qualities not possessed by the sense perceptions from which the coherence is tacitly created. Polanyi exemplifies this by the change of appearance that occurs when a pair of stereo pictures is transformed into a stereo image. As opposed to the original pair, the stereo image has a marked depth and also shows firmly shaped 'solid' objects. The coherence thus has new sensory qualities (Polanyi and Prosch 1975). *The semantic aspect* of tacit knowledge is an act of giving meaning. In isolation from each other or from the focal target, the subsidiaries do not make sense. On the contrary, the focal target on which they rest is the meaning of the subsidiaries (Polanyi and Prosch 1975). As seen, there are three centres of tacit knowledge: the subsidiary particulars, the total target and the knower, who links the particulars to the focal target. We can think of them as forming a triad. But the knower can dissolve the triad by merely looking at the subsidiaries differently. For example, the performance of a skill can be paralysed if we turn our attention away from its performance and concentrate instead on the various motions that compose the performance (Polanyi and Prosch 1975). Polanyi uses this to argue for the existence of two different kinds of awareness that are mutually exclusive: a *focal awareness* and a *from-awareness*. You can be aware of certain things and either focus on them directly or see them as functional parts of a superior target. Focal awareness is always fully conscious, but from-awareness can exist at any level of consciousness, even at the subconscious level. Thus, Polanyi's thesis of something guiding the active shaping of recognition during the process involves a two-level or multilevel structure of higher and lower principles. For instance, oral communication includes five levels. At the lowest level is the production of voice sounds. At the next higher level, these sounds are combined into the utterance of meaningful words. By embedding these words into sentences, the words achieve further meaning. By gathering these sentences together into intelligible points, you get even further meaning that the sentences do not have by themselves. Finally, intelligible points must themselves be used towards the attainment of the ultimate focal aim of communication. Polanyi's ultimate focal aim is that all knowledge is either tacit or rooted in tacit knowing. To understand the design process as a whole the tacit dimension seems to be vital. The designer as 'the knower' links the 'particulars' to the 'focal target', both in the process of defining and solving the problem. But exactly how he or she does this is not clear. According to Polanyi, we will never be fully able to understand the design process due to the tacit dimension.

Design as sequential rational thinking

The majority of design models are based on sequential, rational assumptions. The design problem is assumed to be divisible into separate units that can be solved in series or in parallel. The designer is supposed to follow through a certain, predetermined sequence of phases or stages. The Association of German Engineers, for instance, distinguishes between the following five stages.

Definition of assignment. This stage involves analysing problems and assignments, unless a specification is given. It is claimed that creative processes at this stage involve an internal representation by forming analogies (Gardner 1984) that apply a wide range of recurrent themes and patterns to make the new familiar and the old new (Langley and Jones 1988; Torrance 1988). Requirement analysis leads to requirement definition in the form of an operational specification of tasks. Standards are set and the attainment of goals is evaluated against them.

Designing. In the design process, the specification of requirements, in terms of a description of the desired proportions, is transformed into a description that includes the definition of the system structure, data and control flows, and distribution of components. At this stage of designing, cognitive psychologists typically view creativity as a balance between convergent and divergent thinking abilities appropriate to the situation.

Implementation. This involves translating the design into an operational system. Piaget (1981) calls the ability to think in terms of possible and hypothetical relationships *formal, operational thinking.* Creativity in this respect helps designers to think themselves out of the boundaries set by conventional norms and rules. However, rules and constraints are far from being only restrictive to creativity at this stage of designing. As Margaret Boden points out:

Constraints map out a territory of structural possibilities which can then be explored and transformed to give another one ... To drop all current constraints and refrain from providing new ones is to invite not creativity, but confusion.

(Boden 1994: 82)

Documentation.   Adequate use of the 'product' hinges on documentation. This should include specification of requirements, description of design, administrative records and a user manual. This stage of product development does not require creative abilities of any kind but rather systematic, analytical abilities and a certain level of practical experience.

Testing.   Testing is traditionally understood as a comparison of nominal and actual functions in order to prove that a program is free of errors. Testing in a broader sense means evaluation and includes personal assessment of the result by the people involved. In testing a system or a new product, creativity may be relevant to the extent that new, possible functions and users of the product are to be taken into consideration.

Finally, these five main stages are followed by integration, installation, maintenance, service and administration (Corbett *et al.* 1991). The division of designing into clearly defined stages has been intended to render the process transparent and improve project control. The common characteristics of design as rational thinking are as follows:

1   Objectives are fixed in advance.
2   Strategies and stages are fixed in advance. These are sequential operations but may include parallel operations and recycling as well.
3   The stages are handled through the logical thinking of a designer, who is supposed to operate only in accordance with the inputs that are given to him or her.

If there is a one-to-one relationship between functions and physical components, the whole assembly of inputs and outputs can be specified at the start, and each of the components can be designed afterwards on the assumption that if it fits the inputs and outputs, it fits the system (Jones 1980). Many design problems, however, are difficult or impossible to split up in this way, because they require many trade-offs and inter-relationships between the different actors or components of the system in question. Of course, industrial design problems are split up at some point in order to let many designers work together, but the degree of splitting can vary very much from one kind of system to another.

Designing as social interaction

Many psychologists, in particular, have viewed reflection and creativity as a process existing inside the individual person. An alternative to this view has been pointed out by Gardner (1984), Csikszentmihalyi (1988), Schön (1983, 1987) and Schön and Rein (1994) among others. In their view, reflection and creativity have to be considered as parts in a larger system of social networks, social institutions or specific domains. According to them, the designer is only one of several necessary parts of the system. For instance, without a culturally defined domain of action in which creative design is possible, designing cannot even get started. Without rules regarding the design idea or product, it is impossible to differentiate what is creative from what is simply improbable or bizarre. According to Schön, designers work by naming the relevant factors in the situation, framing a problem in a certain way, taking actions towards a solution and evaluating those actions. Reflective conversation is viewed as one of the most fundamental traits of design, but the ways to carry out this process may be very open, as will be exemplified later on. Some design theorists have coined a particular form of conversation called 'dialogue'. Reflection is a mental process in which you 'take a step aside of the route' followed so far, and critically consider whether you should continue to follow the same route or change it.

According to the interaction paradigm, the designer is part of an active reciprocating process of shaping new ideas, methods and products in a continuous dialogue with peers in the design team as well as with other participants in the social network that constitutes the field of the design context. The means of dialogue are not necessarily restricted to words but may be related to material objects, too, as pointed out by Henderson:

> What goes on in the mind is tied to material existence and material practice. Engineers, designers and drafters participate in tangible actions that construct their visual culture, their way of seeing, literally and figuratively.
>
> (Henderson 1998: 204)

Sketches, mock-ups and posters are examples of such physical means that are part of the designer's *visual culture*. As such, they may play a dynamic role in the teamwork as a shared interaction space (Suchman 1988). What are the possible functions of the dialogue in the design process?

First, dialogue enables people to step back from the solution of specific problems and reflect upon what lies behind them – that is, the more or less conventional assumptions or rules not normally questioned. According to Schön:

> The designer is always in conversation with the design situation. Design rationality is always, in part, a function of the product of that

conversation, as the designer seeks to grasp the meanings of his moves, and of others' responses to his moves and to embody his interpretations in the invention of further moves.

(Schön and Rein 1994: 172)

Conversation is interpreted more broadly than ordinary talk between two or more people. In Schön's terminology, you can converse with 'the situation', with 'the materials' or with 'yourself'. The conversation can be carried out in the mind of the designer himself, or it can involve interaction between the designer and other social actors, for instance, other designers, users or particular experts. This reflective act may initiate learning on one or several levels (Bateson 1972; Schön 1983, 1987; Isaacs 1993).

Second, as the participants of the design process begin to listen to each other, the dialogue may transform existing patterns of perception and thinking and transmute them into new levels of collective creation. The designer's inquiry, Schön claims, does not yield generally applicable laws, but can be interpreted as 'reflective transfer' (Schön and Rein 1994). The new situation is never totally identical with the familiar one. The designer may use analogies between them, but only if he or she critically reflects the limitations of this 'transfer'. Another way to look at functions of dialogue is Beck's (1994) distinction between *generative* and *strategic* dialogue. *Generative* dialogue offers an environment where participants can generate or create a collective meaning or worldview. *Strategic* dialogue, on the other hand, focuses on specific problems and how to find specific solutions to these problems within a given worldview. Banathy (1996) suggests that the two types of dialogue may be connected into a communication mode that he terms 'design conversation'. According to Banathy, the generative dialogue should precede the strategic dialogue in an ideal design conversation:

> Generative dialogue becomes the core process of transforming the group into a designing community. Once the group feels it has reached the stage where it has created a collective, cognitive map for itself, generated a shared worldview, and attained shared consciousness, then, and only then, should the group turn to the tasks of system design by engaging in a strategic dialogue.

(Banathy 1996: 219)

In the generative phase of design, the group operates in a relatively formless and open conversation, exploring the participants' different experiences and attitudes, and trying to find a common basis for the more strategically oriented phase of the design process. If the dialogue succeeds, the process of generative dialogue gradually moves the group from unstructured, open conversation to a structured, task-oriented conversation.

How to use ideal types as analytical tools

Design theorists often seem to favour one of the above-mentioned ideal types of design. However, the complexity of real-life design activities makes it more relevant to use different ideal types as analytical tools to study the visual, rational and communicative attributes of various design activities. None of the above-mentioned ideal types is sufficient to give us a comprehensive understanding of the dynamic relationship between the design process and the relevant aspects of the design environment. The methodological point here is that the three ideal types of how to design may function as different 'lenses' or 'searchlights', and thus help to clarify the relatively complex processes of performing design activities in practice. Such a process may enable the researcher:

- to choose certain *key elements* of designing and describe these key elements in relation to the particular institutional background or context. Particularly if more than one 'searchlight' is used, opposite or conflicting elements in the design procedures could become more visible.
- to *compare relationships between types of design processes* and, for example, the institutional setting of the design in question, the kinds of artifacts used, and the characteristics of organizations in various contexts.
- to analyse the *tensions and conflicts* between different ways of designing, particularly during periods when new ways of designing compete with conventional ways.

The following analysis is based on two surveys carried out by the author in 1984–5 and 1998–9. The former survey included in-depth interviews with twenty-six industrial designers representing fifteen Danish construction, mechanical and electronics companies. The latter survey included thirteen industrial designers representing seven Danish companies, and the sample was similar to the previous survey except that a fewer number of designers and companies was selected. The seven companies selected in 1998–9 were also part of the sample in 1984–5. Eight of the thirteen designers interviewed in 1998–9 had also been interviewed in 1984–5. The remaining five designers interviewed in 1998–9 were young, experienced mainly in using three-dimensional computer-aided design systems. Results from similar investigations made in other countries are also incorporated in the following analysis to supplement or extend the survey data.

Creative aspects of design practice

Intuition versus reason

Several investigations of industrial designers, including the author's own, indicate that intuition is a common theme that arises when designers are asked to describe and explain how they work. For example, Nigel Cross (1995) quotes industrial designer Richard Stevens:

> A lot of engineering design is intuitive, based on subjective thinking. But an engineer is not happy doing this. An engineer wants to test, test and measure. He's been brought up this way and he's unhappy if he can't prove something. Whereas the industrial designer, with his Art School training, is entirely happy making judgements which are intuitive.
>
> (Cross 1995: 106)

The experience that educational background influences this way of considering intuition as a more or less valid method to use in design practice is supported by other design studies as well. However, Stevens' statement can also be interpreted as a rather *stereotyped legitimacy* of the art- or craft-trained designer's professional self-conception: 'We are more intuitive and better at design than the rationally educated engineers.' Similar statements can be found in the author's interviews with craft-trained industrial designers. For example, a craft-trained designer expresses his joy in using imagination:

> I don't use higher mathematics. I use my imagination. For example, we had an engineer with 25 years' experience . . . but he wasn't able to get things to work. I need my creative abilities, my ideas and then my imagination.
>
> (Rasmussen 1985: 103)

But is that all, one could ask? Is good design no more than creative abilities, ideas and imagination? Are designers restricted to choosing between reason and intuition, as many appear to assume, or is the challenge to transcend and overcome this dichotomy and combine intuition and reason as two complementary aspects of the same practice? Christoffer Jones has argued for the latter position:

> The briefest study of how the most successful artists, engineers, scientists etc. work and think, suggests that they have one thing in common: they have found ways of avoiding this split, ways of combining reason with imagination, and being both creative and practical, of knowing when it is rational to be irrational and when it is rational to work by experience. To reconcile what seem to be opposites, to resolve contradictions, is the essence of design.
>
> (Jones 1984: 135)

Industrial designers between objects and symbols

Contextual knowledge of potential users of the design, materials and the ways of doing things is essential to the competent industrial designer. This was made very explicit by one of the industrial designers interviewed by the author:

> I think very much of the physical conditions in relation to which it has to work. It is critical for me whether it is steel or aluminium. Is it supposed to be polished and really appear impressive, or will it just be painted and put away where nobody can see it? It is obvious that the materials have a decisive role in a very early phase of the project, depending on whether it's in brass or in steel.
>
> (Rasmussen 1985: 123)

This interview was conducted in 1985. Has this ability declined in importance since then? Interviews conducted in 1999 with young industrial designers reveal that they still recognize the importance of this ability. One industrial designer described his image-creating ability thus:

> I can imagine the finished product right from the beginning of the design process. I can see the single units of the product as well as the product as a whole. I can even make units rotate in my head.
>
> (Rasmussen 1999: 11)

These quotations indicate that the supposed visibility of the end product influences the designer's choice of material, form and line, as well as colour and texture, very early in the design process. Very rarely does any part of a designed object serve only one purpose. It is frequently necessary to devise an integrated solution to a whole cluster of requirements. Because design tasks are multidimensional, they are also highly interactive. Skilled industrial designers seem to be very well aware of their particular contextual knowledge. One industrial designer in the sample explains his contextual abilities as follows:

> I know our production methods. I have got it into my body and experienced how to work up the object on the machine. It is a very important starting point, I believe.
>
> (Rasmussen 1985: 124)

Some skilled designers stated that often they were able to foresee how production people would react to their ideas *without* even having discussed the idea with them. One designer explains:

> I can see the whole assembly line, the production machines, and how the production people assemble the units of the product. I can see all that for me in my head.
>
> (Rasmussen 1999: 11)

In doing this, each designer brings personal knowledge to his or her object-world deliberations. This knowledge is part of the know-how that enables them to bridge the gap between mental imaginings of possible forms and the practical context of the immediate object. Within a single domain of industrial design, designers can adopt a variety of *work practices*. Such a phenomenon was clearly articulated by one industrial designer in the sample:

> I believe that we work a little differently. I know that some prefer to make sketches and lines immediately. Personally, I prefer to let it 'rumble' in my head before I begin to draw or make sketches on paper. I prefer to see the ideas in my mind, before I really begin to draw them. I like to have a couple of days during which the things begin to take form. That means I get an image of the product I am going to make.
>
> (Rasmussen 1986)

These different facets of work practices are not usually made explicit in formal presentations, nor are they prescribed by any set of formal rules. They may derive from differences in educational origin or in personal knowledge and cannot be learned by 'reading books', as one skilled designer in my sample explained:

> You cannot learn to know the system from the inside by reading books. The knowledge of how it is to weld in different situations is not something you can learn by reading it. It is learned by practical experience ... If you are skilled, you always possess certain advantages compared with a person who has no practical skills. And then it doesn't matter if you are pattern maker, locksmith or engine fitter. Everybody has an advantage.
>
> (Rasmussen 1985: 124)

But what does he mean by 'knowing the system from the inside'? Of course, the knowledge of 'how it is to weld' in different situations is *one aspect*, but perhaps not the most important one. If the skilled industrial designer has not done any welding for a couple of years, his concrete know-how about welding may turn out to be at least partly obsolete. He might therefore be thinking about more than just knowing the concrete methods of welding when he says that 'everybody (skilled person) has an advantage'. As one interviewed designer describes it:

> It does not matter so much which kind of craftsmanship you have learnt. The important thing is that you have learnt to use your fingers to take things apart and put them together again ... I can imagine the design products and see what is behind the surface, because I

have got the experience to take things apart and put them together again.

(Rasmussen 1999: 5)

Several designers in the sample pointed out the importance of being in close contact with the production people:

> They also have some demands to make, which I try to integrate into my design. It is really important that we as designers listen to those who are responsible for the practical realization of our idea. If you don't walk down sometimes and take a look, you miss the grass-roots contact with them downstairs. It is important to keep in close contact with them, because when you design and plan, you prepare the background for them. If I decide that it's got to be welded, then it is really necessary for me to have an idea about how it is easiest to do it . . . and this is only possible if you yourself are down there a lot.

(Rasmussen 1985: 134)

In 1999, a similar opinion is still widely met:

> When we get an idea, we contact the production people and they might suggest a little correction here or there . . . It is essential to involve them several times during the design process.

(Rasmussen 1999: 14)

The informal talks with the production people were considered much easier to carry out if the designers were familiar with their language and ways of thinking, and were able to enter into their culture. Design issues are often full of uncertainties. In fact, both priorities and objectives may change during the design process as the implications of the suggested solutions begin to emerge. The description of a design problem cannot contain an exhaustive list of all the possible solutions to such problems. More emphasis should be placed on the dynamic tension between formulating design problems and creating design solutions than on achieving a static and exhaustive formulation of design problems and design solutions. As Bucciarelli points out:

> Object worlds are not congruent. Interest conflicts, trade-offs must be made among different domains, and negotiation is necessary. Design is a social process as much as it is getting things right within object worlds.

(Bucciarelli 1994: 83)

Competence within an object world is not sufficient to ensure the quality of the design result. Industrial designers must also be able to describe and explain their knowledge to other people from different object worlds who do not possess the same familiarity with the designer's own object world and the technical possibilities it offers for design solutions.

Industrial design as teamwork

Many studies of the design process have focused on the activities of individual designers. However, teamwork is becoming of greater importance as design has become more and more related to other kinds of activities going on in companies. An example of this trend is the transformation of sequential engineering into *simultaneous and concurrent engineering* or *integrated product and process design* (IPPD). These approaches require increased teamwork between industrial designers and members of other departments in the company. A growing number of studies of design teamwork have consequently taken place during the 1980s and 1990s. Many studies of design teamwork have focused on 'successful teams' from a management perspective (Hachman 1986; Manz and Sims 1987; Safizadeh 1991; Katzenbach and Smith 1993; Levi and Slem 1995; Ullman 1997). According to this perspective, successful teams would perform their tasks with the minimum resources necessary. However, this definition focuses only on the specific task and not on the successive development of the social and individual qualifications of the team. Sundström *et al.* (1990) suggest a more comprehensive set of criteria for successful teamwork. According to them, when a team performs a task successfully, it can perform the next task assigned to it better. In other words, teamwork cannot be regarded as successful unless the task is fulfilled *and* the members' technical, social and personal skills improve as a result of the teamwork (Katzenbach and Smith 1993).

One aspect of competence development is the ability to *collaborate*. According to Ullman (1997), collaboration means more than just working together. Ideally, every member of the team should be able to manage several 'problem-solving styles', depending on the demands of the concrete situation. Working as a member of a team introduces different social dimensions for the designer in comparison with working alone. As pointed out by Nigel Cross (1995), the design team will contain various social roles and relationships that will affect the design process in some way. Some of these roles may be formally established. For instance, a higher authority within the organization may appoint a team leader, and each participant in the design team may be assigned a particular job role.

The industrial designer is part of a subculture of interaction within an infrastructure of the firm. The word 'interaction' suggests a process of mutual exchange in economic as well as in social terms. Interactions are utilitarian acts guided by the economic interests of the firm. But they are social, too, in the sense that reflective critique and trust in the value of each other's work are essential to the result of the design process. There must be 'room' for rethinking concepts, shifting images and changing specifications and constraints, as the industrial designers develop their concepts and images during the design process. One of the designers in the sample described an example of such an interactive process:

> Sometimes you have got a problem you feel you can't solve. Then I ask two or three persons that I know have some experiences on the subject to join a common brainstorming session. Then I just sketch the idea for them and we talk about it for a while before we go back to our own places again.
>
> (Rasmussen *et al.* 1989)

Sketching is essential for getting ideas across to other participants of the design process. Some designers engage in discussion through the use of sketches and mock-ups, both with one another and with those who are going to produce, sell or use the design product. Bucciarelli (1994) notes that sketches are valuable for creating a basis for the designer and others to generate a set of more exact plans that may be further modified collectively or individually. A designer describes his use of sketches as follows:

> It happens most when you joined a meeting or when two people stand in front of the screen and talk. You talk really with a pencil in your hand and a piece of paper in front of you. And then you make sketches, usually three-dimensional drawings that make it possible to look at the perspective. Not only a plan but a drawing in which the plan is extended in the space, and then you have your object. We are doing sketches if we have recognized something 'critical' inside the object. We make a sectional view in which you take that 'critical' problem and sketch it, and then it is just as you look in the middle of it . . . It is very important for us to do that during a design process.
>
> (Rasmussen 1999: 7)

This interactive use of sketches and mock-ups serves the function of knitting people together who have different interests and experiences – for instance, people with user experience or shop experience, such as welders and tool-makers (Binder 1996; Brandt 2001). Interpretations and disagreements may take place over, on and through these visual representations, which can be seen as the building blocks of industrial design. As Kathryn Henderson has pointed out:

> They are the components of the social organization of collective cognition and the locus for practice-situated and practice-generated knowledge.
>
> (Henderson 1991: 449)

The sketches and mock-ups serve as means for organizing the collective process of design by acting as 'glue' between designers and other participants in the design process. Collective brainstorming of this kind may suddenly create a very enthusiastic atmosphere and perhaps even a 'solution'. As one designer describes it:

> You are three or four and suddenly you draw with arms and legs and then we say: 'we do that and that'. I just make a drawing of it. This is the way we do it.

(Rasmussen *et al.* 1987: 15)

The acts of communication serve the purpose of mutual orientation and interpretation. The members of the design team do not merely give or carry out messages or orders. They discuss and share experiences, too, regarding the social and functional aspects of their projects.

Design as a visual and social activity

Visual culture

Latour (1986) has pointed out that visual culture is not a metaphor, but a literal worldview that determines how members of a certain culture see the world and make it visible: 'A new visual culture redefines both what it is to see and what there is to see' (Latour 1986: 9–10).

It is well documented that designers and engineers think visually (Arnheim 1969; Ferguson 1977, 1992; Vicenti 1990; Sacks 1993; Bucciarelli 1994; Henderson 1998). But how is the capacity to visualize learned? One of the designers interviewed by the author reported that his visual abilities were already well developed in childhood. As a child, he was always very eager to take different kinds of objects apart and put them together again. During his engineering studies, he was never taught how to visualize the problem in a three-dimensional perspective, although some teachers sometimes requested their students to try to do this. After being employed as industrial designer, nobody told or showed him how to do it, but they more or less expected that he had this ability. Is visual ability then a kind of tacit knowledge? The designers interviewed were able to describe the kind of images they had, but not *how* they created them. They were not able to spell out the visualizing process in explicit steps. According to Polanyi's idea of tacit knowledge, the designer may link the particular elements of the object to a focal target of a 'critical' problem in the process of both defining and solving the problem. But exactly how he or she does this is not clear. The single elements do not make sense isolated from each other, but only in relation to the focal target of the product that is going to be designed. By shifting focal awareness from one sectional view to another, the visual designer is able to get behind the layers of the development problems. Just as oral communication according to Polanyi includes the five levels described earlier, the visualizing interaction involves a many-levelled structure of higher and lower principles. At the lowest level there is the visual recognition of the elements of the object. At the next lowest level isolated recognition is combined into meaningful, visual patterns. By embedding these patterns into an image the patterns achieve further meaning. In gathering several images into sectional views, one obtains even further meaning. Finally, the sectional views can be used to attain the ulti-mate focal aim of the communication. The *focal awareness,* by means of which the designer focuses on the sectional view – for instance, when two designers are discussing 'critical' points – is of course important in order to reach a common solution of the problem. But the *from-awareness* may be just as important, as soon as the focal awareness of this sectional view is released. For instance, some designers often seem to get good ideas when they are doing anything else than designing in front of the computer screen. As one designer describes it:

> It is typical, that the solutions come to me in all other situations than in front of the screen. That is very typical for me, at least. But it may be different for other designers.
>
> (Rasmussen 1999: 4)

One possible interpretation of the phenomenon described above is that the designer's from-awareness takes over as soon as the focal aware-ness is released from the design problem. The point is not that from-awareness is more 'creative' than focal awareness. The point is that they interact and support each other. This relationship is hardly recognized in sequential, rational design thinking. Here, focal awareness is assumed to play the main role when a design task is divided into separate parts to be solved in series or in parallel processes. Predetermined sequences may restrict the influence of from-awareness, if the focus is limited and design behaviour becomes pure routine. However, even in the most sequential, rational design process, there may occur redefinitions of design problems and transformations of the external world into internal models in the designer's head, and the other way around. Such kinds of transformation may be difficult or impossible to carry out without using both kinds of awareness. For instance, in formal, operational thinking, where the designer is supposed to be able to think in terms of possible and hypotheti-cal relationships, both from-awareness and focal awareness are essential in order to transcend conventional ways of doing things.

Viewing the design process from the perspective of social interaction, it is possible to deepen the understanding of the relationship between from-awareness and focal awareness. If designers are members of an active, recip-rocating process of shaping new styles and products in a continuous dialogue with both peers in the design team and other partners in the design process (customers, representatives of marketing and production, etc.) then they participate in tangible actions that construct the internal interaction between focal and from-awareness. The relationship between focal and from-awareness may be essential in order to create sufficient space for a many-levelled social interaction, in which participants of the design process use sketches, posters and mock-ups as means to communicate visual thinking. Banathy (1996) stresses the point of using *generative dialogues* as the core process in transforming the design group into a 'designing community' before it jumps 'into a strategic dialogue'. One reason may be that the generative dialogue helps the participants in the design group to transform the individually varied from-awareness into a gradually more and more overlapping, common, visual 'space' of creative interaction.

Creativity and time pressure

Several studies of industrial design work in the 1990s (Bucciarelli 1994; Henderson 1998; Rasmussen 1999) have reported an increase in work intensification and time pressure. One of the Danish designers interviewed described the change over the last 10–15 years as follows:

> In the 1980s the design team could simply make a decision that we would work really hard on this or that project. It didn't matter if this meant working over the weekend because we just wanted to finish the project. The head of the design office accepted that we could work at a relatively relaxed rate afterwards. Not that we only worked a couple of hours a day, it was just that no time pressure was put on us for a while. Now (1999) we feel that time pressure constantly. There is virtually no time for lunch, because you have so much to do in one day. It is really pressurized, and this may increase the possibilities of making mistakes.
>
> (Rasmussen 1999: 26)

Time pressure is not a new experience in the design office. The new tendency in the 1990s is the constant time pressure that gives no opportunities to recover after a period of intensified work. The average lead-time for product development has been halved during the last 10 years in several design offices in Denmark. Designers have less and less time to reflect and work with various possible solutions in parallel processes. How does this increased and constant time pressure affect the designer's capacity to work creatively?

> From a qualitative perspective it is better to work with three or four units in parallel, just because they are mutually connected. But now we have to focus on just one unit, and make decisions about that alone. These decisions impact on the other units, it is true, but the

number of possible solutions are limited if we work in that way. If we didn't have the time pressure – as we have now – we could have worked in parallel with several units at the same time and have experimented and tested many more possible ideas.

(Rasmussen 1999: 17)

As the above indicates, constant time pressure may influence the work process in several senses. First, ideas might not be followed up or checked out because of lack of time. Second, even if the idea is taken forward, the limited time available for experimenting with several units simultaneously restricts the complexity of ideas that can be tested. Third, as several authors have pointed out (for instance, Poincaré 1952; Csikzentmihalyi 1988; Johnson-Laird 1988; Henderson 1998), being creative requires time. For instance, Johnson-Laird stresses that some levels of creativity depend on the time constraints involved and the opportunities to revise and nurture the outcomes at different stages of the process. Even though flashes of sudden insight might occur, the creative process as such is not considered to be something that can be speeded up without limit. Creative outcomes may turn out to be a time-consuming process, particularly if a really new design is supposed to be developed. Of course, time pressure as such does not necessarily have a negative effect on creativity. Some designers experience time pressure as a big challenge that they try to meet. However, if time pressure is not just temporary but is rather an everyday experience (as it seems to have become in several design offices during the 1990s), this may influence both the physical and psychological working conditions in such a way as to reduce motivation and the time required for creativity in design work.

Networking and isolated design work

Some industrial designers feel a lack of knowledge about what their colleagues in other design teams are doing. One of the middle managers in a Danish design office describes his experience as follows:

I know, of course, what people in my group are doing, but I don't know what they are doing on the other side (of the passage in the design office). And I believe that it is even more restricted if you go out and ask a designer out there: 'What is your colleague beside you doing?' I believe that he will have difficulties to answer that question ... We talk very little about the projects.

(Rasmussen 1999: 28)

On the other hand, geographical distance seems to have less and less influence on membership of design teams. The following example from a Danish design office illustrates this phenomenon:

> Three people here participate in an international development project that is managed by a project leader from one of the other companies of our concern. These three people have nothing to do with our company. They are doing something that nobody else here (in the design office) knows about. I believe that will be more and more general in use in the future.
>
> (Rasmussen 1999: 31)

In principle, there are no physical borders any more. As the above-mentioned example indicates, prospective design teams may consist of members from various design offices situated in various companies, regions and/or nations. Such fragmented design teams may use electronic means of communication as well as occasional face-to-face meetings. But they might have no relationship to the design office, which functions as a 'guest house'. The paradoxical situation seems to be that some industrial designers do not have the slightest knowledge about what their colleagues sitting next to them are doing, while at the same time they are involved in intensive electronic dialogue with colleagues in other companies. How will such changed patterns of communication influence efficiency and creativity in industrial designing? The lack of communication among members of different design teams may have some negative effects, as one designer in a Danish design office describes it:

> If you know what your colleagues on the other side of the passage (in the design office) are doing, and you get a problem that is very similar to what they have been dealing with already, then you may be able to save time if you go and ask him about it instead of doing the same work as he did once. Perhaps we should give that a thought.
>
> (Rasmussen 1999: 29)

In other words, the risk of reduced (or no) communication between members of different design teams is that a lot of duplication might occur. On the other hand, internationally established design teams may challenge conventional ways of doing industrial design and perhaps foster new ideas to transcend culturally determined boundaries, *if* they are managed in a manner that allows sufficient openness and time to explore new ideas. Perhaps the biggest risk to the full use of the opportunities set by 'designing without borders' is the constantly increasing time pressure on industrial designing.

Creativity and the acquisition of work process knowledge

Creative design practice depends on availability of time to rebuild, modify and reorganize the daily work experiences through informal and formal dialogues with colleagues. However, if the design office of the future is becoming the target for an increase in Taylorist management principles, the accumulation of work process knowledge will be seriously restricted. The *explicit* aspects of work process knowledge – such as crucial connections between different functions within the company, shared understanding of the various roles, as well as the flow of information of the product from the raw material to retail outlet – will be difficult to accumulate for the individual industrial designers due to constant time pressure and social isolation from other people except their own design team. The *implicit* aspects of work process knowledge will also be difficult to accumulate. For instance, young, relatively inexperienced industrial designers will have difficulties targeting an implicit understanding of collective models of how design work is carried out in practice, if informal interaction patterns with elder and more experienced colleagues are seriously restricted or eliminated. Creative work process experiences are not automatically transformed into work process knowledge. They have to be reflected on, discussed and reframed in relation to one or several collective models, before the transformation occurs. Relenting pressure to reduce the lead-time of the design process may be competitive – in the short term. But if this means a reduction in opportunities to acquire and reframe creative work experiences, competitive advantage will be seriously reduced in the long term. For the challenge of responding to constantly changing market conditions calls for design based not only on quick-wittedness and advanced technology, but also on a creativity which draws on accumulated work process knowledge.

7 Creating work process knowledge with new technology in a financial services workplace

Norma Lammont and Nicholas Boreham

Contemporary researchers such as Halal (1996), Read (1996), Tenakasi and Boland (1996) and Fischer and Nakakoji (1997) argue that the economy is characterized by firms employing specialized knowledge workers, who require new kinds of skill and who work with new technology in new kinds of organization. With their intellectual capital the key to their employers' success, the way in which their knowledge is constructed in the workplace and shared with colleagues becomes an important issue for research (Fleck 1997). In the past, economic debates often assumed that the knowledge that drives industrial innovation is created externally to the production process – for example, in scientific research laboratories sponsored by universities and governments. Today, however, a significant part of this knowledge is acknowledged to be created by the workforce themselves. Referring to this way of knowing, Gibbons *et al.* (1994: 3) introduced the concept of 'mode two knowledge', which they define as knowledge created in a context of application by practitioners who are collaborating to solve a problem. The increasing importance of this knowledge can be attributed to the growth of new kinds of commercial organization that depend crucially on their capacity to respond quickly to market demands. For in these organizations, the knowledge generated by employees who deal directly with customers is essential for commercial success. And an essential element in this way of knowing is knowledge of the overall work process.

The debt collection agency

To explore the process of creating and sharing such knowledge in an organization whose operations are almost entirely based on new technology, an observational study of the debt collection department of a major finance house was conducted. Located in a large commercial centre, the department functions as a self-contained agency, which can be called 'Lewisham's'. The department deals with private and commercial debts incurred with the parent finance company. It also collects debts for clients such as utilities, mail order firms and other mass-marketing organizations, which accumulate large numbers of bad debts. Debt collecting is a highly competitive industry, with different companies vying for the business of clients. New technology has been introduced to maintain a competitive position in the market, and at Lewisham's the work is performed with two computer-based tools, 'Melissa' and 'JAWS'. Melissa is an automatic dialling system that incorporates a database of debtors' home telephone numbers. The software dials its way through the list until a debtor answers, whereupon it allocates the call to the next available debt collector. The system maximizes the number of debtors who are connected to a debt collector each working day, and restricts the time allowed for each call to three minutes (although collectors may 'extend' calls if necessary). The other piece of technology, JAWS, maintains a record of each debt and the company's attempts to recover it. This record is updated by the collector after completing a call.

Lewisham's delegates a significant measure of autonomy to its collectors. Unlike many teleworkers, they do not work under close supervision following scripts written by copywriters, but construct their own dialogues with the debtors who are, rather surprisingly, known as their 'customers'. There is no formal vocational preparation for this career; telephone debt collectors acquire most of their expertise on-the-job. Apart from the new technology, their expertise is without doubt the principal asset on which the company's competitive advantage depends. However, the fact that the collectors work individually raises the problem of explaining how individual knowledge generated through one-to-one interactions between collectors and debtors can become an asset for the company as a whole. Some researchers postulate an explicit 'organizational memory' as the mechanism by which experience is transferred between individuals and groups within enterprises (for example, Howells 1995). This assumes that essential knowledge is captured, archived and made systematically available to all. At Lewisham's, however, no such attempt at knowledge elicitation has ever been undertaken, nor have collectors' personal techniques for persuading debtors to pay their bills been codified. Indeed, consistent with many previous studies of practitioner expertise, the collectors find it difficult to explain their technique to others verbally, and in this sense much of it may be described as 'tacit' (Haider 1992; Meerabeau 1992; Maeve 1994; Grant 1997; Garrigou 1998). The richness of the affordances (Henning 1998) offered by the technical objects, spatial–temporal dimensions, particular forms of discourse and social relationships in the working environment make codification of the debt collectors' knowledge all but impossible. Yet a body of work process knowledge has clearly accumulated within the company. As described in the introduction to this volume and in many of the chapters, this knowledge is partly tacit and partly verbalized, partly individual and partly collective. It encapsulates information about the overall work process of the agency, but none of it is the inert knowledge found in textbooks because it is part of the activity managed by

Melissa and JAWS. In this chapter, we explain how work process know-ledge at Lewisham's is generated and shared between debt collectors in the course of their work with the new technology.

The data on which this chapter is based were collected during a 3-month period of participant observation at Lewisham's. The debt collectors – all female – worked an evening shift from 5.00–8.30 pm. In the observation period, three trainee collectors began an intensive 12-week training designed to bring them up to the level of experienced staff on the evening shift. The mainstay of this training was listening while experienced staff held telephone conversations with debtors and negotiated repayment agreements. The first author attended these training sessions with the newcomers, and then worked as a collector alongside the regular employees. The participant observation was supplemented by focused group discussions with collectors, and unstructured interviews with the trainees, experienced collectors, team-leaders and the Collections Manager.

Our account of how individual experience becomes work process know-ledge shared by the organization as a whole is based on the theory of the social utilization of artifacts. Vygotsky (1930/85) viewed technology as essentially a means of communication, and maintained that the higher intellectual functions develop through the way in which such artifacts enable men and women to regulate their activity. As knowledge and skill develop through experience with new kinds of technologically based work process, the ways in which people think and act accommodate themselves to the functions and limitations of the artifacts in use. This view was developed further by Leontiev (1976), who asserted that a tool is a product of human culture, a social object and a means by which human thought is developed and expressed. To explain the development and transmission of knowledge and skill in society, Leontiev postulated the progressive acquisition of socially constructed capacities through operations with tools (both material and intellectual). More recently, Zuboff (1988) has developed this line of thought by arguing that the new information and communications technologies 'informate' work by making processes, objects, behaviour and events more visible, knowable and shareable. Rather than simply automating discrete tasks (such as typing or calculating), they rationalize an entire procedure and make it socially available (Hirschorn 1984; Appelbaum and Alpin 1992). Building on these insights, the present chapter will argue that the two computer tools introduced to Lewisham's make the tacit knowledge acquired individually by employees available to all, thus converting individual experience into collective memory.

The account of tool use by Vygotsky, Leontiev and Zuboff assumes a model of the worker as a socialized member of a community whose knowledge and skills are collective and constructed interactively in the workplace. Recently, this perspective has received new impetus from social anthropologists such as Chaiklin and Lave (1988) and Ingold (1992; 1996), who have developed a theory of the interactive construction of shared meaning and understanding. In the view of these writers, knowledge and skill are constructed by the workforce, or rather by groups of workers acting together through mutual observation and reflection (Rose 1991; Fischer and Nakakoji 1997; Raelin 1997). Researchers within this paradigm conduct their analysis at the level of the team or group (Lei 1997) or the entire organization (Kramlinger 1992; McNaughton 1996; Raelin 1997), arguing that context (in the form of collective culture, patterns of socialization, modes of communication and management styles) is critical to the shaping of collective learning and knowledge. Thus in the 'knowledge-creating company', individual learning crystallizes as part of the organizational knowledge system embedded in complex socially created networks (Nonaka 1991; Nonaka 1996). Within this framework, communities of practice which make use of tools do not undertake cognitive work and *then* use tools – rather, the cognition is embedded in the way the tool is used, and the tool structures the thinking.

It is important to recall Leontiev's (1976) insistence that tools are not just physical artifacts (such as screens or computer programs) but incorporate a 'social utilization scheme'. This is the tool's operating procedure, elaborated socially during collective work. It is attached to the tool in the sense that this is how the tool is perceived within the culture in which it is used. The utilization scheme is assimilated by any new member of the workforce who uses the tool in that social context. In this way, technology-in-use becomes the means by which the work culture reproduces itself and transmits knowledge. Using technology helps to determine the individual worker's cognitive structure. Using a tool in a workplace, the new employee acquires the social utilization scheme, which guides his or her thoughts along the pathways the collective work process has already trodden. As Verillon and Rabardel (1995: 87) put it:

> [Instruments – tools and their utilization schemes] have assimilatory capacities: they enable repeatability of action by ensuring its adaptation to intraclass variations of objects and situations. They have accommodating capacities enabling their application to different classes of objects and situations ... they confer signification to the situations in which they are mobilized.

Changes in skill requirements for debt collecting

Before the introduction of new technology such as Melissa and JAWS, debt collecting was conducted with paper files and the collectors dialled their own numbers on traditional handsets. At first sight, the core activity of present-day collectors is no different: to speak on the telephone to debtors in their homes, to persuade them to pay some money to

Lewisham's acting as agents for the creditor and then to negotiate the repayment schedule. However, on more detailed examination, it emerges that the essential nature of the work has altered significantly. One influential factor is the new reward system introduced at the same time as the new technology. Collectors are paid a basic wage and a bonus. To determine the bonus, each collector is now set a target amount of cash to collect over the coming 4-week period, calculated on an average of his or her incomings over the last 6 months. If a debtor agrees to a schedule of repayments and then defaults, the difference between the value of instalments set in any 4-week period, compared with the cash that actually comes into the office, is counted as a 'debit performance' for the collector concerned. When a new arrangement is established with the debtor (usually by another collector), the latter and not the original collector will be awarded the bonus for any money that eventually arrives. Consequently, the crucial skill of debt collecting is not just to secure a verbal agreement to make a repayment; it is to create a genuine commitment on the part of the debtor to adhere to the arrangement that has been made. In order to achieve this, experienced collectors know that it is essential to control the interaction with the debtor firmly and assertively from the start. The crucial interpersonal dynamic is to be proactive rather than reactive.

Controlling the interaction from the outset of the call depends on another new skill requirement arising from the new technology – the ability to 'get the picture' of an account quickly. When a call is answered, Melissa transfers it to the first available collector and displays the debtor's information in the JAWS workspace on the collector's workstation monitor. The collector has just a few seconds to decide tactics for dealing with the debtor, and this requires the ability to get the picture of the account immediately – in other words, to perceive the significant pattern underlying the many pieces of data on the screen. Experienced collectors see the account as a whole with a past and a future, and use experience to guide them; for example, 'fresh' debts are known to be the easiest to collect, while ones which have been recycled around several agencies are notoriously troublesome. The swift comprehension of the screen-based information is a perceptual skill similar to that described by Harper and Hughes (1993) in their study of air traffic controllers, who also need to grasp a particular air traffic configuration quickly and maintain it in their working memory.

In addition to these new skill requirements, however, there has also been a significant amount of deskilling. Lewisham's acquired the new technology in direct response to the challenge of competing debt collection companies who introduced the same or similar systems themselves. The other companies had become more aggressive in their approach to debtors, and in order to survive, Lewisham's also became more ruthless. In the past, when speed of working was not at such a premium, collectors had been encouraged to adopt a 'firm but fair' attitude towards debtors. Accordingly, they had developed what can loosely be described as counselling skills. While the aim was obviously still to collect the debt, a collector would take pride in helping the debtor cope with his or her financial predicament. For example, if the debtor had multiple debts, the collector might enquire about the whole range of liabilities (some of which might not be the responsibility of Lewisham's) and negotiate a scheme of repayment that was affordable within the overall context. Under the competitive pressure of modern debt collecting, however, such kindness is viewed simply as lost income. 'Counselling' has been discouraged by management, and the pressure to deal with a call within the 3 minutes Melissa allows the collector has effectively eliminated it.

The narrative as social utilization scheme

In the present section, we consider how the application of the two computer tools to debt collecting has *informated* it (Zuboff 1988) – this, it will be argued, is the means by which the knowledge acquired by individual collectors at their workstations becomes available to the entire workforce, and is a central process in the creation and use of work process knowledge. The new technology has informated debt collecting, in the sense that it generates information about the overall work process (that is, the productive and administrative processes through which the organization accomplishes its work). It can record, play back and make visible the processes underlying many different debt collecting operations. Thus it increases the transparency of work activities that were once partially or completely obscure, hidden in the private jottings and personal memories of collectors who worked with paper files and their own portfolio of customers. An important feature of the new technology from this point of view is the 'narrative', the reports typed into the JAWS database by collectors to record what occurred during telephone conversations with debtors, and what action was taken as a result. Over time, the notes entered into an account in the JAWS database accumulate into what is often a lengthy history of attempts to recover the arrears. Because Melissa assigns each newly connected call to the next available collector, not necessarily the one who handled the account when the debtor was last contacted, the narrative is constructed and read by many collectors – all the staff of the agency, if the case goes on long enough. While the original intention of Melissa's designers in assigning each call to the next available collector was to ensure that all collectors were fully occupied, the unintended outcome has been that individually constructed meanings become the understandings of the group of collectors as a whole.

It should perhaps be emphasized that the entries collectors type into JAWS do not contain rules, how-to's or inductive generalizations about debt collecting which might be used to instruct others. No such entries were observed during the 3 months of participant observation. Rather, the meaning of the entries is indexical; they possess significance only in the context in which they are used. For example, words are often used performatively in the narrative – that is, as tools to move the action on in particular ways. In constructing the narrative, terms such as the following are used: DNB (I do not believe it) and !!! (incredulity). These marks and symbols convey the feeling-state which a particular collector might have experienced when talking to a customer, powerful emotions conveyed to others who have not participated in the conversation but more significant in this context than an explicit description of fact. In this way, the tacit aspect of interactive skill becomes available to the whole group. However, as the sense of an index depends on the circumstances in which it is used, these entries can be interpreted only by being involved in the culture that gives the signs their significance, and to this extent they constitute a private language constructed and shared by members of the agency.

To illustrate this, let us see how an experienced collector compiles an entry about a disputed debt. The interpretation of the significance of this narrative, due to the indexical nature of the signs, depends on having worked in the actual environment and is therefore likely to be closed to the reader. Nevertheless, we will try to demonstrate the meaning of these indices by drawing on the experiences of the first author who worked there herself. Each section of narrative must be read from the bottom upwards, as the software adds the latest entry to the top.

> **20.10.95 PAT: TEN DAY DELAY**
> **20.10.95 PAT: WILL SEND PROOF**
> **20.10.95 PAT: ANYTHING**
> **20.10.95 PAT: RTD GOODS VALUE, 300 SO RECKONS DOES NOT OWE**
> **20.10.95 PAT: PLUS**
> **20.10.95 PAT: TEL CUST DISPUTES BALANCE. SED ALREADY PAID**

(TEL means telephoned; CUST means customer; SED means said; RTD means returned)

Here, Melissa has telephoned a customer about a debt owed to a mail-order company, and has allocated the call to a collector named Pat. The debtor disputes the negative balance on her account, maintaining that she has returned goods to the value of the outstanding sum of £300, and offers to send proof. Having worked in this environment, the first author interprets the indexical terms as follow. Pat accepts the debtor's excuse, on the basis of her knowledge of the nature of the debt, the business carried out by the client and her experience with previous disputing debtors. The ground knowledge which enables this construction to be placed on the narrative is that disputed catalogue debts are often relatively small sums, and have often been unsuccessfully recycled round a number of debt collecting agencies. They may be the result of clerical errors (such as failure to acknowledge returned or missing goods), or other breakdowns of communication between purchasers and the customer-service department. On the basis of this knowledge, Pat's instinct is to play the debtor on a long line. So she initiates a 10-day **DELAY** code on the account. During this **DELAY**, which gives the debtor an opportunity to send in her proof, no further calls will be made to her number. Any ensuing postal communication from the debtor will be dealt with by another department, which will remove the **DELAY** and take appropriate action on the account. However, should the required proof fail to materialize, the system will automatically reschedule the account for further action once the 10 days have elapsed. If this happens, the section of narrative reproduced above will appear on another collector's workstation and convey not only the bare facts of the case, but how Pat weighed the evidence and managed the case. This is not only constructing the work process, it is sharing knowledge of it with others. The entry also gives crucial insights to the next collector on how to handle the call Melissa assigns her if the 'proof' has not been sent in. As Nonaka and Takeuchi (1995: 63–4) say: 'Apprentices work with their masters and learn craftsmanship ... through observation, instinct and practice.' In this informated environment, the craftsmanship is being advanced by such a process.

The content of the narrative is not a simple report on an interaction with a debtor, but a round of negotiation with a machine-based system of temporal accountability (Suchman 1993: 117). The interface in JAWS takes the form of command menus that are invoked in order to activate processes in the program that will create certain results. Staff strive to achieve an average rate of on-time arrivals for payments, and they are dedicated to achieving, with a new debt, either a full balance or a first payment within 7 days, or with an existing arrangement, prompt payment as agreed. Discipline is administered through the medium of the computer system: details are entered into JAWS by the collectors when they initially set up a schedule of instalments, and other entries originate with the computer when a payment fails to arrive, when a **DELAY** code lapses, and in response to a number of other eventualities. Entries are also compiled by the finance department as payments arrive, or by regional offices if payments are made direct to doorstep collectors. All these entries serve both as a resource for colleagues, and as the audit trail for the essential work of getting the cash back. As we have indicated, the tacit knowledge which individuals acquire while doing this work is made visible by the way the new technology operates and becomes available to all who participate in the activity.

Now let us consider the following narrative which has been constructed by several collectors. In the first extract, the computer has dialled a number which is answered. However, the debtor herself is out; the collector Naomi speaks to her mother. As before, the narrative is read from the bottom line upwards:

21.10.95 NAOMI: AS WD NOT SAY WHO WE WERE
21.10.95 NAOMI: TEL CUST NOT IN SPOKE WOMAN VERY STROPPY

(TEL CUST means telephoned customer; WD means would)

A major constraint on debt collecting with new technology is the legal restrictions in the Data Protection Acts of 1984 and 1998, which require the confidentiality of the debtors on the database to be maintained. Since calls to a debtor's home are often answered by others, collectors must first ensure that they are speaking to the debtor him or herself before discussing an account. In Lewisham's, this problem has been dealt with by creating a fictitious member of staff, 'Pat Matthews'. Should the debtor not be at home, a message is left that Pat Matthews telephoned, asking that the call be returned. Any collector may be called upon to play the part of Pat Matthews when receiving the resulting inbound calls. Consider the following extract:

21.10.95 NAOMI: SED WD NOT PASS ON PAT MAT

When asked to take a Pat Matthews message (PAT MAT), the debtor's mother asks for further information about the caller's identity. Without this information, she refuses to pass on the message. Obedient to the Data Protection Act, Naomi will not disclose the nature of the company's business, as this would compromise the debtor. When pressed, she reluctantly agrees to disclose the company name and places a 2-day delay on the account:

21.10.95 NAOMI: TWO DAY DELAY
21.10.95 NAOMI: MESSAGE LEFT FOR CUSTOMER TO CALL BACK
21.10.95 NAOMI: SO GAVE HER CO NAME

This record of Naomi's predicament is plain to see for all other collectors who access this case, as is her way of dealing with it. It embodies a sophisticated set of dealings which appear almost impossible to describe in terms of rules. For example, her description of the mother as 'VERY STROPPY' is not an attempt to record a fact, but a warning for any colleague who might subsequently deal with that account – a performative utterance. Naomi inserts a 2-day **DELAY** on the account, giving the debtor an opportunity to return the call. However, as the story unfolds, the debtor does not return the Pat Matthews call, and the system redials the number after the 2-day **DELAY** has expired. This time the call is allocated to a collector called Irene. Once again, the customer is unavailable, so Irene leaves another Pat Matthews message with the mother. She then updates the system and places a further **DELAY** on the account. Reading as before from the bottom up:

> **25.10.95 IRENE: TWO DAY DELAY**
> **25.10.95 IRENE: MESSAGE LEFT FOR CUSTOMER TO CALL BACK.**
> **25.10.95 IRENE: TEL CUST NOT IN SPOKE TO WOMAN 7.30**

The following day, Joanne takes an incoming call from the debtor's mother ('non-customer', in Lewisham's jargon) with whom Irene left the 'Pat Matthews' message. The mother wants to speak to Pat Matthews (who Joanne realizes is Irene) and complains that she was rude to her.

> **26.10.95 JOANNE: SED WD GET HER CALL BACK**
> **26.10.95 JOANNE: SED IRENE RUDE TO HER YESTDY**
> **26.10.95 JOANNE: INC CALL. NON-CUST SED WANTED IRENE**

(INC means incoming; NON-CUST means non-customer; YESTDY means yesterday)

Although brief and to the point, the narrative entry assists Irene in formulating her response when she returns the mother's call:

> **27.10.96 IRENE: GAVE NAME. SUGGESTED CALL/WRITE DISCUSS W LIZ**
> **27.10.96 IRENE: EXPLAINED RULE & FOLLOWING MANAGER INSTRUCT**
> **27.10.96 IRENE: HUMILIATED COS ASKED HER READ PAT MAT BACK**
> **27.10.96 IRENE: TEL. SPOKE WOMAN CLAIMED I WAS RUDE & BOLSHY**

(MANAGER INSTRUCT means manager's instructions; W means with; COS means because)

Irene returns the non-customer's call, and learns that the complaint is that she was asked to read back the Pat Matthews number when the message was left. She found this humiliating, and accuses Irene of being **RUDE** and **BOLSHY**. Irene explains that asking recipients to repeat the number is company policy, and in doing so she is acting upon instructions from her manager. Although the narrative does not elaborate on the non-customer's response, it is apparent that the recipient is not satisfied with this explanation. Irene suggests that the non-customer contact **LIZ** (the Collections Manager) to discuss this matter in person. The entry **GAVE NAME** indicates that Irene provides the caller with the appropriate name, job title and location of the person to whom she can direct her complaint, should she wish to pursue the matter.

These narrative entries will assist Irene in any account of her actions she might have to give to the Collections Manager. She will be able to cite Naomi's narrative entry, which independently describes the non-customer as **VERY STROPPY**, in support of her own version of the encounter if the manager questions her behaviour. The entries capture the kind of complex interactions that are occurring all the time at Lewisham's, providing a powerful way of immersing newcomers into the work process knowledge that is embedded in the norms of interaction in this particular workplace.

Knowledge creation and transmission with Melissa and JAWS

In Lewisham's, by standing proxy for the actions of colleagues who previously dealt with an account, the narrative furnishes collectors with a framework for perceiving its history and likely future. The social utilization scheme for the computer debt-collecting tools Melissa and JAWS is embedded in these narratives. The transactions recorded therein are objects which represent whole sets of institutionalized processes, such as recording the actions taken both by the computer system and the collector, setting up payment schedules and sending routine letters. The narratives do not *determine* the sequence of a collector's actions, in the sense that the Fordist automatic assembly line determines the work of a car assembly worker. Rather, a collector will treat a narrative account as one resource among others that can be utilized to organize work activity. He or she must make sense of the narrative and then organize the information into an instrument that helps and makes possible the work of collecting debts. Looking at the narrative, and comprehending the events recorded in it, draws her attention to problems which need to be anticipated. The narrative makes available, transforms or otherwise manages organized social activities. The records placed there organize, and are organized by, the circumstances in which they occur. They are not external to social activity, but subject to the same range of circumstantial and interpretive contingencies as the actions and circumstances they describe.

The problem introduced at the beginning of this chapter was that the knowledge created in the workplace is a major asset on which companies depend for profit and competitiveness, but is difficult to transmit in codified form due to its tacit component. The explanation proposed here for the fact that Lewisham's generates a great deal of work process knowledge at the organizational level is that tacit knowledge can be transmitted without being codified through the power of new technology to informate. The information stored in the system does not consist of codified knowledge such as rules, how-tos or principles for debt collecting, but a complex of indexical and performative meanings that enables individual lived experience to become available to the whole workforce.

It is important to appreciate that this work process knowledge is not just *stored on* the computer system. It is also constructed through the *use* of the computer system, a tool which simultaneously becomes the physical procedure for processing information and the social utilization scheme which gives the procedure its meaning and purpose. It is through this crucial process that work process knowledge is constructed and exchanged. Operations carried out with the technology achieve their distinctive character by being part of the organization of the work – by being intertwined with the language with which actors conduct their affairs, produce arguments and justifications and acknowledge one another's worlds. Boland and Tenakasi (1995) liken communication in such 'communities of knowing' to a language game played in a local culture, where the ability to take the perspective of another into account is essential.

The argument that knowledge created in the context of work is difficult to replicate in other environments has led to claims that there are limits to the contribution of learning organizations to economic development. For example, Dunphy (1997) suggests that the concept of the learning organization may be little more than a powerful emotive symbol which excites enthusiasm in devotees, but has little substance in fact. Similarly, Alvesson (1993) describes corporate competencies as an institutionalized myth and emphasizes the janus-like nature of knowledge work, which pays lip-service to the struggle for rationality yet contains multifarious rhetorical strategies and contradictions. Conklin (1992) argues that experience accumulated in the firm (or its organizational memory) cannot be communicated by workers under traditional, extensively formalized managerial procedures, and Lam (1997) asserts that the socially embedded nature of work-related knowledge impedes cross-boundary collaborative work and knowledge transfer because, as Senker (1993) points out, it can only be transmitted through personal interaction. One inference that can be drawn from the present study is that the transmissibility of work process knowledge may be greater than these researchers suggest, if new technology is interpreted, not as an external driver of change, but as a tool whose use is constructed partly by the work process itself. In this view, technology becomes a social accomplishment, and the social practices through which the participants recognisably and accountably orient themselves to it in the course of its everyday use, become the means by which the tacit knowledge of individuals becomes a knowledge of the work process which can be shared by the organization as a whole.

8 Dimensions of work process knowledge

Maria Teresa Oliveira, Ana Luisa Oliveira Pires and Mariana Gaio Alves

In addressing the question of how work process knowledge grows and develops, this chapter will consider three different dimensions of this complex process: the organizational, the educational and the individual. It will also investigate the implications for the construction of vocational identities. Our starting point is the concept of work process knowledge developed in the EU project WHOLE (Boreham and Lammont 2001). Thus we mean by work process knowledge the capacity to carry out work tasks by mobilizing different kinds of knowledge, not the codified knowledge recorded in textbooks, nor the habits acquired automatically on-the-job, but a new construction out of both ways of knowing that is generated in the course of solving problems in the workplace (Boreham 2002). The chapter has three sections. The first focuses on changes in the organization of work, its articulation with the construction of work process knowledge and the development of individual competencies within work contexts. The second section deals with the challenge of helping university students to construct work process knowledge in preparation for the world of work. In this section, we also present the results of some studies into the relationship between higher education and the labour market. The third section concentrates on how the development of work process knowledge is related to the construction of professional identities. In the conclusion, we bring these three dimensions together in an account of how work process knowledge is developed.

The construction of work process knowledge in the context of work

A new paradigm of work is emerging, characterized by more technological, organizational and human-resource flexibility. This is a response to the increasing competitiveness within a business context characterized by uncertainty and unpredictability, often accompanied by technological innovation. However, the introduction of new technologies to promote flexibility and modernization does not ensure commercial success. According to Kovács (1992: 27), a company often

... hopes for improved competitiveness without having to make changes in its structure, production organization and/or human resource management. But the use of new technologies does not by itself eliminate existing organizational handicaps; on the contrary, it may even aggravate them. Modernizing equipment cannot substitute for modernizing the organization.

For Kovács, there are two strategies of modernization. The technological strategy relies strongly on the introduction of new production technologies, while the other strategy focuses on the quality of human resources, on 'intelligent' organization, on optimization of information processes and on the effectiveness of relations established between work teams at all levels of the organization. Present-day conditions demand this flexibility in order to meet the challenges of competition, quality, shorter time-to-market, customization, product innovation and diversification (Kovács 1992). Flexibility brings organizational structure and human factors to the centre of the picture, and to achieve it company structure becomes simpler (with fewer levels of hierarchy, decentralization of decision-making and responsibility and increased participation by individuals in decision-making). Functional co-operation is improved and more effective information and communication channels are established. The work force is given additional autonomy and a wider range of skills, individual and collective learning are recognized as factors of paramount importance for organizational development and training performs a fundamental role. As argued elsewhere in this volume, these trends require employees to acquire work process knowledge, and this in turn demands the integration of formal knowledge acquired in education and training systems with informal knowledge acquired within work and life contexts.

The study of non-technical competencies – often known as personal, social or transversal competencies – has attracted attention in the last few years mainly because these competencies are transferable to different situations if conditions are favourable. It is claimed that these competencies facilitate performance throughout the whole of working life, allowing the individual to cope with changes in work and increasing occupational mobility. In a review of the literature on non-technical competencies, Pires (1995) found that different authors define them in different ways. Amongst the most significant concepts in this domain are creativity, flexibility, autonomy, teamwork, communication and language competencies, and the ability to learn in different situations and contexts.

Language competencies are particularly significant, as flexible models of work organization recognize the power of language. In participatory management, where all workers are expected to engage fully in order to create an enterprise culture, language plays an important role. Of course, all businesses involve language activities. The novel idea, however, is the recognition that language is a factor of production, a source of productivity, an instrument of management and a vector of social mobilization. Language then becomes a central concern in work organization in order to foster the involvement of workers, their active participation and consensus building in decision-making, and more importantly, for encouraging them to show initiative and critical awareness about the production process (Borzeix 1995). The new role for language competencies in transformed work situations is related to the decrease in manual operations on products or objects and the increase in the use of signs, codes and symbols in the workplace. In technologically developed societies, the work process is continually undergoing rapid change due to the development of new information and communication technologies, telematics, automatization, robotization of production and the growth of the service sector. Consequently, the role of language in the workplace has shifted both quantitatively and qualitatively. Generally speaking, the importance of written or spoken language has increased in all new jobs, while the transformation of matter and physical work has decreased. Nowadays, the labour market demands skill in the symbolic competencies necessary to read a table, a diagram or a report, to write a note, to fill in a questionnaire and to synthesize information, and this holds true for all levels of employment. In short, production, communication and interpretation are closely interlinked.

Development of competencies in work contexts

Within the conceptual frameworks of situated learning and communities of practice, organizations may be seen as contexts for the development of competencies (Lave and Wenger 1991; Wenger 1998; Evans 2000; Evans and Hoffman 2000). The new models of work organization are creating new opportunities for learning at work, and these in turn are leading to increased recognition of the importance of informal, situated and experience-based learning processes. The company, with its potential for learning, can stimulate the individual and collective learning of its employees, and thereby promote its own growth. Thus we are witnessing the dissolution of traditional boundaries between learning and work. The space-time for production, insofar as it contributes to the development of individuals' competencies, may become a privileged space-time for learning, promoting individual and collective learning by the participants.

Several studies have focused on the learning potential in work situations (Zarifian 1986, 1992, 1995; Madelin and Thierry 1992; Mallet 1995; Onstenk 1995; Gama 1997). The emergence of the 'learning organization' concept stresses the importance organizations have in promoting individual and collective learning. This type of organization is a very rich learning environment, and as such should be considered an educational organization as well as a business environment, as it has the potential for optimizing the learning abilities of those directly involved (Madelin and Thierry 1992). On this view, learning is not only what happens within designated training activities, but also within the framework of the production process. That is, learning occurs in informal contexts, and is generated by production itself (Gama 1997).

Onstenk (1995) points out that learning is gaining growing importance, especially with respect to competency and qualification building, alongside continuous change in work organization and the introduction of new production technologies. For Onstenk, the paradigm is characterized by the existence of the work team as a fundamental unity, replacing the individual function, and by the need to generate problem-solving strategies to cope with the highly unpredictable nature of work. In this way, the new kinds of work organization and new production concepts require types of competence quite different from the traditional ones. It is within this context that the need for a wide range of non-technical competencies is needed, in addition to specific professional and procedural knowledge.

Stressing the importance of contextual learning in real-life situations, Onstenk (1955: 35) observes that

> ... learning in workplaces should not be confused with training in workplaces, as the latter has an explicit pedagogic structure, namely training objectives and programmes, and requires the active participation of the trainer and the use of didactic material, training tasks and evaluations ... Learning in workplaces is a multidimensional process that can be analysed in terms of different functions inherent in work activities and situations themselves.

The author identifies the learning potential of the work situation as the result of an interaction between the individual's characteristics (qualifications and experience, acquired competencies, aptitudes, willingness to learn, motivation), the learning opportunities offered by the labour market (characteristics of the functions performed and the work environment) and the availability of training in the workplace.

Learning conditions within organizations

A number of factors may be deemed important for the acquisition of competencies in the workplace. These can broadly be understood as a combination of general and technical knowledge, attitudes, behaviours and skills. The factors important for their acquisition include work organization, organizational culture, organizational climate, the specific features of communities of practices, entrepreneurial communication and the kind of relationship established, the degree of autonomy and responsibility conferred on the actors, work complexity and the incentive system, among others. Rolo (1996) investigated the problem of learning in work contexts and stresses the following requirements:

- that an organization is open to its surroundings and provides rich learning experiences that increase job satisfaction;
- that work tasks are engaging, so that employees feel a need to participate fully;
- that team work is adopted as a way of developing a participatory culture in which collaboration and problem solving are positively valued;
- that there are opportunities for the learning process to develop autonomously and take advantage of informal spaces for learning; and
- that the development of positive relationships among the actors is encouraged, as well as the stability of the work force, mutual knowledge, personal affinities, local knowledge, an active role within management and informality of relationships.

Further ways in which organizational and employment factors can contribute to personal and professional development are discussed by Gama (1997). Company management should themselves be engaged in learning, thus creating a favourable climate for the engagement of the employees. Learning projects should be designed to increase interaction between the individual and the organization. The engagement of workers in the company's projects, especially problem-solving, should provide them with a sense of completion and achievement. Learning should be context-specific (emphasizing learning processes such as self-evaluation, team work, task forces and involvement in planning). To create learning situations such as these, the organization must commit itself to organizational change of the kinds described, especially a new distribution of tasks and responsibilities. At the same time, it is essential to ensure that the development does not become a permanent and continuous instability. It is of crucial importance to find a coherent balance between change and stability, in order to establish conditions for learning to take place (Mallet 1995).

Time management is also fundamental for learning, as understanding what is happening in the workplace requires time for reflection and discussion. It also demands a different type of relationship with colleagues than the usual command and control relationships. As Mallet (1995: 15) points out, 'an organization subject to a permanent urgency, and thus pressured to distribute the work to the best existing skills (the individual who does it better, does it faster) will not promote learning opportunities'.

Adult learning and the development of work process knowledge

Learning is strongly dependent on reflection. As self-reflection and the attribution of meaning are essential parts of the construction of work process knowledge, attention must be given to individual preferences for the rate at which things are learned and experienced.

> Acquisition of knowledge about the work being done, in a reflective and critical way – action backgrounds, features and objectives – requires superior learning ability on the part of the workers, openness to reflection and feed-back and opportunity to think about problems faced at work, in order to promote an exchange of view on operating procedures and learning to learn.
>
> (Onstenk 1995: 35–6)

The role of experience and reflection in the adult learning process has attracted much attention from educational researchers (Pineau 1989, 1991a, b; Finger 1989; Dominicé 1990, 1991; Josso 1988, 1989, 1991). In order for experience to become learning, it has to be rebuilt, modified and reorganized. To be reflected on, there must exist a cognitive process drawing on language and thought. Distance and critical integration are also needed. The learning dimension of experience depends a great deal on the individual cultural resources that allow the making of meaning; to become learning, it has to be reflected on, thought about and symbolized so that it can produce an echo (Dominicé 1991). This mental reconstruction requires consecutive thinking and cognitive perception and is thus abstracted from the phenomenon accessible for experience (Fischer, Chapter 9 of this volume). According to Meneses (1996), by analysing practice, the actor constructs a professional role and this allows him or her to adopt a social position.

Adult socialization processes are based on intentions and initiatives. The adult, with his or her personal agenda, can resist attempts at socialization imposed from outside if he or she does not recognize them as significant. Thus the individual has a decisive role in his or her own learning process. The concept of educational autonomy is fundamental – it is individual initiative, motivation, autonomy and interest that engages in the learning process, within a context of educational potential (Pain 1991).

Learning from experience requires new management styles and new patterns of participation in the workplace (Gama 1997). Participation is essential for creative production. According to Gelpi (1989), this kind of approach is not compatible with bureaucratic and hierarchic productive structures. This reinforces the view that learning in the workplace is closely related to the way the work itself is organized.

The construction of work process knowledge at university

Today, many if not most university graduates are no longer employed in 'graduate' jobs but enter the general labour market. This creates challenges for higher education, as it is no longer sufficient to prepare individuals for specific kinds of employment. The current trend in the higher educational system is therefore to empower young people with a wider range of competencies acquired on broadly based courses, emphasizing the development of a general disposition for self-directed learning (learning to learn) and a new set of non-technical competencies, which are deemed fundamental throughout the entire active life of the individual. A crucial part of this endeavour is the acquisition of work process knowledge.

The non-technical competencies, which were discussed earlier, are developed through processes of identification and socialization in the varied contexts of the individual's life (personal, educational, social and professional) during a lifespan consisting of work experience, involvement in projects, practice and study. Harrison (1996) analyses these kinds of transferable competency in detail and suggests that the activities they entail can be used to provide a bridge between educational provision aimed at developing vocational competencies and provision that aims to develop learning to learn.

The concept of work process knowledge presents a challenge to higher education, which is traditionally oriented to the acquisition of specialized knowledge and technical competencies. It is possible to create favourable learning contexts for the development of work process knowledge within formal systems of higher education and professional training, but it is necessary to rethink traditional learning models and strategies, and especially to introduce new dimensions such as the following:

- a stronger articulation of formal learning with work-based learning;
- the adoption of active learning processes which include the development of higher-order thinking skills in problem-solving situations;
- the encouragement of experiential learning;
- an understanding of the contexts and processes of work in the modern economy through continuous personal and collective reflection.

Language and the processes of education and training at the university

One of the many responsibilities of the modern university is preparing teachers for the field of vocational education and training ('training the trainers'). At the same time, there is a general trend towards university–company partnerships, aiming among other things to exchange knowledge, and to benefit from collaboration in research and practice. In the context of these developments, we turn to the role of language as a medium for developing the cognitive, personal, social and cultural competencies needed to enable the reflection and self-assessment of work experience implied by the acquisition of work process knowledge. While knowledge of this kind is developed through personal experience of the actual work situation, as Fischer (Chapter 9 of this volume) and Lammont (2000:6) have emphasized, direct experience itself is not enough, and needs to be mediated in some way. Language is of course an important way of mediating direct experience, but the necessary language competencies do not arise spontaneously. Consequently, it becomes necessary to develop uses of language that will support the acquisition of work process knowledge.

The interdisciplinary field of language and work is not yet well defined or much studied, and as a result is not a common aspect of professional training. In fact, this innovative approach to language studies in education still meets some resistance from practitioners due to its complexity (Lazar 1998). Some teacher trainers in the vocational field fail to grasp the importance of the systematic study of language and work, but in this they are overlooking the significance this field of study has acquired due to the rapid transformations that are occurring in society. The introduction of new technologies in the context of far-reaching socio-economic change presents us with the challenge of understanding the societal preconditions for these transformations, and the social purposes that are met by the introduction of the new technological tools. It is therefore crucial to create a pedagogy for developing competencies embedded in a language (about work, in work or as work) which has an emancipatory role, empowering the individual to change his or her own professional behaviour.

Work inevitably entails problem-solving and decision-making, activities dependent on higher-order thinking and reflection. To solve a problem in the workplace, it is necessary to identify it as a problem, to diagnose it, to reflect, to formulate hypotheses, to build up dialogues, to argue, to make inferences, to communicate the results, to suggest transformations, to learn and to act. All these in varying ways involve the use of language. In addition to the primary language, each trade and profession has its own scientific and technological second language, with many specific terms and localized areas of meaning, all of which need to be mastered.

Developing higher education curricula that include studies of language and work is no simple task. The complex relationships between language and work are dealt with in many disciplines, including psychology, sociology, linguistics, pragmatics, ergonomics and cognitive science, all of which are useful theoretical models.

Learning the language of work is more than a matter of acquiring functional language skills. Because these skills are embedded in specific work contexts, there is also a need to develop reflective awareness of one's own learning style, an appreciation of how collective learning takes place in companies and to create actual opportunities for learning within the company environment. All three are essential. In a recent study, Oliveira (1998) describes how language is dealt with in pre-service courses of training for vocational science and technology teachers and trainers in Portugal. The empirical results show that the issue of language is ignored by roughly two-thirds (68 per cent) of the sample. Moreover, the trainers of teachers and trainers who do explore language issues in their courses seem to focus on the use of language as a teaching tool rather than as a learning tool. In particular, it seems that they do not recognize the extent to which language is a tool for thought and has an important connection with work.

Graduates' evaluation of their initial academic education

An exploratory study was carried out into the way university education makes use of placements in the world of work. The survey (Ambrósio and Alves 1994) gathered data on the training and professional development of a sample of graduates and assessed needs for continuing professional development in the Portuguese context. The study also contained findings about the demand for non-technical competencies in the labour market, and the strategies used by graduates to acquire them.

The sample consisted of graduates of two degree programmes in administration and two in computing with at least 5 years' professional experience. The results show that the individuals recognized that they were required to possess non-technical competencies in order to carry out their professional work, and that they further recognized that such competencies were developed by practice in specific work situations. The strongest expectations were 'responsibility' (65.1 per cent), 'auto-nomy/initiative ability' (45.6 per cent) and 'team-work ability' (32.9 per cent). When questioned on how they had developed these competencies, respondents reported that the most important factor was 'practical experience' (88.4 per cent) followed by 'training in the workplace' (18 per cent). Most individuals agreed with the proposition that these kinds of competencies were developed in work contexts. Significantly, they did not mention initial formal training as the source of these competencies.

Other results of this inquiry relate to the usefulness of the initial stage of higher education and participants' involvement in continuing training after receiving a degree. Half the subjects (50.5 per cent) were enrolled on degree courses at the time of the inquiry or were taking additional train-ing. The majority (80 per cent) declared that they were working in a pro-fessional area for which they had had adequate initial academic education. Again, the majority (85 per cent) responded that they applied knowledge and competencies acquired during the initial stage of higher education in their present work. This suggests a high level of satisfaction with initial aca-demic education as a preparation for the world of work, at least in these subject areas. The majority considered that initial academic education taught them to exercise 'self evaluation' throughout their professional life (78.6 per cent), and contributed both to an 'improvement of their career status' (67.3 per cent) and 'professional mobility' (58.5 per cent).

It is worth emphasizing, however, that a large number of subjects (75.5 per cent) thought that, despite the vocational importance of knowledge acquired in initial academic education, there are other types of knowledge and competencies that are very useful to the efficient performance of a professional activity. Practical experience seems to them the best way of obtaining and developing both technical knowledge and non-technical competencies (83.2 per cent). They also mentioned the significance of a period of probation in the workplace (36.6 per cent) during which they reported that they acquired and developed non-technical competencies such as responsibility, initiative and teamwork ability.

Continuous training opportunities for higher education graduates

In 1993, we carried out research into continuing training opportunities for graduates in Portugal. Training of this kind is provided at universities and other institutions (companies, government bodies, professional associ- ations and research centres). For each provider institution, we classified training opportunities according to occupational areas, number of courses, the timetable, the budget, the type of certification and criteria used in the definition of the target group (such as area of initial training, age and pro- fessional experience of trainees). On analysing the data, we felt entitled to raise some serious questions about the relevance of the courses provided by these institutions to the needs of those who were not continuing in a well- defined field of higher education. On the whole, universities seemed to privilege courses oriented towards fundamental research while neglecting the need to provide specialist courses in applied fields, although there were some exceptions. The provision of continuous training for graduates in the non-university institutions, on the other hand, appears to have had a more vocational character. Non-university institutions privileged close links between training and work context, and seem to have been meeting voca- tional needs neglected by university education.

Institutional evaluation of the relationships between universities and the labour market

The internal evaluation practices of 31 universities in eight European countries were studied in a project carried out between 1996 and 1998 involving Finland, France, Germany, Italy, Norway, Portugal, Spain and the UK (Dubois *et al.* 1998). We focus here on the results relating to the education–labour market relationship and its contribution to the construc- tion of professional competence. The results clearly indicated that universi- ties' evaluation of their education–labour market relationships was undeveloped in comparison with other fields of evaluation (such as the evaluation of their research or teachers' performance), and often had a discontinuous, informal and optional character. In Finland, France, Portu- gal and the UK, the evaluation of the relationship between work and train- ing is included in the formal, regular institutional evaluation systems of the universities (Ambrósio and Alves 2000). In other countries, however, it is mainly a voluntary and quite informal process, although interest in this type of evaluation seems to be increasing. Moreover, when an evaluation was carried out, it was usually restricted to studies of the match between the supply of and demand for graduates, based on recruitment and vacancies data. This overlooks the opportunities offered by more sophisticated forms of analysis, such as the contribution by the university to the development of the environment and analysis of curricular provision in the light of the needs of the labour market. In the light of this study, it appears that there are serious limits to the extent to which changes in the labour market are being reflected in changes in higher education provision, at least in Europe as a whole. The most common indicators used to evaluate success in placing graduates in the labour market were 'facility/difficulty in getting a job', 'correspondence between job and training' and the 'satisfaction/ dissatisfaction of graduates with their academic education'. It seems to us that it would be also important to analyse the process by which graduates actually gain access to the labour market.

The development of work process knowledge and the construction of professional identity

The development of work process knowledge is necessarily linked to the individual's activity at work. The process is not limited to secondary or higher education, to work organizations or on-the-job training. Work process knowledge requires the development of technical and non-technical competencies, which are not only the result of formal or informal learning (in school or professional context), but also related both to the individual personality and to the social context.

Construction of work process knowledge: relation to the multiple dimensions of individual life

Occupational identity is part of social identity. This means that it is the result of multiple dimensions (personality, gender, age, ethnicity and cultural, political, professional background), which may be combined and articulated in several forms in the process by which the identity of the individual is structured. The 'social trajectories, the interactions they provoke, their projects and their responsibilities play a decisive part in what the individual performs over lengthy periods' (Le Bouedec 1988: 19). Mobility or job instability and uncertain professional situations might bring about changes in identity. According to Sainsaulieu (1996: 201) 'in accelerating professional mobility, social identity is profoundly disturbed'. Changes in personal or social dimensions might also have implications for occupational identity. This interrelationship is quite evident when we analyse, for example, occupational identity upon entering adult life, the way it articulates with matrimonial and family life, or when we analyse how the delimitation of gender identity determines the development of different roles played by boys or by girls. Thus, in short, representing the construction of work process knowledge as dependent on the construction of identity means that it is not independent of the diverse and complex life experiences of the individual.

Construction of work process knowledge: a process of constant structuring

Competencies are constructed out of multiple social contexts, educational trajectories and training on the job, within an overall process of constructing individual, social and professional identity. In turn, work process knowledge is constructed in a constant and dynamic process which encompasses formal education and training, the work organization and, in a broader perspective, social context and personal life. Occupational identity is the result of self-reflection on the relationships between different work scenarios and different life situations. According to Dubar (1991) this process occurs in four main stages, based on an ideal linear model of career development. In the first stage, which corresponds to the initial training process, the individual builds his or her first occupational identity; in the second stage, through the integration and progressive learning of personal competencies and qualifications, identity consolidation occurs; in the third stage, acquiring responsibilities leads to the recognition of identity; and in the last stage, which continues till the age of retirement, individual identity reaches its peak. According to Dubar, two fundamental confrontations commonly occur during these stages. One is that what the individual considers him or herself to be different from the identity assigned to him or her by others. They are inseparable identity elements, although difficult in terms of their mutual articulation. The other confrontation is between the prior life history and the individual's plans for the future, on one hand, and the social system in which the individual is embedded on the other. This approach to identity goes beyond a strictly psychological approach. Professional identity is created in the interaction between both the psychological and the societal structure. Thus, 'identity is a phenomenon that emerges from the dialectics between individual and society' (Berger and Luckman 1991: 195).

Work process knowledge involves non-technical competencies that mobilize psychological contents (affective and cognitive) as well as social, cultural and behavioural contents, all of which are built up over an individual's entire life in relation to the construction of his or her identity. Knowing the work process is an unfinished process and the state of awareness it produces is permanently in a state of reconstruction, in the sense that its development is strictly related to the identity building process. This occurs throughout the whole of a person's working life, and involves an interaction between the personal and the social, the educational system and the training system, work experience and career development.

Conclusion

These reflections have led us to the conclusion that no form of certification can be taken as evidence that an individual has acquired all the work process knowledge needed for the specific performance of an occupational role. The evidence we have assembled supports the conclusion that in the construction of such knowledge, at least three essential and interdependent dimensions are to be considered.

The first dimension represents work process knowledge as a result of experiential learning from day-to-day events in organizations. Accordingly, it is necessary to explore all the modalities that make it possible to improve learning in work situations. This is because the transformation of the work experiences into learning experiences is not a direct or automatic process, but involves a process of constructing, modifying and reorganizing knowledge. As Pires (1998) observes, it is necessary to confront experience and proceed through a process of analysis that gives it meaning. As part of that process, language is a resource for developing cognitive, personal, social and cultural competencies that will permit reflection on one's performance at work which promotes the construction of work process knowledge (Oliveira 1998).

The second dimension represents work process knowledge as a result of the formal processes of learning and competency development within universities. If, as we have argued, there is a need to develop work process knowledge in graduates in order to prepare them for the world of work, we must regard higher education not just as a space/time for the acquisition of technical knowledge, but also as a space/time that contributes to the process of personal development. This developmental process must be understood both as 'personal' (development of individual capacities) and 'professional' (transformation of professional activity using the newly obtained resources) (Le Bouedec 1988: 263).

The third dimension is related to the difficulty of separating 'work process knowledge' from several factors related to a subject's identity and his or her personal and social life. Occupational achievement implies competencies, attitudes, personal capacities and values that are in part the result of the socialization process throughout social and family life. As Alaluf (1986: 145) points out, 'many aspects of the behaviour of the worker lie outside the scope of the employer. He or she belongs to other social groups whose influence arises outside the company door.'

The articulation of the organizational, educational and individual factors needed to generate work process knowledge is a complex undertaking, requiring a coherent and integrated strategy for developing human resources in companies and in the workforce as a whole.

9 Work experience as an element of work process knowledge

Martin Fischer

Work process knowledge is constructed in use out of theoretical knowledge of the work process and direct experience of work itself. The aim of this chapter is to clarify the concept of work experience in this context. Many meanings of the term 'experience' have been articulated, especially in the German debate about experience-guided work. Views on the importance of work experience as a basis for competence range from assigning it very little importance in the early days of computerization to the assumption that experience is the sole basis for learning. By undertaking an epistemological analysis of the nature of experience, this chapter argues that it integrates an aesthetic, a practical and a rational dimension. Experience, however, does not provide understanding of facts and generalizable procedures. Ignoring the complex nature of experience may therefore lead to simplistic human resource development strategies. In particular, learning through experience needs to be enriched by theoretical understanding – a process leading to the acquisition of work process knowledge.

Work experience in the context of new forms of production

Up to the end of the 1980s, German studies of change in the nature of skilled work – especially in the context of computer-aided production – were based on the assumption that work was becoming increasingly abstract. Publications in the field of industrial education and training pointed out the importance of guiding the new work processes by systematic, theoretically informed planning (e.g. Korndörfer 1985). The traditional, experientially based way of learning skills through craftsmanship and apprenticeship seemed to have embarked on an irreversible decline. In recent years, however, something of a reversal of this position has occurred. The terms 'work experience' and 'experiential learning' are enjoying a return to favour. This occurred first in the context of sociological surveys of the field of computer-aided skilled work (e.g. Malsch 1984, 1987; Böhle and Milkau 1988; Böhle and Rose 1992), then spread to research and development into the shaping of work and technology where the important new term 'computer-aided experience guided work' (CEA) was coined (Martin 1995; Fleig and Schneider 1995). This also impacted on the ongoing debate about vocational education and training (Dehnbostel and Peters 1991; Dehnbostel *et al.* 1992).

One of the main assumptions of this debate was that experiential learning plays an important role in the development of competence, even in computer-aided work environments. However, at the same time, it was realized that many different meanings are attached to the term 'experience' within the academic literature. These meanings are drawn from a diverse range of sources, including the everyday use of the term experience, phenomenology and even philosophy. In fact, the term 'experience' threatens to become an all-purpose and therefore meaningless token. The aim of the present chapter is to work out a more precise definition, and on the basis of this to assess the contribution of work experience to work process knowledge (Fischer 1995:158–78; Peters 1991; Siebeck 1994).

The primary characteristic of experience which has to be considered in the present context is that it is ultimately the *personal* experiencing of facts, events and persons. This definition determines (and delimits) experience in two directions. First, it establishes that there are situations for which there can be no experience. For example, the behaviour of atoms cannot be experienced, and there can be no experience of many technical and natural laws. Nevertheless, these are a vital part of many work situations, such as the handling of electrical phenomena and chemical reactions. Second, experience can never be independent of the subjective view, and thus cannot be equated with knowledge in its generalized, objectified form, as for example, in the laws of the natural sciences.

Experience and sense perception

Establishing a connection between experience and *personal* experience, however, does not mean that experience is equivalent to sense perception. While accepting that experience is founded on the senses, as argued by the British empiricists of the eighteenth century (above all Locke and Hume), it must also be acknowledged that only a whole person can experience – with all his or her senses, and also with the thoughts and emotions acquired in the course of a lifetime. To experience a fact goes beyond immediate sense perception. In order to explain this it is useful to distinguish between *immediate sense perception* and *imparted sense perception*. The latter is based on imagination, thoughts and emotions, and is a determinant of the adult's philosophy and understanding of the world (Gußbacher 1988). In immediate sense perception, on the other hand, objects of the outer world do not exist as an exterior unity but are fragmented by the particular senses that are attended to. Thus the sense of vision perceives the colour and the form of an object, the sense of touch signals the specific weight, warmth, cohesion and shape, the sense of smell perceives the fragrance and so on. Each sense perceives its respective section of the object. For this reason, the subjective unity of an object is not captured by immediate sense perception. The sense of vision does not capture the burning smell of an overheated engine, while the sense of smell cannot detect a tear in material, and detecting a loose screw might depend upon the sense of touch. And so the holistic perception of an object or 'holistic cognition' which is crucial for computer-aided image or pattern recognition is not a function of sense perception itself, but presumes the use of intelligence which goes beyond that.

The use of thoughts and emotions in imparted sense perception to construct the unity of an object depends on the ability to create images of the object and store them in memory. On the level of immediate sense perception, a machine is at first nothing but a conglomerate of shapes and colours. It is only on the level of imagination that this conglomerate comes to represent a machine, just as other sense impressions may be interpreted as a tree, a table and so on. In this process the individual contents of sense perceptions are recalled as images and are reproduced as the subjectively established unity of an object. It is only in our imagination that simultaneously hearing and seeing a machine are integrated into a unitary perception.

Experience and memory

The imparted sense perception with which an individual observes the world and which is the origin of his or her experience depends on the capacity to remember images of the experienced object. Aristotle has already pointed this out: 'Many memories of the same object generate the capacity of an experience' (Aristotle 1978: 980). In Aristotle's view, experience derives from sense-perception by way of memory. Memory is the mechanism that delivers sense impressions to the conscious process of thinking, and it is the latter that eventually constructs the unity and identity of an object. The proposition put forward earlier, that experience is personal, can now be expressed more precisely: experience consists of the mental reproduction of personal experiences. The important consequence that follows is that we all need to engage in activity in order to form experience out of impressions. In relation to this point, Piaget (1973: 93) has criticized a definition of experience that represents this as a passively acquired image. He has always pointed out that the creation of basic experience structures requires a continuous organizing activity on the part of the subject. One of the dimensions of this activity is, as we have argued, the memory of the image of the object that the subject has acquired so far.

Experience as a process of mental reception and production

The foundation of the activity of experiencing or having an experience is thus as follows. The individual is simultaneously aware of the object he or she is experiencing and of his or her knowledge of that object. The individual now realizes whether the currently experienced object and the remembered image of it correspond. If the new impression of the object and the activated images of it do match, the individual perceives that the object has remained unchanged over time. This does not mean, however, that the individual has had a *new* experience of the object. What has been experienced is not the object *per se*, but the existence of the object in time. This implies that having a new experience depends on finding a discrepancy between the object as it is currently experienced and its previous image. Thus in experiencing an object, the basic process is to revise or amend previous images of it. In the end, the individual has gained knowledge of a new facet of the object.[1]

The dialectical account of experience introduced here, which represents having an experience as a simultaneous act of reception (of the object) and production (of the enriched images of the object), was first articulated by Hegel:

> This dialectic movement that consciousness is performing on itself, not only on its knowledge but also on its object, insofar as the *new true object* emanates thereof, is in principle what is called experience.
>
> (Hegel 1807/1970; author's translation)

Hegel tries to point out the interdependence of subjectivity and objectivity within the process of having an experience, and argues at the same time that comprehension or understanding are fired by the activation of subjectivity. In this respect, he criticizes both the empiricism of Hume who regarded immediate sense perception as the decisive part of comprehension, and Kant's idealism, which attributed comprehension to the subject as the producer of its images. Modern psychology has even produced empirical evidence in support of Hegel's rapidly sketched ideas. Rubinstein, for example, reports that:

> Experienced grinders are able to distinguish spaces of one to two thousandth of a millimetre of width with the naked eye, whereas human beings are usually only able to distinguish spaces of one hundredth of a millimetre. Steel founders can perceive even the finest shades of the light brown colour which are indicators for the founding temperatures. Workers in pottery and china industries who have to determine the quality of their products according to their sound, develop a sensitive 'technical ear'.
>
> (Rubinstein 1973: 92)

Neither naïve and immediate sense perception, nor the subject's acquisition of concepts independently of experience, produces such performance. As research by Rauner and Zeymer (1991) shows, sense perception, enriched by experience, is superior to 'inexperienced' perception, demonstrating that experience comprises both reception of the objective and production of enriched concepts of it. When experiencing the world, the formative process of experiences simultaneously absorbs views and ideas, thoughts and emotions. And so we can adopt the definition that: *Experience is the personal experience of an objective reality with all the senses* (this is the argument against Kant), *and simultaneously it is that experiencing which is imparted by mental performance* (this is the argument against Hume).[2]

Up to now, we have discussed concepts that are recalled and modified during the process of having an experience. Some of these can be visual images that are not available in verbal forms. The production of experiences can, however, absorb more than mere visual aspects – concepts are usually linked to names and terms (see Oliveira, Pires and Alves in Chapter 8). As language is a central part of society, experiences are socially as well as individually constructed. This aspect of experience was highlighted in the context of the political education of workers in Germany during the 1970s. Brose in his survey of work experience (1983: 15) and Negt and Kluge (1972: 23ff) defined the term 'experience' in the Hegelian way outlined above. And according to the argument we have developed above, Negt is absolutely right when, faced by critics who see experience as more or less an immediate sense perception, he insists that experiences 'are in a certain sense collective moments of dealing with reality, which society produces ... This is why the term experience always contains a general element which goes beyond the totally individualized, coincidental and purely subjective perception' (Negt 1978: 44).[3]

Experience and aesthetics

Especially in the case of education and work in technical trades that make use of instruments or other technical artifacts, experience has an aesthetic dimension.[4] A fact is not only perceived as new or known, it is also experienced as beautiful or ugly, as pleasant or repulsive. Fascination and aversion for technology characterize the experience of technical artifacts, but this dimension of experience has been neglected by many (exceptions include Gerds 1989 and Dieckmann 1994). Efforts have therefore been made to reintegrate the aesthetic dimension into vocational education practice and research, in order to compensate for the instrumental orientation usually given to vocational education and training (Brater 1984).

Aesthetic experience is always to a varying degree part of the personal experience of individuals, whether explicitly recognized or not, in both work and education (Gerds 1989). This is true for the object of experience as well as for the generation of concepts.[5] And, as will be shown below, the aesthetic dimension of experience does not necessarily contradict the practical, instrumentally oriented rationality of experience.

The reason for the existence of aesthetical rationality in experience lies in the above-mentioned quality of sensory personal impressions to which experience is linked. Experience is neither immediate sense perception (accompanied by basic emotional conditions), nor scientific reflection (abstracting from experience and impression). It occupies an intermediate position between unprejudiced perception and abstract reflection, and it is this that brings it within the domain of aesthetic impression. 'The experience of subjects is decisively determined by the historically changing forms of reflexivity itself' (Dieckmann 1994: 241) – an example being the remodelling of the automobile in the course of time, reflecting the changing (social and individual) perceptions of beauty in a car.

Intrinsic and extrinsic experiences

There are also secondary or vicarious experiences. Experience can be based on the experiences of others – regardless of whether it occurs in verbal, written or visual form. Thomas Binder (1995), in a study of a company that manufactured steel springs for railway carriages, has shown how the use of video films in the factory produced experiential learning without direct experience of the manufacturing process itself. However, in order to speak of secondary *experience* at all, two factors are necessary. First, the event in question must be imagined in the medium from which experience is about to be taken. Imagining means that the objective reality of the fact is always present in its mediated presentation – and that it is not abstracted from the start (cf. Adolph 1983, 1984 with reference to the use of media and models in vocational education). Second, the recipient must have the capacity for imagination so that he or she can reproduce and imagine the actual experience.

Experience and practical doing

After having shown how experience is imparted by the act of thinking, the question might arise once more how experience is different from thinking, especially from scientific thinking. Remember on the one hand that some scientific objects are not accessible by experience. On the other hand, experience is embedded in doing: gaining experience does not mean that something is passively happening to a person, least of all in professional life. The following are important for experience by qualified workers.

- Experiences are *accumulated* during practical doing, because the subject is interested in the conditions and prerequisites of his or her acting, in the acting itself and finally in the consequences of the acting. The subject draws his or her attention to the acting, becomes physically and sensuously involved and mentally duplicates the sequence of acting and memorizes it.

- During practical doing, experiences are *sought after* because the subject ignores or only partially knows the prerequisites or the consequences of his or her acting and wants to learn them. This dimension of experience is especially emphasized in the surveys by Böhle and Milkau (1998), Böhle and Rose (1992) and Böhle (1995) and in Germany has led to the concept of 'experience guided work', where technical equipment is designed in a way to allow workers to gain experience during the work process.[6]

One is easily tempted to regard experience, and above all the accumulation of experiences, as an ancillary effect or concomitant of practical doing. This is, however, not the case. The fact that experience is not an automatic consequence of practical doing is evident in all those cases where subjects have accumulated no experience at all, in spite of practical doing. To put the argument more forcefully, the accumulation of experiences presupposes that the subject wants to get acquainted with a fact, wants to make it his or her concern and wants to make practical use of it. This is yet more support for the idea that experience encompasses more than a coincidental and isolated hotchpotch of sense perceptions. The content of experience is rather the context that is important for achieving one's goals. In general, this context can be described as follows: when such and such things happen, then such and such things follow and, with regard to practical acting it can be added: '... then such and such thing has to be done'.

The result of experience is thus knowledge of action. This includes the significant context for action in a form that can immediately be put to use for the purposes of this action. In this context, some writers point out the opportunistic character of expert knowledge (Hacker 1992: 34ff; Dahmer 1994: 138ff). This means that experts try out this or that action depending on what they think is appropriate for the solution of a practical problem. This trying out is not only a deduction from some principle of action, nor an induction from exploring and interpreting the situation. Rather, an intertwining of deductive and inductive approaches can be noted which – to an outsider – seems to be a process of jumping between the different ways of problem-solving. It is therefore appropriate, as emphasized by Waibel and Wehner (1994), not to view the pre-planning of action and experiential knowhow as opposites, but as entering into a dialectical relationship.

Experience and how it is coded

The immediate usefulness of practical acting is expressed in the way in which experiences are retained and remembered. The above statement that the content of experiences takes the hypothetical form 'If this happens, that has to be done', does not mean that experiences are known consciously as sentences. Experts often have difficulties in expressing their thoughts with words. This phenomenon has rightly been emphasized (especially in the Anglo-Saxon community) in the so-called tacit knowledge debate (Polanyi 1966; Dreyfus 1972; Dreyfus and Dreyfus 1986; see also Rasmussen, Chapter 6). However, the undoubted phenomenon of implicit knowledge has sometimes been unjustifiably promoted to being, first, *the* most important property and, second, to a general unfathomableness of expert knowledge (Fischer *et al.* 1995:123).[7]

At this point we would like to suggest that experiences are memorized in various forms – the spectrum ranges from attributes of objective reality conceived by the senses to codified (and partly also written) work rules. In general, the criterion of immediate usefulness for practical actions also influences how experiences are coded. For example, experience of the proper functioning of a machine's clutch can hardly be found in a verbal form. The recall of a sensory impression is considerably more vivid here than verbal description. (Try to find words to describe a properly adjusted clutch!) On the other hand, experiences have also been recorded in verbal forms – and this is especially true when experiences merge into generalized findings: for example, 'Metals are electrical conductors'. In a study of skilled workers, the meaning of this sentence proved to be a mixture of a factual statement of experience and of 'book learning' in the majority of cases (Fischer *et al.* 1995). Such a sentence is basic underpinning knowledge for maintenance personnel, and it is coded as a *sentence* – and not as a memory of this or that kind of metal which had the property of an electrical conductor. There is no need to carry on experiencing this property over and over again. Much more research work is still to be done with regard to the different facets of knowledge and experience within various occupations. Experience plays different roles in diagnosis in maintenance situations and in planning action (Malsch 1984, 1987; Dahmer 1994; Waibel and Wehner 1994), and the situation might also differ with regard to metal-, electrical- and chemo-technical kinds of work).

The transmission of experience

Experiences can be transmitted and are often passed on to others. Thus experience has – apart from its individual and social qualities – a collective or group-specific quality (see Rogalski, Plat and Antonin-Glenn, Chapter 10 and Rasmussen, Chapter 6 in this volume). This can be shown by the way in which maintenance procedures developed in a company are preserved and passed on (Fischer *et al.* 1995: 154ff). The limited explicability of experience and its embedding into the feelings of maintenance workers is not only due to the individuality of experience, but also because the contents of experience are at least partially collective knowledge. They are passed on by cues such as: 'do you see ..., do you realize ..., do you feel ..., do you hear that ...'. In this way, evaluations of meaning of a phenomenon are not transmitted as theoretical statements but are immediately absorbed by the field of sense perception of the acting person.

In the course of time, the worker does not only gain sensory experience of the functioning of machinery such as the clutches made by different manufacturers or of different types, he or she develops a personal idea of the proper operation of a clutch which is then transferred to other types. Volpert has rightly pointed out this phenomenon as a cognition and recognition of 'shapes of a term' (Volpert 1988). Here again, general ideas (e.g. the idea of a well-functioning machine clutch) are linked to sensed characteristics of technology and of technological processes. These circumstances form the basis for communication between skilled workers. There is a common stock of experience values relevant for their work. Most of the time the mere hint of an experience value is sufficient – explanations are mostly neither required nor could they be simply given.[8]

Experience and knowledge

Experiential knowledge is action knowledge, and as long as the goal of action can be reached by experience, experience is sufficient for practical purposes. With regard to experience as a *practical attitude* to reality there is therefore no reason to ascribe limits to the value of experience. Here, everything depends on which ideas and which thoughts are stored in experience and which manifest themselves as practical feelings towards the world. Another question is experience as a means of winning experiences – if the subject aims at acquiring the meaning of a fact:

> Although *perception* starts from *observation* of sensory materials it does not stop short at these, does not confine itself simply to smelling, tasting, seeing, hearing and feeling (touching), but necessarily goes on to relate the sense-perception to a universal which is not observable in an immediate manner, to cognize each individual thing as an internally coherent whole: in *force*, for example, to comprehend all its manifestations; and to seek out the connections and mediations that exist between separate individual things. While therefore the *merely sensory* consciousness merely *shows* things, that is to say, exhibits them in their immediacy, perception, on the other hand, apprehends the connectedness of things, demonstrates that when such and such circumstances are present such and such a thing follows, and thus begins to demonstrate the truth of things. This demonstration is, however, still defective, not final. For that by which something is hereby supposed to be demonstrated is itself *presupposed*, and consequently in need of demonstration; with the result that in this field one goes from one presupposition to another and lapses into the progress of infinity.

> This is the standpoint occupied by empiricism. Everything must be experienced.
>
> (Hegel 1830/1970, Vol. 10, addition to §420, p. 209)

Here experience can be seen in a different context than the context of the immediate action. It is the logical reconstruction of how the subject theoretically acquires the world, i.e. first asks why a fact is as it is – instead of already having correctly or incorrectly answered the question. The standpoint of experience is only limited in this connection: the mere recording of perceived objects and facts within the modality of experience places the phenomena into the form of a dependent relationship without already having mentioned the reason for such a dependence. 'If such and such thing happens, then such and such thing follows' – this is the form of recording experiences. Such a recording of perceived matters can be correct – albeit lacking proof of a diagnosed correlation. As soon as the subject applies experience *instead of a proof*, then, as Hegel remarks with good reason, the progress to infinity is the consequence – one cannot completely finish reflecting on the true sense of a word: each 'if' we commence with presupposes a previous 'then'. And each 'then' we finish with consequently triggers a new 'if'.

Experience and learning

On the basis of experience, in successful cases, people learn how to deal with something properly on a practical basis. The answer to the question why a fact is as it is, presupposes a mental reconstruction of natural laws and technical standards, as well as the interests and purposes related to the fact. This mental reconstruction is not a content of experience but requires careful thinking and finally cognitive perception, and is thus abstracted from the phenomenon that is accessible to experience. Supposing that both cognitive perception (i.e. explanations of the phenomena of the world of work) and its application in the guidance of practical action are aims of vocational education, then experience has a double rating within the framework of such learning processes.

- Experience is the starting point for cognitive perception. Above, the term experience was introduced as the personal experiencing of connections which are important for one's own action. Thus experience contains two major prerequisites for perception: the knowledge of a fact, and the motive to handle the fact practically. It is, however, very rarely recognized in practical teaching and learning *what the knowledge of a fact is all about* and *what* the student can *do* with it. This is why the learning process cannot refer to the students' experiences. Research approaches based on the concept of 'situated learning' (for a critique, see Samurçay and Vidal-Gomel, Chapter 11 in this volume) have revealed weaknesses in this approach; Holzkamp (1993) uses the term 'Teaching-Learning-Short-Circuit', to point out that students do not or only very conditionally learn what the teacher teaches them. Recent findings in the field of learning research (e.g. Lave and Wenger 1991; Holzkamp 1993) have drawn attention to the fact that what students learn least is the *contents* imparted by teachers. Moreover, they learn to interpret the instructional *situations.* The Californian group of researchers around Jean Lave have again and again pointed out the situation and context relations of every kind of teaching.[9] Thus on the way towards cognitive perception the experiences which are part of the learning process and which are accumulated during the learning process should, first, be acknowledged by the teacher and, second, be studied in co-operation with students.

• Cognitive perception qualifying for practical acting again leads back to experience. This means that vocational knowledge and skills are not only the application of learned contents. Twenty years ago Dieta Simon pointed out in her study of learning during the work process that knowledge acquired during initial and continuous vocational training is not simply applied during the work process (Simon 1980: 66). Work is also taken advantage of as a kind of experience-area where school knowledge and work-relevant knowledge and skills are transformed. Under the conditions of computer-aided production, however, these experiences are limited – as shown in our empirical surveys; at least they have undergone drastic changes. Above all, skilled workers from the field of metallurgical occupations have difficulties in practising those forms of sense-related experiential learning, which in former times helped them to cope with the problems emerging during their work (Fischer *et al.* 1995: 157ff). The consequence is that students require an area of experience, i.e. the opportunity to accumulate experiences, in order to cope with specialized theoretical knowledge. This need of skilled workers – *making* experiences instead of *having* experiences – is what Böhle (1995) means when he speaks of experience-guided work, also under the conditions of computer-aided production.

Conclusion

It is now time to draw these arguments together into a conclusion. This is that experience supports the creation of work process knowledge by integrating aesthetic, practical and rational action. To command experience is a matter of the past, reaching into the present. In the process of real experience making, concepts of past events are remembered and modified. This entails consequences for future acting: the richer the stock of experiences, the less strangely are new events experienced by an individual. Experience is based on sense perception, but it is not confined to it. Experience means impressions of whole persons. It contains ideas and concepts, thoughts and emotions and thus is not identical with immediate perception.

The recording of experiences is mainly done according to their usefulness, i.e. some experiences are better coded one way, others in other ways Experience *per se* is conscious, but it is not necessarily consciousness alone that exerts a certain influence on practical action.

Experience has implicit and explicit aspects, but they are not fixed – the implicit can become explicit. The participants in our surveys could perform a verbal reconstruction of experience-related acting in the majority of cases. Difficulties, however, were apparent. The reasons were:

- The verbalization of experiences is extremely difficult as soon as it comes to the definition of sensory qualities. Circumlocutions are mostly found here which do not fully capture direct sensory impression.
- Work on complex problems, requiring conscious activity, becomes automatic in time. This practical feeling houses the generalizing thinking; it is, however, no longer present in language.
- The experience in question is not a socially communicated issue. If there has never been a social need for a verbalization, the subjects do not command (at first or at all) the words for the description of a phenomenon.[10]

Experience is not teachable as such, but educational processes may support the acquisition of experience – best done by giving students the opportunity to make experiences and to reflect on them. The media are not at all excluded from this process. Moreover, the object of experience must always be present for the student. What can be explored by experience, however, is not only a question of the adequate medium but also of the knowledge level of the student (Samurçay 1994).

Our discussion of the term experience has emphasized the three dimensions highlighted by Dieckmann (1994): aesthetic rationality, practical rationality and cognitive rationality. All three rationalities are partially encompassed by the term experience which covers a fairly wide range.

- Experience has an aesthetic dimension; it goes beyond immediate, unsophisticated feeling. It is, however, not identical with artistic shaping or artistic connoisseurship.
- Experience houses practical rationality; it is, however, neither identical with practical acting nor to be seen as a mere ancillary of practical action. On the other hand, the situation could occur where experience is insufficient for coping with a task. In this case, one has to abstract from experience in order to attain practical results.

- Experience is the basis for cognitive perception, not in the sense of an original source (this would be immediate sense perception), but in the sense that one knows the fact in question and one wants to do something with it. Experience is thus necessary for the course of perception, especially the one leading to competent practical acting. It is, however, narrow minded to take experience as a proof that everything must be just as it has been experienced.

The frontiers of experience have been clearly delineated. The strength of basing action on experience lies in the fact – already pointed out by Dewey (1934) – that compared to a mere aesthetic rationality, mere practical rationality or mere cognitive rationality, all three of these dimensions are intertwined in experience. This attribute of experience – the ability to interconnect the dimensions of knowing, feeling and acting – is important in relation to the acquisition and use of work process knowledge. We consider work process knowledge as a specific type of knowing, developed by practitioners in order to cope with modern (and very often computerized) work processes (Fischer 2000). This kind of knowing is characterized by its object – one's own work within the framework of in-company work processes including the life-world of a company or institution. An understanding of modern work processes requires a merging of theoretical knowledge and experience-based situated knowledge (Fischer and Röben, Chapter 4 in this volume).

The role of experience in relation to work process knowledge can be regarded as two-fold (see Figure 9.1): first, experience paves the way for

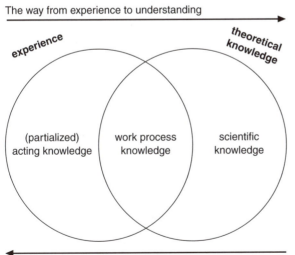

Figure 9.1 Experience as an element of work process knowledge

understanding (Kade and Geißler 1980); second, experience enables one to integrate theoretical knowledge into practical acting in the context of work.

Notes

1 ' "To make an experience" ranges from a familiar situation becoming problematic within personal experiences to a renewed mastering of the matter' (Engler 1992: 41).
2 In recent times Aebli (1980/1981) and Schön (1983) have developed their own approaches. They also postulate the dialectic relationship between experiencing and acting on the one hand and reflection and learning on the other hand.
3 In a review of a study by Shilling (1988), Jones (1994: 6) has vividly demonstrated how value-laden and culture-specific experiences are and can be: Teamwork in a Japanese factory, which was shown as a video to English youngsters as an example of best practice, triggered an entirely different perception of teamwork: 'Teamwork doesn't mean sweating your bollocks off for some lousy job.'
4 Not to speak of the private world of skilled workers and apprentices where the quality of acquired experiences and experience-making is documented by a multitude of accessories, rites and customs.
5 The aesthetic dimension of experience has been especially emphasized by Dewey (1934: 278). However, he did not – and this is decisive here – derive it from artistic experiences but as part of experience as a whole. Dewey already set the pace for Engler's concept (1992: 205) who emphasizes that it is not only the objects of experience which possess an aesthetic quality but above all the experience we make with them: not only the automobile as such possesses an aesthetic quality but the act of looking at a car, driving a car, producing a car.
6 In the field of vocational educational science the 'seeking of experiences' has been discussed with keywords such as 'experimenting learning' or 'experimental act of perception' (Eicker 1983; Rauner 1985). Experiences are sought insofar as a re-linking to experience is necessary if the thoughts already found in the experiment are to be revised (Rauner 1985: 18). The seeking of experiences is thus different from coincidental trial-and-error procedures. However, it differs as well from the use of a scientifically oriented experiment in vocational education where abstraction takes place from the experience of real work and technology in favour of the exploration of a principal context of consequences (Fischer and Lehrl 1991: 204ff).
7 In the meantime, however, further research activities have been launched on the topic of implicit knowledge (Berry and Broadbent 1984, 1987; Boreham 1995; Reber and Lewis 1977; Reber 1989). A very concise overview is given by Boreham (1994). He supports the presumption of a dual cognitive architecture and examines how the relations between implicit and explicit processes of thinking are reflected in different (from unconsciously to consciously controlled) thought patterns. In my opinion, this view defines experience as a comprehensive category which contains both explicit and implicit thinking. Moreover, in future research the *content* of knowledge has to be taken into account with regard to implicit and explicit modes of knowledge. Whereas it may seem understandable that a person is able to ride a bicycle without verbally knowing the rule how to keep balance, one can hardly assume that this person is also able to solve differential equations out of the sphere of signs and symbols.

8 Renan Samurçay has pointed out in more detail that 'pragmatic concepts' (concepts used in action) serve as a mediator for the transmission of experience within a community of workers (see Samurçay and Vidal, Chapter 11; Roglaski, Plat and Antolin-Glenn, Chapter 10).

9 The following results from various studies and empirical surveys shed light on this statement: for example, one study was about learning and application of (elementary) mathematics at school and in extra-scholastic situations, e.g. in a supermarket, in the kitchen and so on (Lave 1988). It could be shown that a good performance in mathematics at school does not automatically lead to good calculating results in a supermarket and that vice versa weak mathematics students scored flawless results in the supermarket. On the other hand, it became evident that students who always scored correct results during mathematics lessons did not always adhere to the mathematical techniques offered by their teacher but – unnoticed by the teacher – applied their own, safely mastered techniques (e.g. regrouping, adding, subtracting instead of multiplying and dividing) in order to prevent their being disgraced during the lessons.

10 In contrast to European languages, the languages of desert-dwelling peoples have numerous words for *camel* – obviously a social necessity in their environment (cf. *The Cambridge Encyclopedia of Language 1997*, p. 155). On the other hand several languages cannot match the many words European languages have available for all kinds of vehicles (car, lorry, bus, tractor etc.) and might just have one word for all of these. An intercultural language comparison reveals that the question of verbalizing experiences also has a socio-cultural dimension apart from the objective and individual dimension.

10 Training for collective competence in rare and unpredictable situations

Janine Rogalski, Marielle Plat and Patricia Antolin-Glenn

Direct work experience is not an effective way of developing competence in dealing with rare or unpredictable situations. In such situations, contingencies and work roles are drastically different from what those involved might previously have experienced. This is especially the case in risky and dynamic environments such as aviation, nuclear power plants, chemical processes and anaesthesiology. The same is true for dealing with emergencies such as large forest fires, fires in fuel depots and gas pipes, pollution, floods and earthquakes, which in France is the responsibility of Public Safety Firefighters. As these risks will never go away, there is a need to train personnel in how to deal with them, quite apart from the need to do all that is possible to prevent them. This is a complex issue from a political and a technical point of view (Amalberti 1996).

Managing these situations requires collective activity, involving a group of operators organized in teams. By 'operator' we mean any actor involved in the complex activity of managing a complex, dynamic environment at any level in the chain of command. The teams may be permanent ones (as is generally the case in process-control rooms) or alternatively their composition may vary (as with crews in civil aviation and operational command posts in the context of public safety, for instance). Operators have to be competent enough to avoid 'collapse of sense making' (Weick 1993) and not to be overwhelmed by the severity of the situation, as has been observed in accidents on offshore oil installations, the managers of which are not usually either selected or trained to deal with emergency situations (Flin and Slaven 1995).

Operators generally have few, if any, opportunities to acquire competence by directly experiencing such situations, nor for developing into competent teams by sharing multiple experiences. In contrast to commonly experienced situations, they cannot access episodic memory of the work process in order to deal with unusual situations (Baerentsen 1996) or disasters, such as aviation accidents, nor can they benefit from indirect experience.

Simulation is a well-established method for developing operational knowledge in rare situations, and its effectiveness has been established within certain limits (Samurçay and Rogalski 1998). In the past, the main use of simulation for training focused on the procedural training of individuals who may work as individuals or as members of teams such as aviation crews. However, as research into collective work has emphasized, the individual competence of the members of a team does not ensure the competence of a team as a whole in collectively tackling a new and difficult situation. Indeed, acting collectively may be the most crucial aspect of performance, as it is central to the process of managing the situation.

In this chapter, two empirical studies will be described in order to tackle two issues: how does collective competence in dealing with rare or unpredictable situations develop through simulation, and how do instructors, when trying to develop collective competence, divide training interventions between technical operational knowledge on the one hand, and collective activity itself, on the other?

These studies were undertaken in two contrasting working environments, aviation and crisis management. We will describe the two domains in the next section, after which we will introduce the main concepts and methods for analysing collective competence development.

Collective competence and work process knowledge in risky dynamic environments

Aviation and emergency management: two different examples of dynamic management

Whatever typology is used for categorizing dynamic environments, aviation and emergency management will fall into contrasting categories. Empirical research has demonstrated contrast on many dimensions (Hoc 1993): the tempo of the dynamic environment; the information and control systems; the labour process; the degree of proceduralization of the action; the nature of the product. Here, we will focus on differences relating to the labour process and the information and control systems.

In flight management, the dynamics of the environment (altitude, speed, trajectory, weather, air traffic) are changing partly independently of the pilot's actions, but are also interacting with them. Today, most aircraft have small crew: typically, two pilots in highly automated cockpits, such as the Airbus A320. Their actions are mediated by a highly complex system, which contains detailed models of the dynamic situation. Computer-based automatic piloting systems act semi-autonomously, as pilots may select the level of automation they prefer at any moment. A complex work organization has been defined in detail for task allocation within the cockpit. It specifies ways for acting through – and interacting with – the automated systems. Finally, during a given flight, decisions depend on the Captain, who is the only 'master' on board the aircraft.

In emergency or crisis operational management, in contrast, the tempo or speed of change is lower. Models of the situation dynamics are 'global' ones. Information from the environment, and interventions in that environment, are generally mediated by human actors who are organized into a complex hierarchical command-and-control system (when fighting large forest fires in France, as many as 2,000 personnel may be involved). Teams located in control posts act as support systems for the Rescue Operations Chief, the person responsible for the operational implementation of the civil authorities' decisions about how the emergency is to be handled. For instance, firefighter officers have no right to decide to start a 'counter-fire' for fighting a forest fire, or to evacuate population in case of chemical pollution. On the other hand, there are many similarities. Distributed co-operation (Rogalski 1994) is required in command posts as well as in cockpits, and someone occupying the position of chief is responsible for supervising the whole task. The work itself is a whole: completing a flight or resolving a critical situation; and the level of responsibility is high. The operators (pilots or firefighters) are highly qualified. Finally, both are given cross training (Volpe 1996); they are prepared not only for their specific role, but also for any role within the team. The question of how collective competence is developed in these situations must now be considered in relation to situational change in both these domains.

Situational change, work process knowledge and professional competence

In aviation, the development of highly automated cockpits led to significant modifications in the flow of information and communication within the cockpit. Numerous studies indicate that mastering these changes and coping with computer-based automated systems is far from easy (Sarter and Woods 1995, 1997; Plat and Amalberti 2000). In emergency or crisis management, the challenge of dealing with rare or unpredictable situations is building up situation-specific configurations of human and material resources – what we have called a *virtual operational device* (Rogalski 1991). In both cases, there is a demand for both work process knowledge and new kinds of vocational competence.

In fact, the notion of vocational competence includes – but is not identical to – *operational knowledge* (Rogalski 1995), a concept developed by French researchers and which is similar to the notion of work process knowledge (see Chapter 1). It involves conceptual knowledge about the 'world to be acted on' (what has to be done) and the 'system of actors' (who is doing what, how and with whom); it also takes into account a dynamic dimension, related to the temporal organization of the operators' activity (the last point is developed in Samurçay and Vidal-Gomel, Chapter 11).

Beyond knowledge, competence has to be seen as a potential for action, which involves:

1   operational knowledge – which is available or may be mobilized;
2   schemes of action for a class of situations; and
3   individual and collective operators' properties (*Eigenschaften*) which enable them to adapt to the pressures of the situation.

Among these properties we may emphasize, first, sensitivity to cues that reveal how the task environment is evolving (needed for situational assessment), as well as sensitivity to cues that reveal what the actors are doing (needed for collective management), as well as what the subjects themselves are doing (needed for self-management) and, second, *resilience* to stressful conditions. A detailed set of properties related to collective resilience to crisis situations was developed by Weick by analysing a dramatic episode in firefighting (the Mann Gulch disaster) (Weick 1993). In the case of collective activity, the issue of collective as well as individual competence has to be considered, but first it needs to be defined, an essential step for identifying how to measure it and build it through practice and training.

What is collective competence? Competence of a team of operators as a unit? Competence of individual operator to collectively perform a task in a class of tasks?

The concept of collective competence is not a simple one. On the one hand, a team – a set of operators engaged in a common task – may be considered an entity: a *virtual operator*, in charge of the task (Rogalski 1991). The competence of this entity may be defined as for an individual operator, as a potential of operative knowledge and properties for generating performance. Assessing collective competence will be guided by the same concepts and tools as for the assessment of individual competence. Implicitly, such a definition implies some stability in the team.

On the other hand, we may focus on individual activities and on interactions developed between individual operators within the team when performing the task. This second definition of collective competence is a verbal short cut, a way of referring to the competence of many individuals engaged in a collective activity. The focus is then on both individual competence related to co-operation, and how individual competencies (both task- and group-oriented) are distributed within a given team. Collective competence can then be considered as distributed competence for collective work. This definition does not imply team stability.

In aviation, *proceduralization* is normally used to enable pilots to deal with a wide range of foreseeable incidents, and also to ensure co-operation itself (Rogalski 1996). At first sight, it seems that developing collective competence entails developing individual pilots' competence in both these sets of procedures. However, this leaves unresolved the question of how procedures become internal resources for promoting collective activity within the cockpit, particularly in the case of rare or unpredictable situations.

In crisis management, the concept of *reference knowledge* has been suggested as a way of representing 'categories of mental representations and operations common to efficient practices, these practices being situated, that is contextualized and personalized' (Rogalski and Samurçay 1994: 43). It includes *strategic knowledge:* how an operational device should be deployed in a complex situation; what tasks have to be allocated to whom; what flow of communication must link actors within the operational device. Strategic knowledge is a resource for dealing with changing situations.

In fact, whatever the level of proceduralization, the twofold mental model required for managing a dynamic situation proposed by Bainbridge (1988) has to be modified to account for collective activity. In addition to a model of the dynamics of the task environment, required to support both individual and collective activity, the model of human activity has to be split into two: a model of the team's actions (considered as a virtual operator) and a model of the articulation of individual actions into the former. Providing operators with mental models of this kind depends on developing work process knowledge, at least in situations where operators undertake knowledge-based activity. Situations may be unforeseen for operators whose competence is under scrutiny, or for the 'community of practice' itself, due to variety and complexity in variables and their interactions in the world of action: this is the case with computer-based automated systems in aviation, due to the internal complexity of the artifacts; it is also the case for open dynamic situations, or crisis, due to the high level of uncertainty and variability, in nature, space, importance and to the low level of modelling.

Resources for collective activity and collective competence

The aim of teaching reference knowledge is to define what may be called a 'common referential' (de Terssac and Chabaud 1990), or 'shared mental model' (Rouse *et al.* 1992), enlarging the cognitive compatibility of actors who have to co-operate with each other. Doctrinal knowledge in particular supplies actors with a common basis for performing the specific tasks devoted to the articulation of individual activities into collective work. This kind of knowledge is a key component of work process knowledge, especially when the structure of the work group varies according to the nature of the situation that has to be managed. Severe incidents or accidents in industrial process control may lead to similar changes; so, developing and training for appropriate doctrinal knowledge would be a key issue for coping with such cases.

Within the set of resources that support collective activity, procedures and methods play a specific role: they are cognitive tools, whose aim is to organize the actors' activity. Other cognitive tools are also quite important, and their mastery is a key component in collective competence. Representational tools – such as maps, diagrams, functional graphs, mimics – are oriented towards representing the state of the world to be acted on. From the perspective of individual activity, operators build up what Ochanine (1992) called *operative images* (schematic and action-oriented); from the point of view of collective activity, they enable actors to construct shared external representations about the world to be acted on, and to develop a better team situation awareness. Situation awareness, as defined for instance by (Endsley 1995), occurs when mental models fit with the main operative features of the situation to be managed.

Thus a significant component of collective competence is if and how such resources are assimilated into team activity – and by individual operators – in order to construct and maintain shared mental models, and bind individual activities into collective work.

Simulation for the development of collective competence for rare or not yet encountered situations

Experience as an element of work process knowledge is analysed in depth by Fischer in Chapter 9. Apart from its limitation to visual images, we agree with Fischer's account of experience and its relationships with a range of issues raised by work process knowledge and professional competence. We would like, however, to underline several points. First, the introduction of a 'dialectic term of experience' as 'an act of reception and an act of production' enables one to understand the role of external representations as operative images produced (by one operator) and received (by another), and the condition of shared operational knowledge. Second, it also enables one to account for the fact that it is possible to transform 'experience of the ancients' into 'knowledge for the beginners', through a process of indirect experience-making (Baerentsen 1996).

The positive role of work experience as defined by Fischer in Chapter 9 is clearly a way of developing competence through action; this is consistent with more general results about 'learning by doing', and 'experiential learning'. From our point of view, however, it leaves unanswered the question of the *conditions* under which work process knowledge and professional competence may develop from practice. This is particularly important where rare or unpredictable situations are concerned. In such cases, work process knowledge constructed out of conceptual knowledge acquired in classrooms and experiential learning in actual workplaces will be too weak to deal with situations well beyond the frontier of the employees' usual domain of action.

Faced with this difficulty, training through simulation offers itself as one possible way of integrating knowledge acquired through explicit instruction with the knowledge constructed by experiencing new situations.

Collective competence development and instructors' activity in simulation situations

When simulation is used to develop collective competence, it can be defined as a system involving a group to be trained (whatever its complexity), a scenario to be played, and one (or more) instructors who fulfil several functions (Figures 10.1 and 10.2 schematize such a system for aviation and operational management respectively). Instructors control the playing of the scenario, and after a while they intervene according to what the group is doing. They may freeze the simulation or replay parts in order to encourage the actors to reflect on their actions. The central role of the instructor is to mediate between the group of trainees and the simulation that is providing them with experience of rare or hazardous situations. Finally, they also play a direct didactical role through their interventions before simulation (briefing), during simulation (on-line interventions), and after simulation (debriefing).

Our analysis of the use of simulation is guided by two questions: 1) what are the effects of simulation training on collective competence, and 2) what do instructors' interventions reveal about group behaviour in these simulations and about what the instructors' didactic interventions are focusing on? In the case of aviation, the results we report are a synthesis coming from very detailed data about six aircrews (detailed analyses may be found in Rogalski 1996; Plat and Rogalski 1999). In the case of operational management, the results come from studies of different groups of firefighters with the same level of experience dealing with similar simulated situations (detailed analyses can be found in Rogalski 1995b; Antolin-Glenn 1997; Rogalski and Antolin-Glenn 1997).

The aim of analysing these data together in the present chapter is to identify common trends or *invariants* in the acquisition of collective competence through simulation, and in the patterns of instructors' interventions. In view of the different kinds of collective task represented, this would provide a way of cross-validating the findings from individual studies.

Evolution of collective competence through simulation

Aviation (civil aviation, highly-automated cockpits, experienced pilots)

The training situation is represented in Figure 10.1, including the expected interactions between the two pilots within the crew. The results concern six crews, whose performance and co-operation were recorded as they were managing a rare and unpredicted disturbance, an engine fire, during the

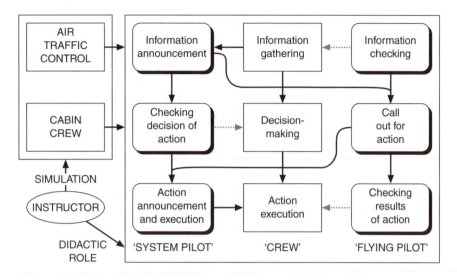

Figure 10.1 Training for piloting highly automated cockpits. The focus is on training crews in cockpit resource management: distributing tasks and ensuring cross-check for executing procedures, as schematized on the right. Instructor plays the role of the other entities interacting with pilots in the crew ('simulation' arrow).

crucial phase of take off. Data were recorded in the middle of the training phase on a full-size simulator (session M), and in the last session, just before the crews' formal assessment for qualification (session L).

Collective performance improved over the simulation sessions, as evaluated by the percentage of correct micro-procedures. Micro-procedures were defined as small but significant units of activity (such as 'gear up', raising the landing gear, or 'take-off check-list', a systematic check procedure).

Correct actions and co-operation (required cross-checking procedures) increased significantly between the middle practice session and the last; incorrect actions and correct actions without the required co-operation on the other hand decreased. Both operational collective performance (the crew as a virtual operator) and co-operation increased throughout the simulation sessions. However, a *décalage* was observed between, on the one hand, spontaneous 'call-out' actions by the crew and on the other hand, the sharing of information. While most of the decision-making and execution of procedures was correct, less than half of them were performed with explicit sharing of information.

Two important aspects of interaction amongst the crew were noted: 1) there was frequent explicit co-operation (cross-checking) when performing procedures, but not always by the pilot who was formally identified as responsible; 2) the pilots shared information tacitly by observing each other's displays more frequently than by sharing information verbally.

These two points indicate that they were using the procedures as a tool for co-operation and sharing control, even if they did not always follow the procedures as prescribed (Rogalski 1996). There were, however, major differences between the six crews studied: out of the total, one was highly efficient and co-operated fully from the first session, while one needed an extra simulation session before they met the standard required for certification. The differences in performance included both procedural knowledge and cockpit resource management.

Operational management of public safety/emergency situations by experienced firefighters

The schema of the training situations is given in Figure 10.2. A series of four simulation sessions was developed to train teams in collective activity.

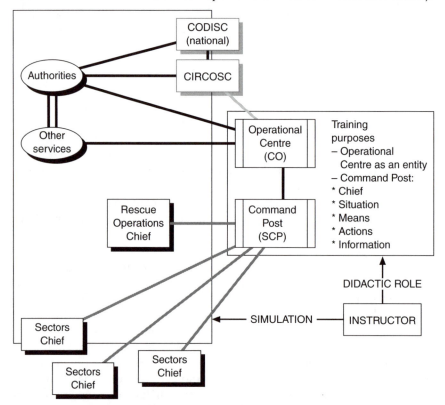

Figure 10.2 Training for operational management. The focus is on training officers in Operational Centre (CO) and in Site Command Post (SCP) to manage the flow of communication (grey arrows), and co-ordinate the design and execution of appropriate manoeuvres to face an unusual emergency situation. Instructor plays the role of the other entities interacting with CO or SCP ('simulation' arrow).

Three teams of firefighters (formed for the purpose of the research from officers who had not previously worked together) were observed over the sessions, and individual questionnaires were completed at the end of each session to elicit the officers' impressions of their performance as a team, their co-operation and the way they fulfilled their individual functions within the team. They had also to record what function was allocated to whom.

On the basis of these results, it was judged that there was an increase in collective competence, although there were important inter-team differences:

- individual perceptions of the allocation of functions within the team rapidly converged (in the first session, there were discrepancies of function identification by different members of the same team, but their number decreased rapidly);
- efficiency in the use of representational tools increased;
- problems in co-operation decreased;
- collective management improved with regard to information management, time management and speed of decision-making.

An important component in collective competence seems to have been the use of representational tools to support collective implementation of a plan of action. It also appears that both individual ways of managing interpersonal relations and individual skills in participating in shared decision-making played an important role in the quality of co-operation and collective performance.

Similarities and differences in learning across simulation sessions

It is clear that a small number of simulation sessions was sufficient to improve competence in collective work in dealing with crises and emergencies in flying aircraft and protecting public safety. Among the skills that were learned were two key components of work process knowledge: who has to do what and what information needs to be transmitted to other members of the team. In addition, the teams acquired the capacity to use cognitive tools (automated systems and procedures in aviation; representational tools in operational management) as tools for increasing collaboration.

Another common finding is inter-team variability. Although confronted with the same simulated situations, marked differences appeared in the performance of the six aircrews and three teams of firefighters. This might be explained by the fact that different participants had different 'zones of proximal development' in terms of their capacity to engage in collective work.

The instructor's role in running simulations

Aviation

The instructor's activity was also analysed, using the same data as presented above, and related to the activity of the crews. Two scenarios were considered: managing an engine fire at take off (called Take Off hereafter), and making a landing approach with automated systems (called Approach hereafter). Instructor interventions were classified as *epistemic* when they were oriented towards the crew's understanding of the systems and procedures, and as *pragmatic* when they were oriented towards the crew's performance. *Co-operation interventions* were those that addressed the co-ordination of different pilots' activity within the cockpit. The orientation of the instructor's interventions regarding the automated systems (the main purpose of the training) was compared with the orientation of interventions concerning the other systems in the cockpit.

Overall, the frequency of instructor's interventions was almost stable from session M to session L (although a little lower in the last session). They were mainly positive interventions which reinforced the crew's action or acknowledged the validity of knowledge previously acquired on automated systems. There was a balance between epistemic and pragmatic interventions. Epistemic interventions were more common when the intervention concerned automated systems, and pragmatic interventions declined in frequency between the middle and last session, while epistemic interventions increased.

Differences between the two scenarios related mainly to interventions about the automated systems. During Take Off, which required following detailed procedures at a rapid speed, the instructor's interventions about the automated systems were mostly made during action and they were mainly performance-oriented. In contrast, during Approach, a significant number of the instructor's interventions were expressed before and after action, and were mainly knowledge-oriented.

Finally, the proportion of interventions oriented towards co-operation itself was low (around 10 per cent of all interventions) and showed little variation. There were more interventions concerning co-operation when automated systems were not involved. It was as if the instructors were focusing on the technical performance of the crew until an adequate level of performance had been achieved, and only then intervened to develop the process of co-operation itself.

Operational management

In this case, the study of instructor's interventions in the simulations was based on a new series of training sessions, using different teams of firefighters (although of similar grades and experience). Training had a similar structure, with four simulation situations led by the same instructor, and with two teams performing in parallel. Data compare the first simulation with the last. Finally, in this part of the study, the role of the instructor now includes, in the simulation phase, intervening in real time (on-line) and, in the debriefing phase, giving feedback on performance.

Both the simulation and debriefing phases contained a large amount of activity by the instructor, with an overall decrease in the total number of interventions in successive simulation sessions, and a relatively stable ratio of on-line interventions (about 60 per cent) to debriefing interventions (about 40 per cent).

Between the middle session and the last, the focus of the instructor's interventions changed dramatically from directly coaching officers in how to handle the simulation to an indirect role encouraging them to take account of each other's actions, thus building their autonomy in collective tactical management. It is possible that this change reveals a significant change in the officers' competencies throughout the series of simulations.

In the aviation training, the instructor's interventions were classified into two main categories: interventions oriented towards trainees' collective activity (what they have to do, what they are doing, what they have done) and interventions oriented towards giving procedural knowledge which the crews are expected to follow.

Overall, the instructor's interventions were mainly pragmatic (about two-thirds of all the on-line interventions) and much less often epistemic. There was no significant change in this between the initial simulation session and the last one.

The nature of knowledge involved in the on-line instructor's interventions differed from session to session: emphasis was initially placed on technical knowledge (middle session) and later on strategic knowledge (last session). A specific type of knowledge which appeared as a focus of the instructor's interventions was called '*experiential knowledge*'. For instance, the instructor might suggest a modification to a trainee's proposed action: 'from my experience, it is better to do it like this'. Such an experiential knowledge is similar to 'rules of thumb'. Such a use of experiential knowledge was also observed in the case of aviation during the debriefing phase, when the instructor underlined the utilization of instruments in the cockpit through personal experience (Dubey 1997: 44).

Interventions concerning representational tools and other resources for collective action were relatively numerous in the middle session (17 per cent) and totally absent in the last session. This is quite consistent with our observations of trainees' activity in the previous study on operational management: in the first session, teams faced difficulties in organizing representational tools (graphical representation of the situation, table of the status of operational equipment, planning for actions and orders), while their use of these tools was skilful during the last session.

Similarities and differences in instructor's interventions in aviation and operational crisis management

The first similarity in the interventions in the simulation practice of both aviation crews and operational command posts is that at the early stages of practice they were predominantly oriented towards the teams' performance. The possibility of comparing the debriefing stage was limited by the fact that the aviation training debriefings were not video- or audio-recorded. However, observations of the debriefing phases indicated that instructors intervened frequently at a general level, their interventions were less contextualized, and they made a quite limited use of the videos recorded during the simulation phase. Debriefing appeared as the occasion for developing crews' understanding of both the procedures they were supposed to follow and their own errors or uncertainties about the new systems. For the operational management training, epistemic interventions were more numerous in debriefing phases than during the on-line simulation.

Interventions directly concerning co-operation activities were infrequent in both the aviation and operational management training. There was, however, in both cases an increased frequency in the last session. This might be related to the difficulties in identifying specific cues of competence in co-operation (Brannick, Salas and Prince 1997). The issue of how instructors might use the cues – identified in a research context – adds yet another difficulty.

In contrast, there was a clear difference in the use of cognitive tools. In the aviation study, the instructors continued to make interventions about the automated systems till the end of the training, but in the operational management training the interventions about representational tools and other resources for collective action had ceased by the last session. In the former case, instructors maintained a high level of on-line interventions, while in the case of operational management, the number of interventions decreased.

Discussion and open issues

Two empirical studies provided data on the development of collective competence through simulation. Similarities were found in both the development of collective competence over the simulation sessions, and in the nature of the support given by instructors.

By the middle simulation session, collective competence appeared to be developing as measured by performance failures, uncertainty in identifying or in performing the assigned roles in the team, and the nature of the instructors' interventions. There was also a marked improvement in team performance and co-operation. New collective competences were being developed regarding the use of shared cognitive tools. In the same way, the instructors' interventions showed a decrease in directly support-ing actors' performance and more emphasis on collaboration.

The participants in these studies were already highly qualified, and the simulation did not provide any opportunity to refer problems to superiors. The question now arises as to what extent this influenced the outcome of the studies. A partial answer can be found in a report on training actors for the collective management of unpredictable events in nuclear power plants. In that study, a simulation was used to improve co-operation between actors occupying different hierarchical levels and functional posi-tions in the plant (Jansens *et al.* 1989). Instructors' interventions were concentrated on developing reflection about collective work, mutual understanding of other's tasks and knowledge of the constraints in the activity. Interviews and observations following this simulation indicated an improvement in communication in the real work situation between actors at all levels and in all functions, and showed evidence of better collective performance.

The examples discussed were cases of dynamic situations which evolved rapidly with a high level of risk. In such domains, collective competence needed for managing rare or unpredictable situations cannot be acquired from direct work experience, as this is too far from the 'target' situations. However, simulation could provide a means for presenting trainees with situations within their 'proximal zone of development' with the support of appropriate interventions by instructor. This can assist operators in devel-oping work process knowledge, articulating knowledge about 'the world to be acted on' and knowledge about 'the organization of the actors involved' while taking into account the fact that the articulations depend on the work situation itself.

Acknowledgements

The studies reported here were supported by grants from the *Direction générale de l'aviation civile* (DGAC), and from the *Institut national d'études de la Sécurité Civile* (INESC). We want to thank Airbus Training, and the École Nationale Supérieure des Officiers Sapeurs-Pompiers, for their welcome and co-operation in observing and recording training simulation sessions. Our thanks extend to trainees for their active participation, and instructors who helped us to acquire the technical knowledge required for performing analyses of simulation sessions.

11 The contribution of work process knowledge to competence in electrical maintenance

Renan Samurçay and Christine Vidal-Gomel

In this chapter, we explore work process knowledge as a component of competence in managing risk in electrical maintenance work. We discuss two aspects of this way of knowing in this context: information flow and organizational constraints. While identifying, eliminating and managing electrical risks, electricians draw upon a range of cognitive resources. Three deserve particular mention: *competencies* – ways and means developed in the trade, *schemas* – invariant organizations of activity for a class of situations, and *instruments* – cognitive tools (Rabardel and Duvenci-Langa, Chapter 5 in this volume; Rabardel 1995; Béguin and Rabardel 2000). Based on data obtained from a series of accident analyses, we compare training situations with real work situations to identify the competence requirements for risk management. The results are then used to discuss the work process content of training, both in the workplace and in formal contexts.

Vocational training and risk management in the workplace

Recent studies and health and safety reports indicate that, while young workers represent only 12 per cent of the French workforce, they are involved in 25 per cent of accidents at work. A research programme was initiated by several French government organizations (including the Ministry of Education and the Departments of Public Health and Occupational Safety) to investigate and recommend appropriate action.[1] There are many causes of accidents, including working conditions, deficiencies in company safety policies, the practice of sub-contracting and lack of competence on the part of the operatives. As far as young workers are concerned, research indicates that two major social and organizational factors often contribute to accidents: their precarious employment status and the practice of sub-contracting (Thébaud-Mony *et al.* 1995). The question of how best to develop competence in occupational risk management through formal training and in the workplace remains open. As Mhamdi (1998) demonstrated, injurability is not only related to the operator's age but also to time in the job, regardless of length of experience in the company. Experience of actual work situations seems to be a decisive factor in determining the likelihood of an accident. However, many studies stress that while work experience is necessary for the development of safe and competent practice, it is not sufficient and specially targeted training is also needed (*Education Permanente* 1995).

In electrical engineering courses in France, technical competence and risk management are taught separately, although these are really two aspects of the same work activity. In the risk prevention part of the training, the knowledge base is derived from engineering sciences, and focuses on safety rules and concepts such as voltage and amperage in order to explain the dangers of electricity for human beings. This knowledge is taught in preparation for a formal qualification. The training uses the latest technical systems, although in real work situations several generations of equipment coexist and do not always conform to safety requirements and the regulations.

The research reported in this chapter was carried out in a company that was reorganizing the way it maintained its electrical systems. The change was in the direction of greater functional flexibility, consistent with the widespread changes in work organization discussed by Boreham in Chapter 1: functions which were previously carried out in separate departments may be brought together within the same team. Previously, operators specialized in either electro-mechanical maintenance or the maintenance of the distribution network. The new structure requires them to work in both fields, confronting them with a wider range of technical devices. At this point, it is necessary to point out a particular difficulty in maintaining electrical equipment. The state of a piece of equipment often reflects the fact that several operators have already serviced it and left errors in place. Each successive operator then has to detect and correct this situation. In the company concerned, the safety-criticality of this problem increased dramatically. When more flexible working was introduced, operators had to service equipment with little or no knowledge of the previous modifications made to the devices and the possible deviations from safety norms this might entail. Although the company recognized the need for multi-skilling, the training programmes that accompanied these organizational changes focused on technical aspects, and gave little or no attention to risk management.

In our view, current methods of vocational training in this field do not develop the capacity to manage risk in situations where safety norms are being disregarded. It is necessary to create *potential situations of competence development* (Mayen 1999), incorporating the following elements:

- the identification of *core tasks* (Norros and Nuutinen, Chapter 3) and the competencies required for dealing with them, especially *reference knowledge* relating to the work process, which Rogalski, Plat and Antolin-Glenn in Chapter 10 describe as classes of mental representations and

operations common to efficient practices, these practices being contextualized and personalized (see also Rogalski and Samurçay 1994);

- the transposition of *core task* dimensions and other dimensions of the
work process into training situations, in order to encourage the development of reference knowledge (Samurçay and Rogalski 1998).

In order to identify the dimensions of operational competence, an
ergonomic analysis of the activity is necessary (Rogalski and Samurçay
1994). In this study we analysed electrical accidents and incidents concerning the maintenance of electrical systems. Accident and incident situations are considered a source of data for core task analysis (Norros 1998)
and for identifying reference knowledge. Reason (1998) distinguishes two
kinds of accidents, individual and organizational. Our focus is on individual accidents. These are 'ones in which a specific person or group is
often both the agent and the victim of the accident' (Reason 1998: 1).
They can have organizational origins (Wagenaar 1998). We define an accident as an undesired event which harms the individual, and an incident as
an event which may have led to an accident if the operator had not recov-
ered it (Faverge 1967). There are often several causes of accidents and
incidents. We focus on both the characteristics of situations that may lead
even experienced operators to fail, and on the identification of deficiencies in risk management.

Electrical maintenance

In electrical maintenance work, the major risk is failing to isolate the
equipment being worked on, resulting in electrocution. To manage this
risk, operators have several technical aids at their disposal, such as diagrams, safety rules, procedures, individual and collective protection equipment, as well as subjective resources such as their own competencies.
Before discussing accidents and incidents in this domain, we will present a
cognitive analysis of the maintenance task.

Schematic analysis of the task of electrical maintenance

The work of maintenance electricians can be schematically broken down
into three phases: the diagnosis phase, the making-safe phase and the
repairing phase.

The diagnosis phase.   Diagnosis in this context has two dimensions: identification of the risk and identification of the cause(s) of the failure. The
former can be seen as an elaboration or updating of the operator's
representation of the situation. Several studies use the term *situational
awareness* to describe this (*Human Factors* 1995). The diagnosis and constraints such as the need to provide continuity of service and the opera-

tor's estimation of his or her own competencies determine the decision whether or not to cut off the power. The power cut can be total or partial, or the operator may decide to work with the device fully powered. The operator also has to generate a hypothesis about the causes of failure (for example, the fact that the emergency stop button is constantly triggered), which can lead him or her to corrective action (in the same example, to replace the emergency stop button).

The making-safe phase. The operator has to be sure that he or she can operate on the circuit safely. Decisions therefore need to be made concerning 'breakdown' (disconnecting the circuit partly, totally or not at all, and at which node), how to check the effectiveness of the disconnection, whether to use instruments, and whether or not to wear protective equipment.

The repair phase. This phase includes fixing and testing actions, when management of risk is critical. For instance, even if power has been cut from part of a circuit, there may still be live elements in the vicinity. The operator must also take into consideration and manage constraints. For example, when disconnecting, the operator must not interrupt any crucial function performed by the company.[2] This is why, in some situations, the power cannot be fully cut. More generally, operators have to manage constraints such as working in isolation and shift work.

Description of an accident

As mentioned earlier, accidents and incidents are critical situations that enable us to explore the dimensions of competence in risk management. In the study reported here, five accidents and one incident were analysed. All occurred during normal work situations. Injured operators were interviewed about the accident to establish what happened, why they did a particular action, how they evaluated the situation, what criteria determined their choice to wear or not wear protective equipment and so on. The analysis was not designed to discover the causes of the accident, as is generally the case in accident analysis for prevention purposes, nor did it attempt to determine responsibility. It aimed at identifying the activity that occurs in this kind of maintenance work.

The following accident can be considered typical of the cases we studied. The company's electrical systems maintenance department was informed of a breakdown – an emergency stop button in an electrical cupboard was constantly being triggered. A pair of electricians was entrusted with repairing this fault. They discovered that the emergency stop button was triggered every time the doors to the cupboard were opened or closed. The button could not be repaired and had to be replaced. They knew that this part was not in stock and had to be ordered. Meanwhile, to allow the continued use of the cupboard until they could carry out the repair, they decided to disconnect the emergency stop button and temporarily replace it with a 'cap'. To perform this operation safely, they cut power to the emergency stop button, thus eliminating the electrical risk. This cupboard (labelled '2' in Figure 11.1) was powered by one of the circuits from another cupboard (labelled '1'). Using the circuit diagram, the operators identified the corresponding circuit breaker in cupboard 1 (labelled 'X') and disconnected it. They carried out an absence of tension control on the downstream nodes of this circuit breaker (control point a). They checked that the code on the cable linking cupboards 1 and 2 corresponded to the cable code in the diagram (control point b). Then they cut the power to the main circuit breaker in cupboard 2, which should have disconnected all the elements in the cupboard. They tested for absence of tension on the downstream nodes of this circuit breaker (control point c). Convinced that cupboard 2 was now disconnected, they decided not to carry out the absence of tension test on the node of the emergency stop button, despite the fact that this meant disregarding a formal safety rule. They considered that this operation, which would have meant removing all the screws of the cupboard's inner door, would take too much time. An operator removed some of these screws but only enough to access the node and disconnect it. In doing so, he simultaneously picked up two live and neutral wires and received electrical burns to the hands. The emergency stop button was still powered due to a latent connection error (bold line in Figure 11.1). The investigation that followed the accident revealed that this connection error was made by a sub-contracted company entrusted with installing the emergency stop button so as to bring the cupboard in line with electrical equipment security norms. The change to the device had been carried out at the request of the department that used the cupboard, without informing the maintenance department and without updating the diagrams of the device.

Why the accident occurred and its implications for competence

We collected data from interviews with six electrical maintenance operators who had experienced an accident or an incident of electrical origin. The interviews were analysed in several ways in order to explore the dimensions of competence in this domain. The first analysis aimed to describe the way the activity was organized as it unfolded, in particular situations. This level of analysis allows us to understand the relations between contextual elements (the state and evolution of the technical system, organizational and time constraints) and the operator's activity in the situation (information gathering, diagnosis, decision, action). A possible explanation of the accident is suggested by the following.

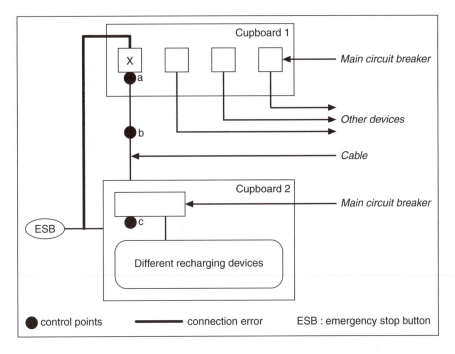

Figure 11.1 Electrical repair problem

- The device had been modified before the operators worked on it, yet there was no record of this intervention. This can be interpreted as a lack of work process knowledge, in that they were carrying out maintenance work without knowing how other sections of the company were carrying out closely related tasks on which their own safety depended. This situation was encountered in several other cases investigated.
- The operators' diagnosis of the situation was based on an inadequate representation of the state of the system. The criteria they used to establish that the circuit was not powered were insufficient to detect the danger. In the total set of accidents studied, three of the four operators required to cut power did so unsuccessfully.
- The operators believed that they were working in safe conditions (they disconnected the circuit breakers and carried out controls). They did not wear their safety equipment and did not test for absence of tension on the node of the emergency stop button because they considered that they were dealing with a 'normal situation'.[3] The same three operators mentioned above acted similarly.

As in the other events analysed, this accident occurred due to errors made in the diagnosis and making-safe phases. Disconnecting equipment is the core task because it constitutes a major means of managing risk.

However, the operators did not know what work processes were being followed in other sections of the company and were consequently unable to detect the risk factors.

In our data we can differentiate between operators who carry out local tests and those who do not carry out any tests at all. In the example given, the operators performed local tests which allowed them to verify the correct functioning of the circuit breakers (control points a and c, Figure 11.1) as well as the correct connection between cupboard 1 and cupboard 2 (control point b, Figure 11.1). Furthermore, cutting power to the general circuit breaker of cupboard 2 protected them from a potential connection error between circuit breaker X and the general circuit breaker in cupboard 2. Although these tests were insufficient to detect the connection error present, they do show that the operators were aware of the possibility of irregular connections in electrical apparatus. This was not the case for the other operators studied, who switched off a device and assumed immediately that it was not powered.

This level of description only allows us to describe the activity in terms of transformation of the state of the system, representation, diagnosis and actions undertaken by the operator. Therefore, we need to build a description of competencies that explains, even partially, all these aspects.

The dimensions of competencies

As pointed out by several authors (Fischer 1998; Boreham and Samurçay 1998; Nardi 1996 and Norros and Nuutinen, Chapter 3), the classic models of expertise based on information processing (IP) theory are too weak and incomplete to provide an understanding of what competencies are and how subjects construct them. On the other hand, situated cognition approaches, which stand in direct opposition to the IP framework, propose a new framework in which activity can only be known 'in situ' and pre-organized elements of cognition are seen as 'retrospective reconstruction'. However, this too is problematic because it represents human activity as being without invariant structure. This is highly debatable, especially when applied to higher conscious level activity and occupational competence.

Inspired by constructivist approaches such as Piaget's theory and Vygotsky's notion of the dialectic development of cognition, it is possible to outline a framework describing the components of competencies in a developmental perspective (Rabardel and Samurçay 1995). Within this framework, the process of development is not seen from a cumulative point of view, but is considered as a result of restructuring by the subject's constructive activities.[4] The proposed framework focuses on the organization of highly integrated elements of human cognition (other elements are discussed in Rogalski, Plat and Antolin-Glenn, Chapter 10). We distinguish four types of entities: representations and concepts (related to objects, their properties and relations), activity organizers (schemes of different levels: rules, procedures, methods, etc.), instruments (artifacts and their utilization schemes) and situations (classes of situations). So a particular activity observed in a single situation can be described as a particular interaction between these more structured entities, made specific by the context and by the subjective manner in which the activity is undertaken. Thus it becomes possible to infer from a single activity the dimension of competencies for a given operator and for a given activity field in terms of core competence. Let us return to our example.

- The operators had to identify the sections of the circuit which needed to be disconnected. In the given situation, they knew that they could not cut power to the whole circuit of cupboard 1 because of the need to maintain a service. Given that they could only disconnect partly (activity organizer: *disconnection scheme*), they acted on the two circuit breakers. Their representation of normal situations integrated connection errors and circuit breaker malfunctions, so they carried out local controls (activity organizer: *verification scheme*). The results of these controls led them to infer that they were dealing with a 'normal' situation. They thus applied a *model of a 'normal' circuit* which respected two aspects: *continuity* and *directions of energy distribution* (considered here as *pragmatic concepts*).[5]
- The operators carried out controls to verify that they were indeed in a 'normal' situation: checking the absence of tension on the downstream node of the two circuit breakers and verifying the cable code. These criteria were insufficient to detect the latent error in this situation. After opening the circuit breakers and performing the controls, they inferred that it was no longer powered. This led them to consider that checking the node of the emergency stop button and wearing protective gloves were unnecessary (rule associated with *normal situations*). On one hand, the formal safety rule requiring a check for the absence of tension was violated here. On the other hand, the controls performed were more precise than those required by the formal safety rule itself: they allow the detection of circuit breaker malfunctions and the detection of some connection errors (related to the connection of a circuit breaker in cupboard 1 to cupboard 2). These controls function as *precautionary measures*.[6]

We focus on the disconnecting operation, which is considered to be a core task for risk management, and on the dimensions of the competencies required to perform it. These are *core competencies*. In short, we postulate that the operators activate the following dimensions of competencies for risk management.

- The set of classes of situations, which may or may not include the representation of abnormal situations such as connection errors. *Normal situations are those which respect safety rules and the procedures adopted in the trade.* For example, to connect a fuse box, the operator has to connect the current upstream of the fuse box with the top of the fuse box. The top is identified by the way the fuse box is opened (from top to bottom). This procedure links topography and the direction of energy distribution. We will elaborate on this notion later. Some operators integrate the representation of connection errors into their model of situations. In the given event, the operators carried out local controls. Other operators (three out of four who had to cut power) did not: they applied models of normal situations.

- Representations, some of which are underlined by the *pragmatic concepts of continuity and energy distribution direction.* Pragmatic concepts were identified based on operators' statements and actions. In our example, the operators' representation of the circuit included the order of elements. This order is organized from upstream to downstream:

  a   the circuit breaker X of electric cupboard 1,
  b   the cable between the two cupboards,
  c   the general circuit breaker of cupboard 2,
  d   the emergency stop button.

  This ordering of elements describes the direction of energy distribution. The representation of the circuit also includes continuity. An important characteristic of electrical circuits is that they are closed and continuous. The disconnecting operation implies a break in continuity, and this is one way for the operators to achieve their goal. Two pragmatic concepts organized their representation of the circuit: to disconnect the emergency stop button, they acted on two circuit breakers because they were upstream and there was continuity between these elements. These two pragmatic concepts organized representations of the circuit shared by all the operators.

- Activity organizers: *disconnection schema* and *verification schema.* The schemas can be defined as invariant organizations of the activity for a class of situations. It seems that operators applied two schemas:

  1   *Disconnection schema.* To carry out a disconnection operation the operators need to consider where the element to be disconnected is situated within the distribution network, and from which element onwards they can disconnect in a given situation; that is, they must integrate the continuity of service constraints. These representations are based on the two pragmatic concepts identified above. Yet integration of the constraints leads the operator to disconnect as little as possible. In the events analysed, all the operators who had to cut power, did so as little as possible. This proved to be *an invariant rule for a class of situations.*

  2   *Verification schema.* Depending on whether or not operators had integrated a connection error into the model of situations, they carried out an absence of tension test. This could have two differ-

ent goals: checking that the disconnection was effective, or checking that the situation was normal. In the example given above, the organization of the activity was the same for the two circuit breakers: checking the absence of tension on the downstream node of the two. *Activity has the same organization.* Based on the results of these controls, the operators inferred that the situation was normal and therefore that the circuit corresponded to their representation in terms of the order of different elements and continuity. When connection errors were not integrated into the operators' model of situations, they inferred that the operation had been effective (i.e. the device was no longer powered).

- Means of risk management. The rule to check for the absence of tension demands that the test be carried out as close as possible to the place where the repair work will be done. For example, in the case at hand, this meant on the node of the emergency stop button. In the four events where this rule should have been applied, it was not (three out of four cases) or its application was informal (the case discussed above). In this example, the operators' local controls can be seen as *precautionary measures.* These practices as a whole are an efficient means of treating certain disorders. They can save time in that they allow the operator to detect and situate dysfunction and disorders in a more precise manner. In our example, they *replaced* the rule. This is not the only case of substitution we observed. For example, another operator stated that he used handling gloves instead of safety gloves when the amperage was low. Thus, operators appear to use a variety of means to manage risks. They could be formal means – safety rules, individual and collective protection equipment, etc. – or informal means, such as handling gloves. Some of these means can function as precautionary measures and replace formal means, when operators consider that they have the same capacity to manage risks, and when they constitute economic practices. We consider all these means as a *system of instruments* (Lefort 1982; Rabardel 1995).

From a developmental point of view, we assume that the classes of situations constructed by operators are enriched by on-the-job experience. This development is parallel to the elaboration of pragmatic concepts and model representations which allow operators to take into account deviations from 'normal' situations and, more specifically, to identify such situations. The classes of situations and pragmatic concept developments are associated with the elaboration of schemes and of more efficient systems of instruments. Some of the artifacts that compose them are the formal safety rules (for example, checking for the absence of tension). Their use evolves during development, depending on the extent to which classes of situations and the pragmatic concepts are elaborated. This use can become informal and can lead to the development of precautionary measures, as in the previous example. This approach is in line with studies by Gaudard and Weill-Fassina (1999) and De la Garza and Weill-Fassina (2000). These authors stress that with experience, operators adapt that which is forbidden so as to set up the regulation and rectification of dangerous situations. Informal instruments supplement the 'blanks' left by the safety rules, as observed by Rousseau and Monteau (1991). The construction of this system of instruments can be considered as instrumental genesis (Rabardel 1995; Rabardel and Duvenci-Langa, Chapter 5).

How can operators' constructive activities be improved?

Both vocational and occupational training programmes tend to focus on normal situations and safety rules. For this reason, the usual kinds of training appear incapable of developing core competencies for risk management. The integration of connection errors and the development of pragmatic concepts seem to be key issues in developing an appropriate conceptualization of safe action. In training situations, instructors present safety rules but are less willing to justify them. Even if operators use informal instruments which allow local controls, the safety rule of testing for the absence of tension remains the best means of detecting connection errors. Mayen and Savoyant (1999) stress that one must understand the need for a safety rule in order to be motivated to use it. Moreover, vocational education and training programmes do not stress the consequences of failing to appreciate the work processes in use in other parts of the organization, especially the necessity for operators to provide records of their interventions to avoid creating a latent error for the future. In a global and systemic approach to prevention, detection of latent errors is a crucial issue and poses a real problem. Reason (1998) describes different methods of detecting them, but stresses that none is foolproof and the best method remains retroactive, i.e. accident and incident analysis. Nevertheless, vocational education and training programmes treat technical and risk prevention aspects independently. For example, in order to disconnect safely, operators need a representation of the distribution of the energy network (the technical aspect). What is needed to treat the problem is to transpose these three dimensions of real work situations into training situations:[7] the importance of understanding the work process in other sections, the integration of the technical and the risk prevention aspects and connection errors. The disconnection operation is a core task for risk management and training must focus on this in order to encourage core competence development.

A second goal is to design a programme of coherent training that covers these three points. In addition to risk identification and disconnection operations, training should also promote safe behaviour (Hale 1984). This last point seems particularly important for electricians, given that they constantly work within a few centimetres of live elements, or in contexts where they must work without disconnecting the device.

Finally, analysis of maintenance activity can assist both trainers and trainees. For trainers, it can provide a better understanding of trainee activity and help them in the debriefing phase (Pastré, Plénacoste and Samurçay 1998). For trainees, it can assist reflection (Rabardel and Six 1995; Mhamdi 1998).

Conclusion

Similar to the findings of Fischer and Rauner in Chapter 12, in this study we found that electrical risk management requires both technical knowledge derived from engineering science and pragmatic knowledge that includes an understanding of the overall work process in the organization. Constructing the knowledge needed to carry out maintenance safely requires the operator to actively relate these two diverse sources of work-related knowledge. In Taylorist organizations, risk is managed by imposing formal safety rules. The alternative approach outlined in this chapter allows us to move beyond the idea of rule following and focus on the development of ways of managing risks proactively (Battmann and Klumb 1993), a concept of preventive maintenance that depends in part on work process knowledge.

Acknowledgement

This study was carried out with support from the Institut national de recherche et de sécurité and the Régie autonome des transports parisiens.

Notes

1 Our study is part of the national 'electrical risk prevention' programme which is in the process of applying European safety norms. This programme considers occupational risk management as an important component of professional qualification.
2 The company's main function is passenger transport.
3 In normal situations all the connections comply with trade rules and are represented on the diagram of the device.
4 On the relation between experience and work process development see also Fischer and Rauner, Chapter 12; Rabardel and Duvenci-Langa, Chapter 5.
5 *Pragmatic concepts* (Samurçay and Pastré, 1995) are developed by operators on the basis of crucial variables of the plant or device they have to manage and control. They are not scientific or technical concepts. They can be defined as conceptual and operational invariant. Operators can name them and talk about them. They can be thought of. They are elaborated *in* and *for* action. On the role of action, see also Norros and Nuutinen, Chapter 3.
6 The concept of *precautionary measures* is a translation of *savoir-faire de prudence*. This concept is developed by Cru (1995) to designate the construction of specific safety skills. They operationalize and complete formal safety rules according to the contextual elements of the situations.
7 The notion of *transposition* is discussed by Rogalski, Plat and Antolin-Glenn, Chapter 10, and more precisely by Samurçay and Rogalski (1998).

12 The implications of work process knowledge for vocational education and training

Martin Fischer and Felix Rauner

The main purpose of this chapter is to discuss the implications for vocational education and training (VET) of acknowledging the importance of work process knowledge in modern employment. Two issues are important here. First, how can the concept of work process knowledge inform the development of VET, and second, how can the acquisition of work process knowledge be supported by VET? Work process knowledge as introduced here is immediately useful for work, but empirical research into skilled production and maintenance work reveals that work process knowledge is not a matter of mere work experience. The acquisition of work process knowledge presupposes a process of constructing and combining theoretical and practical knowledge. This process is made difficult under the conditions of computerization and permanent change. Courses of technical training based on content derived from the engineering sciences do not sufficiently support learners in the acquisition of work process knowledge. Curriculum development in this field has therefore to develop a new concept of the theoretical underpinning of work process knowledge. We examine the new European occupational profile of the 'car mechatronic' to support the case for a co-operative (as distinct from a dual system) of VET, designed to integrate the performance of essential work tasks with the acquisition of work-related theoretical knowledge. This curriculum can be regarded as an attempt to surmount the dualism between the teaching of abstract scientific principles, on one hand, and training for narrow Taylorist work tasks on the other hand.

Work process knowledge

It is widely believed in industrial training circles that much or even all of the knowledge that is acquired in institutions such as school or university can be regarded as 'inert', and this has been supported by empirical investigations (Mandl *et al.* 1993; Renkl 1996). Inert knowledge may be described as a kind of book-knowledge which is not immediately useful for work and which can be difficult to adapt to different work situations. For example, Heinz Mandl and his colleagues found that students of industrial management failed to achieve better results in managing a computer-simulated business enterprise than a control group consisting of students of pedagogy (Renkl *et al.* 1994). Thus it appears that much of the content of vocational courses in institutions might have very little impact on the development of individual work competencies. On the other hand, one of the defining characteristics of what we call 'work process knowledge' is that it is useful in the workplace (Kruse 1985, 1986). The development of a theory of work process knowledge has drawn on many different fields of academic study and professional practice. In Germany, this approach has been revived by an organization of university institutions providing training for teachers and trainers in the technical sector (HGTB).[1] Members of this organization have criticized the traditional content of vocational education and training for intermediate level employees on the grounds that it is derived from degree level engineering sciences. It has been argued that knowledge of the engineering sciences is qualitatively different from the technician or operator's knowledge of how to repair and operate machines. Even the knowledge of a professional engineer has to be regarded as very different from the theoretical knowledge he or she studied on university courses. In both cases, a way of presenting engineering theory is needed with a better orientation towards practicalities. The concept of 'work process knowledge' is a tool for achieving this, and represents a significant change of perspective for VET. Several universities in Germany have begun to establish the academic study of VET as a science (as it is called on the continent) or a discipline (as it is called in English-speaking countries), not only with respect to its didactics but also curriculum content. The adoption of work process knowledge as the focal or core concept of 'VET science' has led to a new and vigorous programme of research activities, replacing an earlier one much more operational in its approach to questions of didactics and teaching environments.

As a working definition (Fischer 2000), we have described work process knowledge as:

- immediately useful for the work to be done (the knowledge that actively informs the work of the skilled worker);
- mostly (although not exclusively) constructed in the workplace through experience and work itself, especially through interaction between individuals and the complex tools they use;
- an understanding of the whole work process including preparation, action, control and evaluation.

This is a definition which needs further elaboration, and this is a preoccupation of many other chapters in the present volume. In the present chapter, we will concentrate on presenting some thoughts about the acquisition of work process knowledge, and about the role played in this by formal systems of vocational education and training. Finally, we will discuss an example of how work process knowledge can be used as the organizing principle for curriculum development.

The acquisition of work process knowledge

On the basis of our research in different sectors – industrial maintenance work (Fischer *et al.* 1995; Drescher 1996), production islands in manufacturing plant (Fischer 1995), chemical laboratories (see Fischer and Röben, Chapter 4 in this volume) and the automobile service sector (Rauner and Zeymer 1991) – we have reached the conclusion that work experience alone does not generate competence in these contexts. When people know how to do something, namely how to carry out a task practically, their competence is based on a complex of the practical, rational and aesthetic aspects of work activity (see Fischer, Chapter 9). It is of course true that socialization into the trade or occupation and direct experience of machinery, tasks, situations and people does enable skilled workers to overcome the difficulties which confront them in the course of their everyday activities in the plant. However, our research has found that even the experientially guided work activity of intermediate level employees is informed by theoretical knowledge (albeit often rudimentary), and that it conforms to rules that can be verbalized and generalized. It is also guided by tacit knowledge which can be made explicit and codified (Polanyi 1966; Dreyfus 1979; Dreyfus and Dreyfus 1986). This finding cautions us against falling into the error of believing that the experience that guides work is no more than unconscious sense perception. Moreover, there is not necessarily any conflict between experience and knowledge.[2] The concept of work process knowledge provides a theoretical framework for explaining how theoretical knowledge and practical experience can come together to guide skilled work.

The work process knowledge used by skilled workers is different from the scientific knowledge which enables professional engineers to design and construct technical systems, but it goes far beyond the simple procedural or how-to knowledge which is all that may be necessary for completely routinized work. In particular, it is more than the knowledge required for a single task or combination of tasks – it also includes knowledge of how the various dimensions of the work are connected together in the context of the whole company. This knowledge has its own independent character. It integrates conceptual models of work organization and lived experience of the world of work, and it integrates knowledge of the engineering principles underlying artifacts and the idiosyncrasies of the machines actually used in the production process.

Vital aspects of this knowledge about the context of the industrial sector include:

- how the company is structured; this includes understanding work processes within the framework of a company's overall work organization;

- the peculiarities of material and equipment ('Every machine has its own peculiarities!' Fischer *et al.* 1995);
- the mechanics, energy and chemistry of the industrial processes;
- the concrete consequences that can derive from specific actions.

Underlying this list are two continua of knowledge and action, running from (at one end) the abstract principles of work organization and production processes, to (at the other end) the concrete realities of specific labour processes, individual machines and batches of materials (Figure 12.1). The former – representing theory – is the essence of engineering knowledge. It also represents what was traditionally taught in vocational education and training colleges in the form of general principles of engineering. The other extreme, direct knowledge of the characteristics of the actual materials and installations in the factory can be acquired only by learning in the context of work. What the concept of work process knowledge adds to traditional ways of defining the curriculum content is that it is these ways of knowing should be integrated within a common process.

Naturally, the two dimensions cannot be considered as totally independent from each other. We cannot deny that the general principles of technical and natural sciences are applied in computerized production installations, and that they are therefore operating in specific plant. However, in the ordinary, everyday operation of machinery these principles are only partly visible to the operators. This is one reason why many skilled workers have an

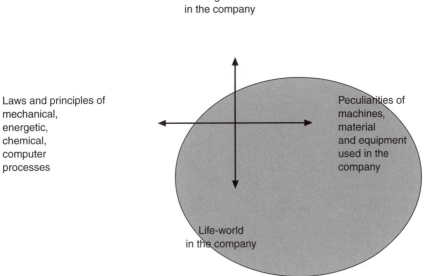

Figure 12.1 Objects of work process knowledge within skilled maintenance and production work

incomplete or even incorrect concept of the technical principles according to which the machinery they operate is functioning. In the normal course of production, it is not usually necessary to possess such knowledge, but this situation is reversed immediately the machine breaks down or unforeseen events occur. In these situations, it may be necessary to imagine what has happened by mentally reconstructing the technical and organizational principles on which the production system is operating (for the implications of novel situations for competence and training, see Norros and Nuutinen, Chapter 3 and Rogalski, Plat and Antolin-Glenn, Chapter 10).

If we conceptualize work process knowledge in this way, then it is obviously going to be difficult for the individual worker to acquire it without any support. In fact, carefully planned curricula are needed in order to:

- relate the knowledge taught in VET institutions more effectively to the knowledge which is really needed at the workplace;
- create an environment for workplace learning so that it is not an additional demand on workers – an extra source of stress and pressure – but is an opportunity for personal development;
- design technical artifacts with regard to user-specific ways of working, in co-operation with future users, and to ensure that they can promote learning as well as perform the work task (Ehn 1985; Fischer *et al.* 1996).

The role of vocational education and training

We now turn to the question posed at the beginning of the chapter: the relationship between work process knowledge and the knowledge learned in VET institutions. The qualification requirements created by the introduction of new forms of work organization, as well as increased pressure to deal with demands such as one-offs and speedier maintenance, require new kinds of competencies and attitudes. In Germany, these are framed within the regulations for qualification as a *Meister*. Initiative in dealing with critical situations and the ability to take responsibility for the quality of one's own work and learning are competencies which cannot be assumed. Our own research (Fischer 1995: 207), as well as research by Walter Georg (1996: 655), has illustrated that the successful implementation of new forms of work organization is not only dependent on job design but also on the motivation, competencies and experiences workers bring into the work process. Participation in change at the shop-floor level presupposes that the worker can anticipate future alternative outcomes and is willing to explore solutions to problems. Thus there are requirements for a general vocational education that encourages learners to develop personal attitudes towards work and an openness to change at work without being overwhelmed by threat and uncertainty. Walter Georg comes to the conclusion that general education provided by schools and other formal institutions of study are of increasing importance, for the very reason that workers within modern production systems have to cope with critical situations and are not able to leave the solving of problems to management.

While we agree with this conclusion, we have to admit that up to now, apart from a few isolated examples (e.g. Fischer and Stuber 1998), the capacity to envisage future and very different kinds of work situation and the development of personal responsibility for managing one's own learning career are probably not being developed by the everyday teaching that we have observed in vocational schools in Germany. The evidence suggests that skilled workers develop a personal commitment to their work – and to working life as a whole – on the basis of life strategies which lead to particular occupational self-concepts (Heinz and Witzel 1995). In a German longitudinal study of 2,000 young people in Munich and Bremen, analyses were carried out of school-to-work transitions and transitions within working life (Witzel and Kühn 1999). The study included mechanics, hairdressers, bank clerks, office-workers and others who had finished their apprenticeships in 1989. It was found that they followed different strategies for shaping their own careers against the backdrop of the demands of their occupations and employment in general. Using a grounded theory approach, an empirically based typology was developed that contained six modalities for shaping vocational identity. These were:

- identification with the company,
- adopting the role of paid worker,
- career orientation,
- optimization of opportunities,
- personal growth and development,
- assuming the role of the entrepreneur.

All these strategies have implications for vocational learning. Those who adopt the role of the 'paid worker' comply with requirements to engage in further education and training if necessary but otherwise regard it largely as a waste of time. In this case, the motivation to develop work process knowledge through learning at work by exploring and analysing work situations must be seen as limited, and if it exists at all, merely extrinsic. On the other hand, those who have definite career objectives tend to develop a more intrinsically motivated approach towards vocational learning, regarding learning in the workplace as a means of shaping their own vocational biographies.

Research on career development shows that vocational identity is not only the result of vocational learning inside and outside of work, but that strategies for developing vocational identity themselves influence learning processes. In Germany, these strategies are related with the personal meaning given to the societal construct of a *Beruf* (occupational profile, such as baker or chemical industry process operator). This affects how one views one's own life and how one regards one's work. For this reason, we suggest that VET has a hidden curriculum that is implicitly creating patterns of interpretation of occupations and the world of work in general. These patterns of interpretation are relevant to the task of transforming school knowledge into work process knowledge (see also the discussion of identity by Norros and Nuutinen, Chapter 3).

Work process knowledge in the car service sector and its role in curriculum development

At the beginning of the 1990s, a sectoral survey on automobile distribution and repair was carried out in the EU FORCE programme (Rauner and Spöttl 1996; Spöttl 1997). The findings of the surveys were quite surprising, even for experts – the differences in organization and productivity of the automobile service sector within the EU Member States, and between Europe, the United States and Japan could not have been greater (Moritz *et al.* 1997; Spöttl *et al.* 1997). On average, the productivity of US automotive businesses is almost twice as high as in Europe. The European countries with the highest productivity are still lower than the United States. Among EU countries the average productivity varies by as much as a factor of three. The reasons for these extraordinarily large differences are not the degree of automation in the automotive business, nor the use of state-of-the-art computer-aided diagnostic systems, but both the way the companies are organized and the qualifications structure of their personnel.

The content and the number of qualifications reflects the degree of horizontal and vertical division of work in the automotive business. In US companies it is usual to employ all-round technicians, while in European automotive businesses there is still a high degree of specialization with a horizontal and vertical division of labour. Greece, with its fourteen different automotive occupations (in authorized dealerships), marks one extreme whereas the United States, with its single grade of all-round technician, occupies the opposite pole. The specialization typical in Europe is shown in Figure 12.2. This hierarchic and horizontal specialization is reflected in vocational training. (For additional discussion of the implications of the division of labour for working practices and the acquisition of work process knowledge, see Boreham, Chapter 13 and Huys and van Hootegem, Chapter 14.) The specialists at qualification level 2 are trained for their roles in separate courses. The general car technicians at qualification level 1 are trained on-the-job for standard service tasks and 'wear and tear' repairs, whereas training courses designed to meet the needs of a problem-solving function are organized for the service technician.

It is proposed to reduce these demarcations by implementing the European occupational profile for Car Mechatronics. The aim is to restructure the curriculum and change the organization of automobile service work in quality service stations. The European occupational profile aims at a

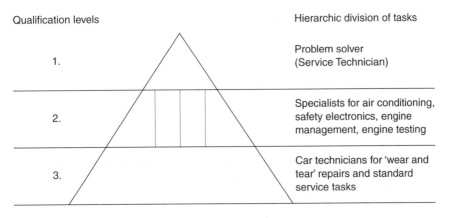

Qualification levels

Hierarchic division of tasks

1.

Problem solver
(Service Technician)

2.

Specialists for air conditioning,
safety electronics, engine
management, engine testing

3.

Car technicians for 'wear and
tear' repairs and standard
service tasks

Figure 12.2 Qualification hierarchy in European authorized dealerships

comprehensive and holistic initial training for the automotive trade, breaking out of the straitjacket which divides mechanical and electrical technicians, while taking into consideration the opportunities and challenges created by new tools, new forms of work organization and the increasing emphasis on enterprise and competitiveness (Spöttl and Gerds 1999; Rauner and Spöttl 2002). The contents of the new curriculum are formulated using a conceptual framework based on the work process. It is no longer sufficient to base the curriculum for technical occupations on a lengthy and detailed catalogue of scientific and technological facts. Instead, curriculum content is selected on the criterion that it is linked to the basic work tasks, and to the knowledge of the work process. Figure 12.3 shows the macro structure of this curriculum.

Thus the new qualification reflects key business and work processes, instead of the structure of the academic discipline. The work process orientation is supported by an emphasis on key tasks and the design of good quality vocational education. The aim of structuring the curriculum around the work process is to ensure that the skilled worker is made more aware of an enterprise's internal organization. While learning and working, trainees are encouraged to appreciate the wider picture: to consider the inputs which other departments make to their own work, the functions of other departments and processes, and indeed all of the company's constituent functions and processes. Work process knowledge is central to the development of organic business processes and it is vital within the overall learning environment of such companies (see Mariani, Chapter 2).

Work process knowledge is an integration of concrete, context-related and empirical knowledge and general, systematic and scientific knowledge. It has a clear relation to the internal work organization, the business environment and the technical systems operating in the company

'Car Mechatronic': Structuring the contents	
Learning areas	**Range of skilled work**
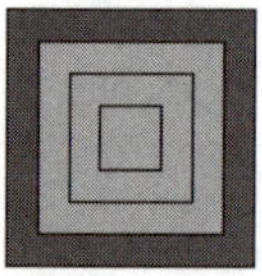 Orientation and overview knowledge	**Learning area 1:** **The car: Basic service** 1. Standard service 2. Repair of basic wear and tear 3. Vehicle maintenance 4. Administrative services
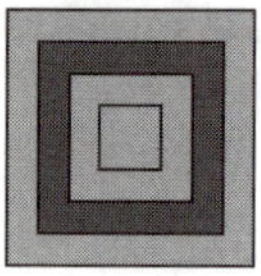 Coherent knowledge	**Learning area 2:** **The car and its architecture: Services and supplementary installations** 1. Standard default extension and supplementary installations 2. Extended services including summer, winter and holiday checks 3. Services
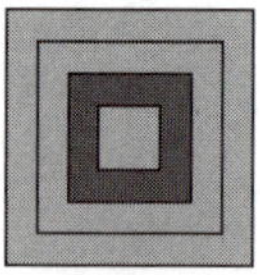 Detailed and functional knowledge	**Learning area 3:** **The car and its modules: Fault diagnosis and repair** 1. Repair of faults (chassis, body, steering) 2. Fault location and repair 3. Repair of parts 4. Special extensions and supplementary installations
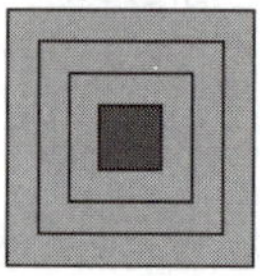 Specialized advanced knowledge	**Learning area 4:** **The car and its construction: Expert diagnosis and repair** 1. Special diagnosis and repair 2. Accident defects 3. Complaints 4. Testing of systems – alternatives

Figure 12.3 Characteristic work tasks and curriculum structure of the core profession 'Car Mechatronics'

(see Figure 12.1). The didactic relevance of work process knowledge is that curriculum content is organized into clearly structured 'learning fields', such as orientation and overview knowledge, coherent knowledge, detailed and functional knowledge and specialized advanced knowledge (see Figure 12.3). Traditional subjects and thematic modules move into the background as an orientation towards work tasks begins to take centre stage. As a result, the mutual relations between complex content-related structures become the focus of attention. The social structure of work and tool-specific aspects also have important roles to play in a work process curriculum. When selecting work tasks as the basis for the curriculum, they are selected for their relevance to work and business processes, in order to ensure that the curriculum addresses the most important challenges the company faces. The selection of tasks should also make sense, in that they should add up to a coherent picture of the work process.

Starting from this basic framework, typical work tasks in the vehicle service sector were determined using various instruments. Fifteen such tasks constituting the work of the core profession of Car Mechatronic are represented in Figure 12.3. They are selected in a way that ensures that:

- comprehensive knowledge of the motor-car as a whole can be acquired;
- internal company work processes serve as framework for structuring curriculum content.

The tasks mentioned in Figure 12.3 aim to develop the skills and knowledge relevant to the occupation through effective learning processes. They are therefore structured to avoid an abstract pattern of information and knowledge transfer, encouraging the worker/learner to be able to recognize broader connections and associations at different levels. Only towards the end of the training will emphasis be laid on more academic ways of knowing. While this goes beyond the knowledge directly required in the workplace, its purpose is to lay foundations for further study. These topics are the basis for continuing technological education; they are important prerequisites for post-graduate studies at technical universities and thus support access to higher education. It is at this point that the strongly vocational orientation of the curriculum is augmented by a gateway to general education.

The car mechatronics curriculum demands changes in the training practices in car service centres. Training tasks are no longer designed to support a Taylorist organization of work (see Figure 12.2) nor to perform the traditional catch-all role of the apprentice. Although there is a developmental structure within the curriculum (novices begin with tasks which are easier to carry out than tasks undertaken during the final stages of the apprenticeship) all fifteen tasks within the curriculum represent essential work tasks which have been considered by experts to be relevant for the future development of the trade (Figure 12.3). The car mechatronics curriculum also demands changes in the teaching practices of vocational schools. Usually, German students in the car service sector begin their vocational training by studying traditional subject matter such as 'electro-physics as applied to power transmission'. That this approach creates a gulf between classroom study and the experience of learning in the workplace should be obvious. As surveys of apprentices in Germany have found, there are enormous difficulties in relating theoretical knowledge learned in vocational schools to practical in-company training, especially among those with the highest levels of motivation (Pätzold 1997).

Conclusion

Work process knowledge can be understood as the result of a process of constructing personal competence out of:

- experiential as well as theoretical knowledge;
- contextual factors, such as the labour process in the workplace, and non-contextual factors, such as a personal identity as a 'professional practitioner' or the general and scientific knowledge embedded in artifacts used;
- ways of implicit knowing as well as explicit communication.

This construction process has become difficult in many modern work environments. 'Making sense of events at the workplace' (Boreham 1995) is something that every practitioner needs to do, but it is increasingly difficult in computer-aided work situations and under the conditions of an extreme division of labour (Rabardel and Duvenci-Langa, Chapter 5).

In this chapter, we have argued in support of approaches to curriculum development which use work process knowledge as the organizing framework for the curriculum. This requires a new perspective on VET (Pahl and Rauner 1998). Future research is required, especially with regard to two aspects of work process knowledge:

- analysing expert work process knowledge in different occupations, as distinct from the knowledge of beginners;
- analysing how beginners become members of their community of practice in terms of acquiring work process knowledge.

It should be emphasized, however, that while drawing up a framework of work process knowledge is a necessary step for curriculum development, it is not appropriate for providing a general education that meets all the learner's needs. All our research has shown that the acquisition of work process knowledge requires the learner already to have acquired an occupational self-concept and motivation, and this is a broader task which must be addressed within a much more general education. Future comparative research under way will indicate whether the different forms of vocational education and training found in different industrial cultures have differential effects on strategies for acquiring work process knowledge.

Notes

1 Arbeitsgemeinschaft der Hochschulinstitut für gewerblich-technische Berufsbildung (cf. Bannwitz and Rauner 1993; Pahl and Rauner 1998).
2 In this respect, it is instructive to compare the work process knowledge approach to the concept of the 'reflective practitioner' developed in the USA by Donald Schön (1983).

13 Professionalization and work process knowledge in the UK's National Health Service

Nicholas Boreham

The concept of work process knowledge represented in the previous chapters is on the whole politically neutral. However, in the case of the established professions we have to acknowledge that such knowledge also has a political dimension. Over the last 150 years, the pattern of employment in the UK has been significantly affected by professionalization, the process whereby occupational groups claim privileges including the exclusive right to practice, control of entry to their ranks and closure of their knowledge base to non-members. In the now extensive literature on the professions, different moral standpoints have been adopted on these issues. Some writers view professionalization as a way of ensuring a high standard of service and protecting the public against exploitation. Others, however, view it as a process of status group conflict in which occupations vie for economic advantage by creating scarcity of much-needed expertise. Whichever view is taken, knowledge is central to the argument, as the crux is the desirability of allowing occupational groups to claim exclusive ownership of certain bodies of knowledge and skill. The situation addressed in the present chapter is one in which several professions are practising within the same organization. If they maintain their traditional closure, then it becomes difficult to encourage everybody in the organization to share their knowledge of work processes in the interests of collaboration and flexibility. The still-rising tide of professionalization thus emerges as a potential barrier to the kinds of organizational change on which many pin their hopes for improved performance. In the following pages, this problem is examined in the context of the UK's National Health Service (NHS).

The NHS was founded in 1948 and is now one of the world's largest employers, with well over a million staff. It is funded by taxes and compulsory insurance contributions, and most of the services are free at the point of delivery. One of several contradictions manifested in the structure of the NHS is that, while the sick person is a whole, the health care workforce is divided into more than a dozen professions, each of which offers a limited range of health care interventions and maintains strong boundaries against the others. The main professions are doctors (subdivided into general practitioners (GPs) and hospital specialists), nurses, midwives, dentists,

pharmacists, opticians, physiotherapists, radiographers, occupational therapists, audiologists, speech therapists and chiropodists. All professionals
employed by the NHS are directly responsible to their NHS line managers,
but they are also answerable to their respective professional bodies, such as
the General Medical Council (GMC), the medical Royal Colleges (for
physicians, surgeons, GPs, etc.), the United Kingdom Central Council for
Nursing, Health Visiting and Midwifery (UKCC) and many more. Professional bodies use legal powers to prevent non-members from practising.
They define the scope and standards of the practice of their members,
monitor the training and qualifications system, control entry to the profession and exert considerable influence on the overall numbers who are
admitted. Above all, they define the knowledge base needed to practise
the profession, and discourage non-members from gaining access to this
knowledge.

In recent years there has been much disquiet about the performance of
the NHS, which is now widely regarded as a 'third-world' service delivering
poor health outcomes. Limited resources remain a cause of underperfor-
mance, but the fragmentation of services due to inadequate co-ordination
of the different professions in the workforce is also a contributory factor.
An example of this can be found in a recent study by Boreham *et al.*
(2000), which collected critical incidents over a 30-month period from a
sample of hospital emergency departments in the UK. Emergency departments are often the subject of litigation for medical error, and in this
study four common situations were found to threaten patient well-being:
delay in beginning investigations or treatment, failure to obtain necessary
diagnostic information, misinterpretation of diagnostic information and
the administration of inappropriate treatments. The root causes of these
incidents were investigated and three latent conditions predisposing to
error were identified. One of these was poor communication between co-
workers due to rigid vertical and horizontal demarcations enforced by the
professionalization of the workforce. While staff understood their specialized roles very well, lack of a shared understanding of the overall work
process could at times result in failures of co-ordination which caused
harm or distress to patients, or which wasted resources.

Mindful of the problem of patients 'falling down the cracks' between
the separate professions and agencies within the NHS, the UK government is currently pursuing the objective of creating a more flexible and
integrated heath care system. The aim is to create a 'seamless service',
although cost cutting is also a major motivation. To this end, the government has encouraged relaxations in professional demarcations and the
growth of multi-professional teams. An essential part of this strategy is to
provide the different health care professions with better understanding of
each other's roles. More ambitiously, a concept of 'collaborative practice'
has been developed, a new concept of health care in which different professions work together in virtually interchangeable roles.

An important role has been assigned to education in bringing about the hoped-for transformation. The influential Standing Medical and Nursing and Midwifery Advisory Committee has declared that 'professional education should ... prepare individual practitioners for ... collaborative working ... to enable each professional to retain certain unique areas of skill and knowledge, while sharing overlapping aspects of knowledge and skills' (Standing Medical and Nursing and Midwifery Advisory Committee 1996: 16). To this end, the government has encouraged the development of 'shared learning', the practice of training different professions together to support team working across professional and organizational boundaries. Many innovations in multi-professional education and training have been introduced, and most emphasize the development of a shared understanding of work process. However, the concerns of the health care professions to protect their occupational interests make them reluctant to accept the implications of these initiatives, and the prospects for bringing about fundamental changes in working practices appear poor in consequence.

Changes in professional boundaries

For reasons of space, we will restrict the discussion to the division of labour between doctors and nurses. At first sight, there seems to have been a significant reduction in the previously rigid demarcation between these two groups. Today, nurses can be found performing many tasks which 30 years ago were restricted to doctors, and multi-disciplinary teams in which nurses work alongside doctors are now common. Many nurses have acquired a new range of advanced qualifications and practise as 'clinical nurse specialists' and 'nurse practitioners', entitled to diagnose and/or treat many illnesses, and they even teach junior doctors how to carry out the treatments in which they specialize. Only 30 years ago, doctors alone received a university-based training, but today all UK nurses are trained in universities, many to degree level, and many take PhDs and conduct research. At first sight, it seems that the professions are drawing closer together in a 'knowledge-based NHS', and that the kinds of collaborative practice the government wishes to see are likely to emerge from this new *rapprochement* and go from strength to strength. However, more careful investigation will reveal that these signs of increasing functional flexibility and the adoption by nurses of research-based practice by no means indicate the coming integration of the two professions, and may in fact be considered indications of the opposite.

Changing professional boundaries in general practice

In the UK, patients seeking medical care must first consult their GP, who will either treat them directly or refer them to a hospital. In the 1950s and

1960s, GPs functioned largely as 'signpost doctors', treating minor ailments and referring large numbers of patients for investigation and treatment by specialists in hospitals. In search of greater cost-efficiency in a costly NHS, however, the UK government has reduced the bed capacity of the hospitals and has made general practice the foundation service, responsible for treating most patients including many who would previously have been referred to hospital (Secretaries of State for Health, Social Security, Wales and Scotland 1989; Department of Health 1994; Handysides 1994). At the same time, the government has ended the age-old system of lone GPs practising from surgeries in their own homes, replacing it with purpose-built health centres staffed by teams of GPs and other health care professionals. These new teams provide a service similar to that of Health Maintenance Organizations in the USA (Handysides 1994).

The changes have transformed the role and workload of GPs, who not only provide treatment for large numbers of patients previously referred to hospitals, but have assumed the clinical and financial management of the health centres. The extra pressure this puts on GPs in a country where there is an overall shortage of doctors has been eased by employing nurses to discharge some of the medical duties doctors used to perform themselves. The origins of this shift in the boundary between nursing and medical practice can be traced back 40 years to the concern felt by NHS GPs about the large numbers of patients on their lists, many of whom attended the surgery with minor ailments. In the 1960s, an enterprising GP Dr Geoffrey Marsh proposed the creation of a new role of 'minor illness nurse' to deal with less serious cases under the direction of the doctor, freeing the latter to concentrate on patients with more serious conditions (about one-third of all consultations) (Marsh 1991). Amendments to the GP contract in 1966 gave them the right to employ nurses, and following Marsh's lead, a small number of GPs took on practice nurses to deal with minor illnesses (Atkin 1993). Initially, practice nurses were employed to carry out treatment-room duties. However, changes in the system of GP payment in 1990 gave financial incentives for carrying out various kinds of preventive work such as immunization, health checks and health promotion. Appropriately trained nurses could carry much of this workload, and GPs started employing them in this capacity in large numbers (Jewell and Turton 1994; Robinson 1993). Today, there is great variety in the role of the practice nurse as they assume more of the work of their hard-pressed GP colleagues. Some work within the traditional role of treatment room nurse, others have taken on extended roles such as managing patients with chronic disease, while others see themselves as nurse practitioners who have taken over medical duties such as the diagnosis and treatment of minor injuries. The role is flexible, enabling the nurse to adapt to the changing demands of general practice under the conditions that prevail locally (Atkin and Lunt 1996).

Changing professional boundaries in hospitals

The boundary between medical and nursing practices has also changed in hospitals. As in general practice, the precipitating factor was a shortage of doctors which resulted in increasing workloads. In the 1970s, junior hospital doctors' grievances over workloads exploded into a strike, the first in the profession's history. As there was no immediate way of increasing the number of doctors, a working party was set up to legalize arrangements for extending the nurse's role to include some of the work of junior doctors. Guidance on the extended role of the nurse was eventually issued by the government (Department of Health and Social Security 1977). However, this can hardly be interpreted as a relaxation of professional boundaries, as the delegated medical duties were tightly regulated and controlled by doctors. The process of delegation was based on a system of local arrangements initiated by senior doctors who found themselves short of junior medical staff. If they identified the need, they would delegate a *specific* medical task to a *specific* nurse, such as ordering investigations, prescribing drugs, defibrillation, suturing wounds, injecting drugs intravenously or inserting catheters. The nurse could perform these duties only after being trained and assessed by doctors and after the employing authority had issued the appropriate certificate. The certificate listed the tasks that the nurse was licensed to perform, and alongside each was the signature of the doctor granting permission to act. There was also a space on the form for the authorities to rescind the delegation, and the validity of the certificate was restricted to the unit or hospital which had issued it.

In their extended role, most nurses continued to discharge their usual nursing duties, to which they added a small number of medical tasks. However, as Dowling *et al.* (1996) discovered, more profound changes were taking place. For example, at times of staff shortage experienced nurses sometimes stepped into the role of pre-registration house officer (intern), taking over the whole of the latter's work and ceasing to perform any nursing duties. Analysis of these role transitions reveals that the traditional demarcations had not always been in the patients' best interest. Contrary to what they had asserted in the past, many doctors now conceded that appropriately trained and experienced nurses could perform some medical tasks quite competently, and in some cases more skilfully than doctors. Ashcroft (1992), for example, argued that many of the medical tasks performed by junior hospital doctors could be performed more competently by nurses. He cited the tasks carried out by Senior House Officers in the labour ward, about 90 per cent of whom were training to enter general practice and would soon leave the unit. The tasks concerned included suturing episiotomies, artificial rupture of membranes and assistance at Caesarean sections. For many of these doctors, the procedures were carried out once or twice only without specific training or supervision, and Ashcroft maintained that a trained midwife who worked in the unit for a longer period would build up greater expertise and could carry out the work more competently. For the purposes of the present chapter, the significant part of Ashcroft's argument is that junior doctors should hand these tasks over to midwives *because they did not contribute to their career development as they would never use them once they entered general practice.*

The accelerated professionalization of nursing

Although nurses have assumed a number of medical duties in recent years, it appears from the preceding that boundary maintenance is as strong as ever. The changes that have taken place are not steps towards collaborative practice, nor indeed cases of genuine functional flexibility. Doctors have taken on new responsibilities, and to ease their workloads have passed on routine work to nurses. In turn, the nursing profession has been happy to take these on, and as we will see, has itself delegated some of its work to lower status groups.

Over the last 30 years, the nursing profession has undergone a major transformation. In historical perspective, this appears to have been triggered by problems of recruitment. During the 1960s, major difficulties in recruiting and retaining nurses occurred, as young women who in previous generations would have become nurses were now opting for other careers. The dropout rate among those who did commence nurse training rose to about one-third, and the cause was identified as the Victorian working conditions that prevailed. For the first few years of a nurse's career, he or she (but mostly she) was expected to perform routine procedures such as changing dressings, making beds and emptying bedpans under a regime which demanded that they carry out instructions without question (Sbaih 1995). Training remained in most essentials the system that was created by Florence Nightingale in the nineteenth century, a ward-based apprenticeship with stern discipline and an expectation that private life would be sacrificed to the needs of the service. In the 'swinging sixties', this way of life seemed unattractive to school leavers. The alternative now open to girls was a newly expanded post-compulsory education system with mandatory maintenance grants, education on equal terms with men and a dazzling array of career openings.

A Committee on Nursing was set up to consider the problem of recruitment and training (Briggs 1972). To make a career in nursing more attractive, it recommended the end of the apprenticeship system of training and recommended that nurses become students in colleges of health supported by government bursaries. They would cease to work during their training, and would instead visit clinical units in a supernumerary capacity to learn by observation and guided practice. Traditionally, basic nursing care – washing patients, toileting them, giving them their meals, etc. – had always been the responsibility of student nurses in the first years of their training. This was now considered a major barrier to recruiting the most able candidates and when student nurses became supernumerary, a new occupational group was created to carry out these duties: the health care assistant. Although wearing a nurse-like uniform, these employees are not nurses. They are recruited locally and given a rudimentary training. Basic nursing care thus vanished from the role of the nurse, and a new occupational demarcation was created.

At the same time as the Briggs reforms, departments of nursing were established for the first time in universities. These recruited school-leavers with good academic qualifications and taught nursing to degree level. Initially, they concentrated on producing nursing graduates to occupy the commanding heights of the profession, such as senior administrative posts, research and university teaching. In time, they also took over the training of non-graduate nurses from the colleges of health, offering a two-year diploma course. Their impact over the three decades of their existence has been profound. Enjoying the advantage of academic freedom, the leading departments have made huge efforts to bring nursing closer in status to medicine while at the same time striving to make it more autonomous and independent in terms of its practice. The pioneering Bachelor of Nursing course established in the University of Manchester by Professor Jean MacFarlane aimed to replace the traditional British system of nursing (a quasi-Taylorist system of task allocation) with the North American idea of 'nursing process', a patient-focused system of care in which a 'named nurse' takes personal responsibility for a patient, making an assessment of the patient's nursing care needs independently of medical staff and supervising health care assistants in providing it. It is true that British nurses have not yet adopted the North American practice of calling their nursing care plan a 'nursing diagnosis'. However, the nursing process is by definition separate from the medical process, both in practice and in terms of its underpinning theory.

Other innovations stemming from the research undertaken by university departments of nursing placed even more clear water between nurses and the doctors. One was the concept of 'advanced nursing' – the development of autonomous nursing skills to a therapeutic level, challenging the long-standing right of doctors alone to decide the patient's treatment. The opportunity which the nurses seized was an increase in the number of patients suffering from chronic illnesses who could benefit from ameliorative treatment with a new range of drugs and techniques. These patients are treated over long periods and there is a need to continually assess their condition and vary the treatment regimen accordingly. Increasing numbers of nurses have been trained for this role: clinical nurse specialists (CNSs). Specialist practice was defined as a clinical and consultative role, teaching, management, research and the application of relevant nursing research. More than 80 CNS roles have been defined, such as stoma nurse, Macmillan nurse, infection control nurse and diabetic nurse. The legal basis for this independent form of practice was created when the UKCC introduced a new qualification of 'specialist practitioner' to be recorded on the professional register (UKCC 1994). Typically, a CNS will spend 40 per cent of his or her time in clinical work, 40 per cent in consultative work, 15 per cent in educational work and the remainder in other activities including research (Wilson-Barnett and Beech 1994.) Care has been taken to emphasize that the role is not ancillary to medicine but an independent form of professional practice.

Further insight into the strength of boundary maintenance between the two professions can be gained by examining the way in which the nursing profession reacted to the arrangements for extending the role of the nurse. Far from viewing it as an opportunity for collaborative practice, many nurses expressed resentment that they were putting themselves at risk by accepting responsibility for tasks that doctors found inconvenient, time-consuming or boring (Shepherd 1993). Criticism of the scheme mounted (Kingmire 1989; Salvage 1989) and it was not long before the nurses' professional bodies formally challenged it. While accepting that nurses could – and should – take over doctors' work, the professional bodies now rejected the idea that they should do so under the licensing arrangement on which the extended role scheme was based (UKCC 1992, 1994). One set of objections focused on the fact that this scheme was task-oriented, which contradicted the new-found professional autonomy enshrined in the concepts of the nursing process and advanced nursing, both of which require that nurses perform their duties at their own discretion. Another objection was that extended role certificates were not transferable between Health Authorities, so that an extended role lapsed if the nurse moved to another hospital, i.e. it was an employer's temporary expedient, not a permanent increase in the nurse's professional authority. Yet another objection was that the scheme did not extend the role far enough, as nurses were still prevented from carrying out tasks that were neither part of their initial training for registration, nor covered by an extended role certificate.

Seeking an end to medical control of the extended role, while also seeking to retain the freedom to perform medical duties, in 1992 the UKCC published new statutory regulations. The new system was known as the *Scope of Professional Practice* and introduced the new concept of the 'expanded' role of the nurse. The difference between 'extended' and 'expanded' in this context is considerable. The new scheme was based on the premise that decisions about the boundaries of practice were the responsibility of nurses alone, acting as individuals. The *Scope of Professional Practice* encouraged them to extend their role if they chose to do so, and to develop their practice in whichever direction they wished. Guidelines were provided to help them make these decisions. Faced with the not inconsiderable political power of the UKCC, the government accepted the proposals and accordingly withdrew the earlier guidelines for the delegation of medical tasks and activities to nurses via an employing authority (Department of Health 1992). The *Scope of Professional Practice* supports the UKCC Code of Professional Conduct, which makes it clear that nurses alone are accountable for their professional practice. It removes legally defined boundaries to what tasks nurses can and cannot do. The sole restriction now seems to be that nurses are expected to be 'clear about the limits' of their own knowledge and skill, and restrict their practice accordingly. However, the general expectation is that nurses will move into new fields of practice, and a commitment to career development and professional updating is stressed. Thus the new guidelines require nurses contemplating taking on a new task to acknowledge any limits to their knowledge and skill, endeavour to make improvements and to satisfy themselves that the intervention they propose to make is in the patient's interests.

The new system has established nurses as autonomous and self-regulated practitioners independent of any form of supervision by doctors. The extent of professional boundary maintenance in the NHS can be judged by the reaction of the medical profession in 1995 when the GMC (the doctors' regulatory body broadly comparable to the UKCC) responded with guidance to doctors on the nurse's extended role. This stated that doctors could delegate medical care to nurses if they were sure that the nurse was competent to undertake the work, but made it clear that overall responsibility for managing patient care remained with the doctor (General Medical Council 1995). At least on paper, the two professions each claim autonomy over overlapping spheres of practice, hardly indicative of a commitment to collaborative practice. Meanwhile, nurses are beginning to develop their work in diverse ways, but as the nurse's scope of practice is limited only by self-assessment, questions of risk and safety are being raised. It has been claimed, for example, that nurses are increasing their scope of practice without undertaking training or acquiring the necessary competence (Hopkins 1996).

Educational initiatives

This analysis of the politics of the changing division of labour between nurses and doctors in the UK suggests that it has not been motivated by any desire by the two professions to join together in collaborative practice. Instead, the drivers of change have been a shortage of medical manpower, which has lead doctors to delegate tasks to nurses while insisting on retaining control of the work, recruitment problems in nursing and the desire on the part of the nursing profession to increase its autonomy and separate itself from the medical profession. Although moving nurse training into universities might have been assumed to bring the two professions closer together, doctors and nurses continue to study separately (apart from a few initiatives which will be discussed below), and are maintaining separation between the knowledge bases which define their status as autonomous professions.

It was stated earlier that the UK government has supported a considerable number of initiatives in the field of shared learning. The hope for these projects expressed by Leathard (1994: 221) is that:

> ... education and training [can] make a notable contribution to the future of inter-professional work through breaking down professional barriers and enabling students and future practitioners to perceive the changing nature of the workplace as a collaborative arena [and to develop] common philosophies of care and a knowledge about what other professionals were doing.

The evidence of numerous research studies, however, is that these initiatives are making little impact on the obvious desire of health care professions to maintain the boundaries between them. In a survey of multidisciplinary education of health professionals in the UK, Pirrie (1999) found that, despite government exhortations, the professions were maintaining a 'strict closure' and resisting attempts to share their knowledge. Knowledge, she found, continued to be 'generated, regulated and maintained within the profession itself, and its relative autonomy preserved' (p. 123). As one of the medical school lecturers she interviewed commented:

> We could move our students into the integrated pattern of learning quite simply, but the research base wouldn't let us do it. That's where the core knowledge is, and that's where the traditions, in terms of the knowledge base lie. They lie within disciplines. And that's about power.
>
> (Pirrie 1999: 120)

A similar picture emerges from a review of research by Barr *et al.* (1999). This analysed nineteen published evaluations of shared learning initiatives. It found that under favourable circumstances shared learning could improve reciprocal role perceptions, but that such outcomes did not invariably occur. 'Nor, on the one occasion when students were followed up, were improvements sustained' (p. 537).

Similar conclusions emerged from a survey of collaborative shared learning for health and social care professionals in both initial and continuing professional education. This identified surprisingly little multiprofessional education of any kind being offered in higher education. Moreover, little of the multi-professional education on offer followed the pattern suggested by the health service agenda, i.e. knowledge sharing for collaborative practice (Miller 1999: 8).

Conclusion

According to the sociologist of the professions, Larson (1990), control of knowledge creation is central to the process of professionalization because it enables occupational interest groups to create monopolies of practice. Other sociologists of the professions such as Abbott (1988) and Collins (1990) go so far as to argue that the bodies of professional knowledge developed in this way are not entirely relevant to practice, serving principally to construct status and create barriers to others practising in the same field. Armstrong (1993), writing in the same tradition, points out that to achieve competitive advantage, a profession must develop a knowledge base distinct from that of its competitors. He cites the development of the modern nursing knowledge base by university departments of nursing, which explicitly distances itself from medical knowledge. It does this by claiming its intellectual foundations in a holistic concept of 'care', which it opposes to the positivism of medical science often called 'the medical model'.

As in other sectors of the economy, management in the NHS has responded to the pressures for improved services by seeking the relaxation of traditional occupational demarcations and more flexible working informed by a shared knowledge base. The research evidence, however, is that educational initiatives in the field of shared learning have failed to impact on professional practice in any significant way. One explanation is the status group conflict explored by sociologists such as Larson, Abbott, Collins and Armstrong, in which professional knowledge becomes a tool for driving professions further apart rather than bringing them together. The case of the NHS reveals considerable evidence that the professional bodies have negotiated changes in professional boundaries primarily to protect their members' employment interests, in particular relieving workloads and maintaining professional autonomy. It is significant that the tasks doctors and nurses have relinquished to other occupational groups are those with the lowest economic value. Thus GPs have delegated minor treatment to practice nurses in order to concentrate on cases previously referred to hospitals, while hospital doctors have delegated medical tasks with no long-term career development potential to nurses. In turn, nurses have assumed responsibility for new kinds of treatment relinquished by doctors while delegating basic nursing care to health care assistants. The public pronouncements of the professional bodies have revealed a greater concern with autonomy than with collaborative practice. Thus while expressing interest in taking over medical tasks, the nurses' professional bodies rejected the system in which their assumption of those tasks was controlled by the medical profession, and persuaded government to give them freedom to determine their own scope of practice. While both the UKCC and the GMC have issued statements supporting flexible working, both have sought to retain control of the tasks they have delegated to others: the UKCC guidelines on the Scope of Practice seek to retain nurse control over the work of health care assistants, and the GMC insists that overall responsibility for managing patient care remains with the doctor.

The implications for work process knowledge are considerable. Although the original definition of work process knowledge was non-political, sharing knowledge of the work process throughout an organization will affect status group relationships. The UK government has put a lot of faith in innovative forms of multi-professional education and training, but as long as knowledge remains an asset in status group conflict, it is doubtful whether this strategy alone will succeed in breaking down professional barriers, developing common philosophies of care and introducing new forms of collaborative practice.

14 A delayed transformation?

Changes in the division of labour and their implications for learning opportunities

Rik Huys and Geert van Hootegem

The development of work process knowledge cannot be achieved through formal vocational education alone. It is constructed in and through work itself. But the need for this knowledge, and opportunities for workers to acquire it, depend on organizations creating new kinds of job with broader roles and more autonomy. 'Traditional' organizations with a strong division of labour fragment work experience and constrain the development of work process knowledge. Such a traditional division of labour is increasingly seen as inappropriate for manufacturing the highly customized goods that modern markets are demanding and many argue that it should be replaced by 'learning organizations'. This chapter discusses the relationship between the division of labour within organizations and the learning opportunities this offers workers. Then it addresses the fundamental question whether a transformation from a traditional to a new division of labour is actually occurring. Drawing on empirical results from a study of the spread of new production concepts in four industrial sectors in Flanders, it demonstrates that the transformation is limited, leaving substantial potential for improving the opportunity for workers to acquire work process knowledge. In a concluding paragraph several obstacles will be identified which limit the transformation towards a new division of labour, the need for work process knowledge and opportunities for workers to acquire it on the job.

What are learning opportunities?

Learning opportunities as the result of job demand and job control

According to Karasek's demand–control model, jobs with high demand and high control offer the best learning opportunities (Karasek 1979). In general, the opportunity to learn in the workplace presupposes that the work is varied and offers new challenges (high demand). It also presupposes autonomy in dealing with the requirements of the task, and freedom to adopt one's own work strategies (high control). Jobs with high demand and high control also reduce the likelihood of stress. The problems and disturbances that occur during work are not themselves the causes of stress. Stress results when the division of labour in the organization creates jobs that do not allow workers to tackle these problems themselves.

These guidelines could be considered fundamental for ensuring the quality of working life. A first requirement for 'good' work is that it does not make people ill through mental overload. A second requirement is that work must allow workers to learn and develop their abilities. This strengthens the position of the worker, enhancing his or her job security in the organization and creating opportunities for promotion. Equally, it enhances employability. If the worker is laid off, learning and qualifications will strengthen his or her position in the external labour market.

In contrast to machines, human beings are able to learn through work. For this reason, the human factor adds value to the process as well as to the product. While they are working, in addition to making a product or delivering a service, employees are accumulating knowledge and skills. These resources are not immediately obvious on the organization's balance sheet, but they are essential for its future development. Work that does not provide opportunities for learning denies the fundamental difference between human and machine, and degrades workers to the status of machines. It is, in this sense, inhumane.

In their division of labour, organizations must therefore take account of both these requirements. To reduce the risk of stress, job control should be commensurate with job demand. The level of disturbances, malfunctions and unexpected events in the workplace must be balanced with an appropriate level of autonomy in dealing with them. However, this balance should not be achieved by minimizing both job demand and job control because high job demand is essential for learning. It is only work that confronts people with problems to solve which offers them the opportunity to improve their knowledge and skills. The combination that must be sought in the design of jobs is therefore high job demand and high job control ('active jobs'). Jobs which constantly present the worker with new challenges offer the best opportunities for learning. As long as the job offers sufficient autonomy, the worker is potentially capable of developing strategies, improving them and changing them depending on the nature of problems encountered.

Seven criteria for jobs with good learning opportunities

Whether jobs have stress risks and learning opportunities is to a large extent dependent on the same factor: the balance between task demand and the opportunities for control. Sociotechnical system theory (de Sitter 1994; de Sitter *et al.* 1997) provides a framework for dealing with both stress and learning opportunities, but we confine ourselves here to learning opportunities. The conditions for maximizing learning opportunities have been identified by the WEBA project using seven questions (WEBA 1990: 9–10, 1995).[1]

Is the job occupationally complete?

A job is occupationally complete if it consists of a coherent unit of work that incorporates preparatory, executive and supportive tasks. Preparing and supporting one's own work is essential for maintaining and developing knowledge and skill. Complete jobs increase the level of control and the complexity of the operations, both of which are relevant to the learning potential (WEBA 1990: 9).

Does the job contain enough organizing tasks?

Organizing tasks involve making decisions about how to carry out work that the worker undertakes in collaboration with others. When the worker has effective organizing tasks to do (such as co-operation with other departments, periodic discussions about procedures or task group meetings) there is an opportunity to express and develop the potential improvement and innovation (WEBA 1990: 10).

Does the job contain enough non-short cycled tasks?

Generally speaking, short cycled tasks have a very limited control capacity. One cannot learn much from repetitive work (WEBA 1990: 10).

Does the job contain a balance of difficult and easy tasks?

The complexity of a task depends on the indeterminateness of the time within which it has to be done and the variability of the environment. Clearly, when work consists of simple tasks the opportunities for learning are restricted. On the other hand, when work consists of difficult tasks, the risk of stress is increased. Consequently, there must be a balance between simple and difficult tasks (WEBA 1990: 10).

Does the job contain enough autonomy?

Autonomy means that work can be adapted to changing demands, needs and circumstances, an important prerequisite for occupational learning. Work that is prescribed in detail offers few possibilities to learn (WEBA 1990: 10).

Does the job contain enough opportunities for contact?

The organization of work has to offer possibilities of contact with others during work. That can come about in different ways: by support (lending a hand), by functional contacts (formal linkages of the work process) and by means of social contacts (not directly related to work). Learning depends to a large extent on others, by helping in the work, by showing them how to do the work or by consulting with them (WEBA 1990: 10).

Is there enough information available on the purpose and result of the work?

Information is necessary to make use of opportunities to exercise control. Without effective feedback on the results of one's work, one cannot learn (WEBA 1990: 10). The instrument developed by the WEBA project team contains guidelines and instructions for answering these questions and for adding up the scores from independent observers to give a reliable overall evaluation of each dimension. Jobs that receive a good score on all seven criteria combine limited stress risks with high learning opportunities (Figure 14.1). They enhance the development of vocational competence. This holds through for all jobs within organizations, from high to low.

The division of labour and its relationship to opportunities to learn in the workplace

What is the division of labour?

Sometimes, the conclusion of a job evaluation carried out as described above is that measures are needed to improve the quality of the work. To make fundamental improvements, an analysis of the structure of the division of labour in the organization then becomes necessary. The reason is that different structures of the division of labour have different effects on learning opportunities. The measures proposed by the WEBA to fundamentally improve the quality of work aim to redesign the structure

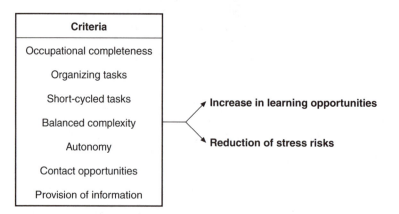

Figure 14.1 Seven criteria to improve learning opportunities and reduce stress risks

of the division of labour. This requires understanding the relationship between the learning opportunities of jobs as defined above and the division of labour implemented in the organization that results in these jobs.

The executive function of a company is to produce certain goods or services. Production, however, depends unavoidably on a number of contiguous functions. For example, production must be planned. New products must be designed in order to meet changes in demand, methods of making the new products must be developed, tools must be made and material ordered and the work itself must be planned. In addition to all this, production must be supported by monitoring quality, maintaining hardware and recruiting and training personnel. Finally, the production has to be managed. Decisions must be taken on an ongoing basis and effective communication maintained if production is to proceed smoothly.

Companies can be viewed as conglomerations of production, planning, support and managerial operations. The division of labour is the way in which these operations are divided, grouped and linked. In a single-trader firm, all are in the hands of one person. However, the essence of the industrial production of goods and services is that the operations take place within the framework of a large-scale organization. This automatically implies splitting them up so that each job covers a small portion of the total production process. Complex organizations rarely do this in a disorderly, *ad hoc* or serendipitous fashion. As a rule, they follow a fixed pattern. There is a recognizable configuration or structure – the structure of the division of labour – which can vary on three dimensions: production organization, production technology and work organization.

Production organization

Production organization is a specific way of grouping and linking the functions of execution, planning, support and management, and the way they are distributed between departments or production groups. Depending on how these functions are grouped or linked, a variety of production organizations emerge, each with its own consequences for the quality of the organization and the work itself. The following configurations are typical.

Concentration vs. deconcentration

Support and planning operations can be concentrated as much as possible into separate staff departments, giving rise to such classic divisions as production planning, product and process development, maintenance, quality assurance, logistics, equipment management and training. These divisions offer their support to almost all the production departments. Alternatively, these operations can be merged with execution or production tasks. In this case, we speak of deconcentration. Each production department is responsible for its own maintenance, quality assurance and so on.

Centralized vs. decentralized decision-making

With respect to managerial operations, firms may choose to centralize decision-making as much as possible at the apex of the organization, or to decentralize it by devolving it to the production units. Decentralized management is characterized by greater horizontal co-ordination, i.e. the direct reciprocal co-ordination of activities; van Amelsvoort (1989: 261) compares this to a canoe which moves forward under the combined efforts of the canoeists. Centralized management implies a form of vertical (in most instances top-down) co-ordination or indirect co-ordination via hierarchical levels of management. This is the familiar staff-line organization.

Ways of organizing the production process

Firms can choose between three basic structures for organizing the production process itself: the operation-oriented structure, the flow-oriented structure and the product-oriented structure (Figure 14.2). These

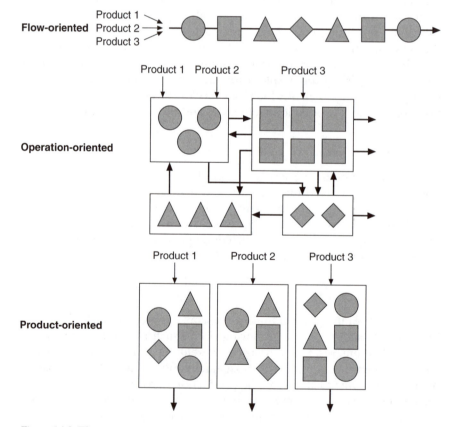

Figure 14.2 The structure of execution: three types

are alternative ways of splitting up, regrouping and linking execution operations.

Operation-oriented structures group identical operations into production groups or departments. Each group or department specializes in a few operations or possibly just one. Orders consisting mainly of non-identical products or semi-manufactures pass through all or a few of these specialist production groups in series (de Sitter *et al.* 1986: 18). The order is relatively open and there are multiple routes and directions. It is this very flexible and unstructured linking that differentiates the operation-oriented structure from the flow- and product-oriented structures. Such flexible operations are the preferred option whenever relatively small batches from a fairly wide product range have to be produced and the production programme is quite varied. But this high level of flexibility comes at a price – a relatively low level of productivity. Production processes organized in an operation-oriented structure are often plagued by long routeing times and large intermediate stocks.

As soon as the sequence of departments is more or less fixed into a single or small number of routes moving in one direction, the operation-oriented structure merges into the second variant, the flow-oriented structure. In a pure flow-oriented structure, all the products go through all the processes in a fixed sequence. The structure is clear and pre-programmed but also inflexible and non-adjustable. The flow-oriented structure is said to be particularly common in companies which produce a narrow product range in large batches. Its strength is said to be a relatively high potential productivity. Its weakness is the limited product mix and restrictions on volume flexibility.

In a product-oriented structure, one product (or product family) is finished or nearly finished in a clearly demarcated processing phase. Thus one production group or department makes one type of product. All the operations and equipment required to produce that one product are grouped together. The link between the processing steps is once again very clear: it moves in one direction, but over multiple routes. The economic advantage of this structure is supposed to lie in its drastic simplification of planning, in shorter routeing times and in reduced stocks. On the other hand, it is difficult to achieve optimal use of the equipment. Advocates of socio-technical systems favour the product-oriented structure because they believe that it is superior to the operation-oriented and flow-oriented structures at meeting present-day market demands for high production volumes, short and reliable lead times and production tailored to the customer's individual needs.

We should note at this point that the execution structures have been presented here in their purest forms. Hybrid forms are quite common in actual practice and the various execution principles frequently exist side by side within a single organization.

Production technology

Some of the operations allocated to a department or production group may be carried out by machines. In certain areas, automatic equipment, computers, robots and so on are taking over an increasing number of operations from manual workers. No consideration of the division of labour can afford to ignore these systems. They must be included in the assessment of the way production is organized, not to understand the intrinsic qualities of the technology, but because first, their level of penetration determines which operations remain to be distributed between humans, and second, the nature of the operations which remain in human hands, and in consequence the skills and knowledge required, hinges largely on the nature of the technical systems used and the way in which they are embedded in the organization. This requires us to make a distinction between inflexible technology, i.e. that which is fixed by the mechanical structure of the machine itself, and flexible technology, which in the first instance refers to programmability. Flexible machines (robots, CNC machine tools, flexible manufacturing systems, etc.) have a wide repertoire of functions at their disposal. They are therefore functional for a large variety of purposes, problems and situations.

Work organization

A proportion of the management, planning, support and execution operations allocated to a department or production group can be taken over by technical systems. Since automation is seldom complete, a number of residual tasks will remain. But automation can also create new tasks for humans to perform, and so the residual and new tasks are grouped together into new jobs. Work organization in this context results in jobs that comprise an overall package of management, planning, support and execution tasks. Such jobs differ from one another depending on the organizational options available, but reaching a sensible conclusion about work organization involves exploring the nature of these functions first.

With respect to execution tasks, a company has roughly two choices: very narrow jobs, i.e. those in which the employee specializes in a single execution task (or even parts of a task), or broad jobs which consist of multiple execution tasks. A company can also opt for segregated or for integrated jobs. The first consist exclusively of execution tasks. The second also include planning and/or support tasks. The descriptions 'segregated' and 'integrated' indicate the composition of the jobs. In researching job composition, then, we are exploring whether production workers perform tasks in the area of quality assurance, maintenance, planning and so on.

How things fit together and affect opportunities for learning

If we look at the division of labour in a company, we must focus on the nature of the production organization, the production technology and the work organization. The way in which the structure of the division of labour becomes manifest in a company is called its production concept. This term covers the entire range of options related to the organization of the production process. Any insight into contemporary patterns of the division of labour must therefore be derived from a description of the prevailing production concept.

The three forms of division of labour are related to how the production organization structures the production technology and the work organization (Figure 14.3). It will be clear that it is decisions regarding the production organization which determine how many of a specific department's tasks remain to be distributed between human beings and machines, and after that, distributed between jobs. Thus the production organization and the production technology structure the work organization. The choices made in these three dimensions finally result in jobs with different characteristics – including different learning opportunities.

This multi-dimensional analytical framework can be used to describe an ideal type of 'Taylorist' production concept and its antithesis, an ideal type of 'new production concept'. In a 'new production concept' the optimal division of labour is estimated as much less than in a Taylorist concept. The transition from an extreme Taylorist to an extreme form of new production concept implies that the staff departments must be split up and distributed between the local departments as a result of the process of deconcentration, each one being allocated to one segment of production. It implies an end to the separation of support and planning departments on the one hand and production departments on the other (at least in part). It also implies that planning and support tasks should be

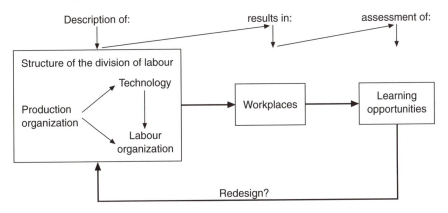

Figure 14.3 The redesign of the division of labour in order to improve learning opportunities

delegated to production departments and become integrated into the functions of the production workers. This leads to a highly integrated set of execution, support, planning and management functions and the dismantling of the staff departments. Integrated production functions are the ultimate result, with decentralization bringing more organizational capacity to the production groups (Table 14.1).

Socio-technical systems theory (de Sitter 1994; de Sitter *et al.* 1997) emphasizes the importance of achieving an optimal design of the production organization, not only to maximize the quality of the work, but also the quality of the organization in terms of flexibility, quality, delivery times and productivity. The seven WEBA conditions developed to measure the learning opportunities of jobs are to a large extent determined by the type of production organization. The functional dependency between jobs and the conditions for co-operation under which people work are the result.

Once the organization is structured in such a way that different units and departments are focused on a specific task in the production process, most of the harm has already been done. In this context, job rotation hardly improves the learning opportunities for workers, because the same kind of tasks are grouped together within the same unit or department. Job enrichment is equally difficult, because workers have no overview of the production process and few possess knowledge about the work that happens before and after their own activities. Even the implementation of 'team meetings' hardly improves learning opportunities, because the scope is restricted.

In order to fundamentally improve learning opportunities, it is necessary to reorganize the production process itself. The most favourable conditions are offered by a production organization of the product-oriented

Table 14.1 Traditional versus new production concept: a typology

Dimensions	Traditional	New
Production organization		
Structure of execution	Flow or operation-oriented	Product-oriented
Structure of preparation and support	Concentration	Deconcentration
Structure of decision and control	Centralization	Decentralization
Production technology		
Type of technology	Rigid mechanization	Automation of integrated production systems with emergence of system regulators
Work organization		
Width of workplaces	Small	Broad
Composition of workplaces	Segregated	Integrated

type (see Figure 14.2). A product-oriented structure groups together all the operations which belong to one type of product. In this structure, a complete set of operations is allocated to groups of workers. This alternative stresses the need to divide the work of the organization into holistic and complete parts instead of dividing it according to specialization. Provided with an adequate technology, task groups should be constructed on the level of the work organization.

Task groups within a product-oriented production organization offer the best conditions for learning according to the WEBA criteria. Such work groups are responsible for a complete part of the process including the organizational, direct production and social aspects. Additionally, the degree of control exercised can be balanced as much as possible with what is required. By simplifying the production organization, control requirements are reduced, as is the autonomy assigned to the group (WEBA 1990: 23). Thus providing better learning opportunities implies a transition from traditional complex organizations with simple jobs to simple organizations with complex jobs (de Sitter *et al.* 1997).

Are organizations changing in the direction of a new division of labour with better learning opportunities for workers?

The need for more evidence

Nearly two decades ago, Kern and Schumann (1984) announced their findings of the trend in the core industrial sectors of Germany (the automobile, machine-tool and chemical industries) towards the adoption of new production concepts. However, their study attracted criticism on the grounds of its small empirical base (Lutz 1988). In an effort to enlarge the data base, a research team from the Soziologisches Forschungsinstitut (SOFI) embarked on a much broader survey of companies within these sectors, resulting in the 'Trendreport' (Schumann *et al.* 1994). The gauntlet was also taken up in Belgium, where a Trend Study was launched in 1991 based on a perception to improve both the methodology and empirical base of these research projects (Huys *et al.* 1995). This study aimed to determine whether the Taylorist division of labour is really vanishing into the past. With a view to achieving maximum comparability with the results of the SOFI research team, the Belgian Trend Study also focused on the automotive, machine-tool and chemical industries, although developments in the clothing industry were studied as well. In the clothing industry, a transformation towards new production concepts might be a way to counter the threat of relocation of labour-intensive production to countries with low labour costs.

A fundamental methodological aim of the Trend Study was to enable the findings for each sector to be generalized. It had therefore to provide a better basis for intersectoral comparison and hence to be applicable to a variety of organizational types. To ensure that the conceptual framework was in fact capable of performing this function, its dimensions (see above) were refined, and an operational instrument was derived from it for field research. The operational instrument finally had to undergo a translation for each industry before we could begin drafting standardized questionnaires for the respective industries. The search for new production concepts called for the formulation of fairly branch-specific questions. However, backing up each branch-specific translation with the same generic framework guaranteed comparability.

The intention was to examine the prevalence of new production concepts within the widest possible range of companies. In the present chapter, we focus on the results of the surveys organized in the four industries mentioned. Details concerning the four surveys are presented in Table 14.2. The information on the automotive industry can be considered complete. All of the Belgian companies agreed to co-operate fully. The approach was particularly successful in the chemical and in the clothing industries, less so in the machine-tool industry. But overall, the response rates can be considered satisfactory.

The approach in the car assembly industry deviated from the methodology in the other branches, as there were 'only' five plants operating in Belgium. Data were collected in all five cases through observation as well as through the study of available documents. Furthermore, in the clothing and the machine-tool industries, the population was restricted to companies with over 50 employees.

Table 14.2 Number of observations of the sector surveys

	Companies[a]	Divisions[b]	Employees[c]	Response
Survey 1 (1992–3) Chemical industry	77	154	11,373	75%
Survey 2 (1993–4) Automotive industry	5	15	32,420	100%
Survey 3 (1994–5) Machine-tool industry	47	104	5,975	33%
Survey 4 (1995–6) Clothing industry	54	123	5,467	90%

Notes

a Large companies often have several plants (i.e. the entire sum of processes concentrated at the same location). One plant may have multiple units, each residing under the authority of a production manager. In the machine-tool industry and the clothing industry, a 'production concept' questionnaire was sent to each 'plant production manager'. In the chemical industry, a questionnaire was sent to each 'unit production manager'.

b Number of divisions on which information on work organization was obtained.

c Total number of employees working in the companies that participated in the survey.

A delayed transformation

Our data support a 'neo' rather than a 'post'-Taylorist or Fordist concept. The changes taking place have in common the fact that they do not change the fundamental nature of the Fordist–Taylorist production system. Table 14.3 highlights similarities and differences between the branches investigated (for a more detailed presentation of survey results, see Huys *et al.* 1995, 1999).

At first sight, the new production concepts have only effected a breakthrough in the machine-tool industry, where the picture of forms of production and work organization shows a consistent movement in the direction of partially integrated jobs, deconcentration and decentralization. But taking the historical evolution of the machine-tool industry into account, it is more correct to refer to timeless craftsmanship in the machine-tool industry than 'new production concepts'. In the automobile assembly industry, there is marked deconcentration and decentralization of the production organization. However, this does not lead to major changes in work organization. An important obstacle to broader and more integrated jobs is the continuing and ever more intensive use of the driven belt as the dominant structure (flow-oriented). The clothing industry is lagging behind in all dimensions of the production concept. In all likelihood, the overwhelming weight of labour costs, especially within sewing departments, is the obstacle which prevents the creation of a new production concept. Workers are brought to full capacity as quickly as possible by tying them to a single operation. Finally, in the chemical industry the large proportion of system regulators leads to many broad jobs. However, a traditional production organization remains in place.

Table 14.3 Summary evaluation of the dominant production concept in four industrial sectors

	Automotive industry	*Clothing industry*	*Chemical industry*	*Machine-tool industry*
Deconcentration	+	−	−	+
Decentralization	+	−	−	+
Product-oriented production	−	−	−	+/−[a]
Integrated automation/system regulators	+/−[b]	−	+	+/−[c]
Integrated jobs	−	−	−	+
Broad jobs	−	−	+	+

Notes
a Product-oriented production is dominant in the assembly shops, not so in the machine shops.
b Flexible automation has made deep inroads in the body shops, but the proportion of system regulators remains small.
c In the machine shops, flexible automation has led to a substantial proportion of system regulators, while the level of automation remains extremely low in the assembly shops.

It is clear that there is a discrepancy between what is often claimed about the introduction of new production concepts and our empirical findings. At the very least, the much-heralded transformation in work seems to be delayed. In the following section, we offer some possible explanations for this.

Obstacles to a transformation

One possible explanation for a delay in the transformation of the structure of the division of labour is that the traditional methods of production are much more adaptable than expected. Our data suggest that improvements in flexibility and quality of production can be achieved without departing from the structural principles of the traditional concept of industrial employment. A second possibility is that the changes which are assumed to be taking place in the market and which were supposed to impede the continuation of the Taylorist production concept have not materialized, or are only present to a limited extent.

In order to explain this 'delayed transformation', the supposed driving forces behind the transformation towards less division of labour need to be critically examined: (1) the supposed market fragmentation, (2) the increasing level of automation and (3) changes in the labour market. Additionally (4), the nature of the employment relationship may contribute to this delay.

Market fragmentation

Though advocates of flexible specialization point to market fragmentation as favouring new small-scale producers, this does not preclude extensive product differentiation by established large-scale producers. While Ford has implemented rigid product standardization in order to standardize operations, product differentiation does not preclude the standardization of operations, as a distinction should be made between 'small batches' and 'short runs'. With short runs, it is difficult to standardize operations. Indeed many industries which operate with short runs, such as the machine-tool industry, have never been 'Taylorized'. However, the flexibility of small-batch production is a matter of frequent changes between standardized models using the same production methods. This process of changeover can be standardized as well, and its implication for the workforce is a variation on the same simple and standardized tasks. Anyone visiting a car assembly plant will notice that the high level of production flexibility is achieved not by some system of autonomous teams, but rather through the more intensive control of the overall production flow made possible by information technology, in which all parts have to switch simultaneously like cogs in a gearbox.

As Shingo (1981: 112) points out, 'the Toyota Production System is not the antithesis of mass production; it is rather the antithesis of large batch production'. This kind of flexibility in no way requires a return to 'craft production' in which 'plants are increasingly engaged in the manufacture of specialized goods tailored to the needs of particular consumers and produced by broadly skilled workers using capital equipment that can make various models' (Katz and Sabel 1985: 297). Rather, it is an extension of scientific management, as the process of standardization includes not merely the execution of predetermined tasks but also the frequent changeovers between them.

Increasing levels of automation

By the same token, increasing levels of automation have often been claimed to establish a fundamentally new relationship between workers and management. As the new production concepts emphasize, workers in automated sectors are no longer potential obstacles to increased productivity but the key to the smooth operation of the process. As such, the system regulator's task cannot be 'Taylorized' as a certain degree of autonomy is necessary for him or her to react to stochastic events. But the importance of this autonomy is overstated in the theorizing about the new production concepts, as this 'new worker' is subject to the pervasive control exercised by information technology through the computer-integrated control of production and personnel information systems. This autonomy is further limited by the increased power delegated to lower parts of the managerial hierarchy (Dankbaar 1988).

Moreover, the statistical importance of this new type of labour is still small, its proportion in the workforce bearing no relationship to the attention it receives from academics and policy-makers. Finally, as the chemical industry shows, this 'new' work is not necessarily transfunctional by nature. And where there is proof of job integration, as in the automotive industry, the range of skills involved consists mainly of the addition of simple tasks without opening up substantial opportunities in the high-technology areas for those concerned. As Jürgens and his co-workers conclude in their study of the automotive industry: 'In our observations in the factories we studied we could not find evidence of a general trend towards an upgrading of production work due to the increase in automation as, for example, Kern and Schumann hypothesized' (Jürgens *et al.* 1993: 284). Indeed, the tasks integrated into production jobs are often subject to standardization and thus acquire the same nature for workers as the usual predetermined production task. The 'enskilling' influence of job integration is in general less than expected.

Changes in the labour market

Changes in the labour market are often cited as a principal cause of changes in the division of labour. This is perhaps most clearly exemplified by the much discussed alternative work organization in the Swedish plants – a form of organization which is often said to have grown out of specifically Swedish situations in the labour market as the title of the introductory chapter in Gyllenhammer (1974: 9) makes clear: 'The Swedish way is best – for Sweden.' Labour market factors which tend to reduce the division of labour include:

- a low level of unemployment (offering workers alternatives in seeking work);
- higher levels of education among the workers, who consequently become less willing to do boring work;
- high levels of social benefits provided by a welfare state and not – as is the case in Japan – by the company in which the worker is employed. This allows workers to demonstrate their frustration, for example, through high levels of absenteeism;
- low wage differentials between companies and sectors, which denies companies the opportunity to compensate for boring work through high wages. The level of wage differences is influenced by the structure of union organization. The emphasis on plant-based unions is more likely to induce high wage differences between plants and sectors (Berggren 1992: 11).

Currently, however, such pressures from the labour market are rather weak in Belgium. Although education levels are extremely high – school attendance is obligatory till 18 years of age – in itself this does not necessarily entail changes in the division of labour. As in the case of the clothing industry, an abundance of well-trained and experienced workers may facilitate the implementation of new production concepts, but it is not sufficient if other factors intervene.

The employment relationship

While the picture emerging from our findings does not support the hoped for reduction in the division of labour, we will add a concluding remark on the implications of the delay in this transformation for the quality of working life and skills requirements. On the one hand, the remaining boundaries in the division of labour do not exclude more skilled work. It is wrong to suggest that such an increase of skill requirements can merely be brought about by less division of labour. As is exemplified by the chemical industry, the continuing rigid demarcation between direct and indirect tasks goes together with higher skill requirements for production workers, as the running of the increasingly integrated and complex processes demands better trained workers. Conversely, a move towards less division of labour is not necessarily welcomed by workers and unions, as many of the changes in the division of labour, although tentative, are attempts by management to achieve work intensification, an aspect of the supposed transformation which is conspicuously absent in the 'post-Fordist' debate. The changes that do occur in some industries with regard to work organization can be viewed as part of a new rationalization strategy that is opposed to the traditional principles of separation and specialization. This remains a rationalization strategy, however, which is aimed at work intensification.

Splitting up staff departments and bringing them into a closer relationship with production results in staff functions coming under greater production pressure. Job integration for production jobs entails broader responsibilities and greater stress for workers. The integration of simple indirect tasks into production jobs makes it possible to cut back staff support, while imposing more responsibilities and stress on workers, as they can no longer afford to be merely concerned with output. Multifunctionality is an attempt to despecialize workers which increases peer pressure within teams and makes it possible to run the factory with minimal manpower. Moreover, a decrease in the division of labour is often considered by unions to be a 'Trojan horse'. There are specific Belgian circumstances contributing to this. Unions are a force to be reckoned with, as union membership in comparison to neighbouring countries remains very high. Fifty per cent of workers belong to a union in Belgium, compared with 39 per cent in the UK, 33 per cent in Germany, 25 per cent in The Netherlands and a mere 11 per cent in France (Visser 1991). The results of the Trend Study surveys indicate that union density among blue-collar workers in Belgium is as high as 86 per cent in car assembly, 88 per cent in the chemical industry, 82 per cent in the machine-tool industry and 90 per cent in the clothing industry.

The power of Belgian unions is reflected in their monopoly with regard to negotiations on terms and conditions of employment, in which they have to be included by law. As such, unions are institutionally very much involved in the policies of the social security system, which they helped to develop, but they contribute equally to a conservatism which protects long-established interests. On the other hand, issues concerning job design and its effects on the quality of work receive low priority on the union agenda. This neglect is exacerbated by the presence of different unions in each plant, and by the fact that the unions compete with each other primarily on the basis of fringe benefits. However, although job design is left to management, a transformation in the production concept inevitably has its effect on the terms and conditions of employment. In this way, although indirectly, unions do have an influence on job design and, in view of their power, on the terms and conditions of employment. They are in a position to block or at least delay a transformation towards new production concepts.

The outlook for learning opportunities

Learning opportunities are an objective characteristic of jobs in organizations. The degree to which learning opportunities are offered by these jobs is dependent on the structure of the division of labour in the organization. In this chapter, we have made this structure of the division of labour (or in other words, the production concept) more explicit by identifying several dimensions along which organizations can vary. A transition towards a 'new production concept' results in jobs with different characteristics, including the more extensive learning opportunities embedded in these jobs.

However, data from large-scale surveys in four industrial sectors in Flanders show that a transformation towards new production concepts has until now only been implemented in a piecemeal way. On the one hand, the traditional production concept in these industries is more effective than presumed and turns out to be more resilient. This means that this conservatism continues to put a break on learning opportunities for workers. On the other hand, the supposed pressures from the environment, be it from the labour market, the consumer market or technology, are not as strong as they are often presented. In this context, it should be stressed that the employment relationship is one of the main factors affecting the introduction of a new production concept, and is therefore an issue requiring further research. It may very well be that a production concept can as such be easily copied and implemented, but the related employment relationship under which this has to occur may not be copied so easily. In agreement with the conclusions of Krüger, Kruse and Caprile (Chapter 15, this volume) this suggests that workers and their representatives should be included in initiatives to introduce new production concepts and the increased learning opportunities they offer. In such efforts, unions should be prepared to reconsider their protection of long-established interests accumulated under the old production concept and to redefine their role under the new one. Insofar as new management practices often involve larger responsibilities for workers without offering them the resources needed to respond to these demands, union opposition to such a 'management by stress' is appropriate. However, this reaction often becomes a defence of the Tayloristic status quo. Unions could move towards a more constructive strategy in which the resources the workers need are demanded on the basis of meeting the demands made on them by new production concepts. One such resource is undoubtedly the opportunity for workers to learn in and through work, which can be realized only if management is willing to alter the traditional division of labour in organizations.

Note

1 WElzijn Bij de Arbeid, short for 'Well-Being during Work', abbreviated to WEBA. The incentive for the development of this instrument was the necessity to operationalize the relevant provisions on well-being in the Dutch Working Environment Act in 1990. In the section of the act concerned are provisions which the employer has to observe in organizing work, designing jobs and establishing production and work methods, all aimed at the advancement of well-being during work.

15 Work process knowledge and industrial and labour relations

Karsten Krüger, Wilfried Kruse and Maria Caprile

Since the 1980s, a wave of change has occurred in companies, reflected in new ways of organizing work and new ways of viewing competence and professionalism. These changes have been attributed to globalization (Castells 1997; Priore and Sabel 1984; Pries 1991) and computerization. The argument is not that the new working forms require a production system based on information and communication technologies, but that these technologies are opening new areas of activity for which new approaches are needed. Finally, social changes (increasing qualification levels, lifestyle changes and demographic changes) have also been identified as a contributory factor. In a study carried out in France, Italy and Germany, Heidenreich (1990) showed that the way in which companies in these three countries treat their highly qualified employees follows a logic that is then reflected in the design of company information processes.

Whatever the current situation in different economic sectors and sub-sectors, and in different work processes and their phases, there is growing interest in the way in which work processes are organized and in the competencies required to carry out the tasks the new kinds of work create. There has been an extensive discussion about the growing importance of 'non-technical competencies' (Harrison 1996), 'soft competencies' (Nyhan 1989), 'transversal competencies' (MacBer 1987), 'social competencies' (Fontana 1990), 'relational competencies' (Folk *et al.* 1998) and 'collective competencies' (Rogalski, Plat and Antolin-Glenn, Chapter 10 in this volume). The recognition of a need for employees to gain greater understanding of the work process must be seen within this general framework.

Although there has been wide-ranging discussion of the reasons for the emergence of these concepts and related pedagogical tools, the actual or potential effects of the acquisition of these competencies and especially the implications of workers acquiring work process knowledge has attracted less attention. The questions at issue concern the social organization of enterprises, within which the work processes are embedded. Specifically, changing the focus of productivity issues to questions of how to organize the work process, and identifying work process knowledge as a key requirement for all workers, will necessarily raise questions of labour politics. The present chapter will examine this aspect of work process knowledge, paying particular attention to the changes that are taking place in social relations in the workplace, and in industrial relations both inside and outside enterprises. The starting point will be examples of projects in which company personnel, particularly management, and an advisory team of work psychologists have attempted to develop innovative approaches to human resource management. Work process knowledge is a core strategic area within these projects, concerning as it does the knowledge and mastery of the whole operational context stretching far beyond the horizon of the individual workplace or group-related work functions.

Industrial relations: the agents and those affected

Even in companies undergoing intensive modernization, there is a marked contrast between reality and what is claimed in policy statements about the benefits of new kinds of work organization, in the context of which we place work process knowledge. For example, the 1997 Green Paper, *Partnership for a New Organization of Work* (European Communities 1997) advocates a work organization based on qualifications, a culture of trust, quality and the full participation of employees, all of which can be bundled together in what is known as the 'European route to the modernization of industry'. The Green Paper claims that such an improved form of work organization would be able to make a major contribution to improving the competitiveness of European companies, improving the quality of working life and improving workers' employability.

In fact, empirical studies such as one carried out by the European Foundation for the Improvement of Living and Working Conditions (1997), as well as experience gained from many practice-oriented projects on the modernization of work organization, show that the growth of improved forms of work organization is very limited throughout Europe. Similarly, recent studies such as Schumann (1997) indicate that even when experiments have been attempted with innovations in work organization along the lines cited, many of these have either been discontinued or kept within narrow limits. A picture thus emerges in which examples of 'better' forms of work organization are rare, even though the vast management literature on the subject continues to argue that it is necessary. The implication of this can only be that in this case we are dealing with an extremely 'compact structure of social restrictions', reflecting a fundamental fact of industrial life – that work is disputed terrain.

Knowledge about work procedures has always been the focal point of rationalization at the company level. The reason for this is that the crux of work organization is the way in which individual working tasks are structured or related to the overall process of producing goods or providing services. The Taylorist structure, based on the standardization and routinization of labour requirements, and the accompanying rigidity and compartmentalization of the horizontal and vertical division of labour, was the dominant approach in the past. However, with the declining productivity of Taylorist forms of work organization, this is now in question. The 'soft skills' that are now in the forefront of debate, such as responsibility and teamwork, are evidence of the struggle that is taking place for the minds of the workers.

It is hardly surprising that work has yet again emerged as disputed terrain. This is because of its dual character: on the one hand its productive and value-creating aspect, and on the other hand, the simple fact, often overlooked in reductive economic analyses, that the capacity to work (and therefore the work actually performed by individuals) is not divisible, because work is an important constituent of personal identity and the individual's participation in life in its widest sense. Much is at stake for this reason. If the form of work organization that is currently accepted by both sides of industry is a compromise which maintains an acceptable balance between completing work tasks, power sharing and distributing wealth between the different actors, then it is clear that every proposed change to the current arrangement will signify both risks and opportunities for all concerned. For this reason, approaching change will initially tend to arouse worries and fears, possibly of a diffuse nature, rather than feelings of optimism. Such reactions should not be seen as external to the process of work re-organization, but as a basic and intrinsic structural factor within that process. Thus, when industrial reorganization is proposed, those representing the interests of workers are forced to adopt a certain initial position in the negotiations: that changes in the form of work organization will inevitably reposition the workers, substantially affecting the relationship between performance and reward that is protected by the current form of work organization. For this reason, the theoretically expected gain in working conditions and quality of life for workers is counterbalanced by the need to protect the status quo. Thus the negotiators' attitude will depend decisively on the opportunities for workers to gain influence or control over the process of innovation. From the management's point of view, the issue is to keep the innovation free of undesirable social consequences, or at least to hold these within manageable limits. The keyword 'culture of trust' is central in this context, indicating one model of social organization by which the potentially conflicting interests of company personnel can be reconciled. Consequently, attention is given to the culture of the working relationships and the institutional composition of the industrial relationships, with their implications for the processes of negotiating change.

If we view employee knowledge of the overall work process as an innovation that is central to many of the current changes that are taking place in work organization, reflecting the transition from an industrial society to a knowledge society, then effective industrial relationships are a prerequisite for bringing about these changes. Equally, as changes are made, there will be major effects on the organization and social quality of industrial relations. In this sense, industrial relations are an intrinsic part of work process knowledge, and not just an external condition necessary for bringing it about.

The Spanish system of industrial and labour relations

Before discussing work process knowledge in Spanish enterprises, a brief account will be given of the Spanish system of industrial relations. The aim is to emphasize the importance of the history and structure of national systems of industrial relations for understanding innovation in work organization, and in that context, the difficulties of developing a shared knowledge of the work process. In the late 1970s, when Spain was consolidating its new democracy, it encountered an economic recession which was partly due to the global economic difficulties of the time (the 'oil crisis') and partly due to the transition from the controlled Francoist economy to a market economy. Then, in the 1980s, came a process of economic liberalization in preparation for entry into the European Community, and the focus shifted from democratization towards safeguarding the economic and social interests of employees. Initially, the two large trade union alliances, CCOO and UGT, were pursuing different policies due to their different political allegiances. In the early 1980s, the employers and the UGT, which was linked with the governing socialist party, signed a series of important national agreements, the *Acuerdos Economicos y Social* which the CCOO refused to sign but did not actually oppose. These reformed the system of industrial relations. At the same time, the government adopted a policy of drastic deregulation of conditions of employment. The following years were marked by clashes between the unions and the government. The government pursued a neo-liberal economic policy which included privatization, but also made efforts to establish a policy of negotiation and agreements between the social partners. After 25 years, the Spanish trade unions have emancipated themselves from their close connections to political parties and an autonomous and stable system of industrial relations has been established. However, below the level of framework agreements concerning minimum standards, there is a very fragmented pattern of agreements on wages and working conditions. Pay agreements at sector and regional levels are often not fully implemented due to lack of worker representation in many companies. At the same time, in large companies with strong worker representation, special company-related agreements are common.

Large and medium-sized enterprises, which have well-developed bargaining structures, are often the pioneers in the introduction of new concepts of work organization, human resource management and training policies. Nevertheless, law limits the influence of workers' representatives within these enterprises. The rights to receive information are minimal, and the rights to influence and participate in the decision-making process are even less.[1] In this context, the strategy of the union representatives in the enterprise is usually a reactive one of defending the limited rights and interests of the workers. Low trust and low levels of membership generally characterize industrial relations in the enterprises and the multiplicity of trade unions[2] operating at company level has reduced their influence.[3] Dealing with in-company problems and organizational assignments has not traditionally been a major commitment by Spanish trade unions, which have tended to be more politically than company oriented. The two major trade unions have centred their strategy on societal problems such as unemployment, the high rate of temporary work and, recently, occupational health and safety. The official rate of unemployment reached its peak in 1994 at 24.3 per cent, but among younger people under 24 years of age it was over 40 per cent. Then, by 1999 the rate dropped to a national average of 15.6 per cent and considerably less in some regions. Unemployment among the younger groups is also falling but remains at approximately 30 per cent. One of the central consequences of deregulation was the spread of temporary jobs. Today temporary work is one of the main characteristics of the Spanish employment system. In 1995, at the peak, 35 per cent of those employed were in temporary jobs, and in 1999 this quota remained at 32.7 per cent.

There is little or no discussion of a new role for workers in the organization processes and for the workers' representatives in the reorganization processes.

The traditional internal structure of Spanish companies is multiple layers of supervisors. This reflects a Taylorist philosophy that has up to now been characterized by a lack of efficiency, disregard for vocational training and a strong distrust of the workers on the part of employers. Public debate on the role of qualified workers in the process of modernization has been minimal. Today, initiatives to change the form of work organization come from the companies and provoke fears of job losses among employees, company trade union sections and *Comités de Empresa* (works' councils). Even where unions within companies enter partial modernizing agreements, these are rarely accepted by the staff. For example, in 1994 Opel wanted to introduce teamwork in its factory near Zaragoza and had already experimented with pilot groups to this end. UGT and CCOO, the two big trade unions represented in the company also agreed to this development. However, the *Comité de Empresa* demanded a referendum among the staff. This referendum led to a rejection of the introduction of team work because the employees were unable to assess the implications for themselves and doubted whether they would be able to control the process of change (Alcalde and Blasco 1994).

The Spanish discussion of new work forms and new human resource strategies

On 15 March 1999, the well-known Spanish daily paper *El País* ran a comprehensive report on a conference on 'The Future of Work' in Bilbao under the headline 'El fin de las jeraquías en el trabajo' ('The end of hierarchies at work'). This was one of the first major newspaper articles on this subject in Spain and it seemed like the discovery of a new landscape, at quite a late stage in comparison to other – particularly northern – European countries. Leading Spanish companies such as Fuchosa, TVA, Irizar, IBM, Ikusi, Maier, Salica, Arteche, Mondragón Cooperacion Cooperativa (MCC) and CAF have either formed alliances with international concerns or have found a significant opening into international markets themselves. 'Internationalization' is obviously a decisive aspect in the re-evaluation of the factor of 'qualified work'. All the companies represented are extremely successful economically; the managers attribute part of this success to the new value placed on the workforce.

TVA, a company which belongs to a multinational concern for the production of automobile components, says that this success required the traditional hierarchic pyramid to be torn down and demanded the participation of the workforce by necessity. The Mondragón co-operative includes a bus manufacturer that delivers globally. The personnel director explains: 'There are no fixed working times for coming and going; there are no bosses and the word "control" is forbidden.' In the Maier co-operative, the entire factory has been divided into individually organized mini-factories and these are linked through an ambitious Internet communications model that ensures complete transparency for all business activity. In the words of the personnel director, 'the power of the company lies in the capacity of individuals, not that of the hierarchy'.

What the balance of power allows

Let us now discuss a project where an attempt to develop work process knowledge and change working practices failed. The aim of the project was to create a system of continuous training in travel agencies for the development of transversal competencies based on the whole work process and the quality management systems. In collaboration with a training school in the sector, a team of specialists drew up a project to introduce quality systems based on work process knowledge in a service sector and undertook a pilot project in a micro-company incorporated in the training school. The pilot project was intended to start up the system, to fine-tune it in accordance with the experiences of the pilot project and to set it out in a manual. To achieve this, it was considered essential to have the active collaboration of the payroll and to involve the company management in all the introductory stages. The aim of this method of achieving controlled participation was to co-ordinate the development of the process and to be able to react as early as possible to any problems that might arise.

In the first phase, the project included the preparation of material on items of quality management, the principles of organizational learning and principles of adult pedagogy; at the same time it included a formal description of the specific work processes carried out by specialists from the school.[4] In the second phase of the project, the aim was that the employees of the micro-company, including the manager, would revise the descriptions of the procedures. The fact that there were only three employees in the travel agency apart from the manager made it possible to achieve the participation of all of the staff. It was also intended to introduce the principles of quality management and organizational learning in parallel, and improve the revised procedures.

The team of specialists had designed a programme of meetings to analyse the actual procedures and the possibility of improvements to them. At the same time, the meetings were intended to serve as training in quality management systems and to encourage processes of change towards an organization based on a shared knowledge of the work process in the organization as a whole. The following steps were designed in the original procedure: diagnosis of previous conditions, key process selection, process description, strategic planning, analysis of competencies, detection and analysis of training needs, daily management, training of continuous improvement teams, problem analysis, evaluation and certification.

Because of the special nature of the project, it was decided to separate the first three steps from the others and to include them in the first phase. The first step was dependent on the management of the training school, because they were ultimately responsible for what was happening in the company within the pilot project. In a third phase, which was developed alongside the second, it was planned to initiate the improvements drawn up in the second phase and introduce the principles of quality management and organizational learning into the daily work of the travel agency. However, the pilot project was suspended in the second phase and the third phase was not started. The meetings were cancelled at the competence analysis stage and the problems with working with the whole staff, including the manager, were so great that it was decided not to continue. The discussion of the two kinds of service processes and the increased transparency of the relevant organizational procedures met with resistance from the manager and this led to a passive attitude on the part of the employees. In this situation, it was considered that the pilot project, which was based on the active, broad participation of the staff, had failed.

Why did the pilot project fail? The idea of basing everybody's performance on a common understanding of the work process was fundamental. This inevitably entailed securing the participation of the workers. In particular, the focus given to this project started with the idea that the knowledge or cultural capital of the workers included technical, social and organizational dimensions. It was assumed that the technical competencies would not be a problem in the process of introducing modern principles of organization into the agency, because they did not presuppose technological innovation. However, it was considered that the social and organizational competencies would be crucial.

The standardization of work procedures is very limited in small and micro-companies in contrast to medium-sized and large companies. Most working tasks are carried out through informal processes, with a large amount of discretion accorded to the people undertaking them. As a result, the labour roles have very little formal definition and their configuration is based on informal, interactive defining processes. The project was intended to standardize some of the procedures and therefore to increase their transparency, which would serve to reveal cases of dysfunction in the processes and allow them to be corrected, accompanied by a redefinition of the roles and a redistribution of the organizational capital. However, when the manager perceived the scope of the change, which would have redefined her position and affected her organizational capital within the company, she refused to continue to participate. The employees, who clearly perceived that the project could contribute to increasing their cultural and organizational capital, were at first willing to collaborate. Nevertheless, they changed their attitude when they saw the negative stance of the manager. The changes foreseen in the organizational structures would have caused a redistribution of influences, power and control and the manager was not willing to accept these rules because she feared that she would lose out and her role in the company would change.

New professionalism: work process knowledge based?

In 1996 a continuous project was begun in the steel industry with the aim of introducing a 'new professionalism', as a drive to restructure the companies in the sector as non-Taylorist forms of organization. The employers' association supported this project. The transformation of markets towards trade internationalization and greater competitiveness between companies throughout the world, as well as the massive introduction of computer technology in production processes, led to a generalized search in the sector for ways of adapting to this changing environment. Without expressing this openly, the project was based on the concept of work process knowledge as the implicit beginning of the new professionalism and a drive towards organizational change.

At the beginning of the project, an analysis was made of ten companies in the sector in terms of their work procedures, the knowledge base and any existing projects for change.[5] This organizational diagnosis also served as a means to sensitize companies towards change and was based on a series of interviews with representatives of all sections of the companies, from operatives to senior management. The analysis gave an initial picture of the complex power structure within the companies, and made it possible to identify the strengths and weaknesses for the application of a continuous training programme to bring about change.

One indicator of the problems associated with developing a shared knowledge of the work process in a company is the lack of organizational development activities implicitly based on this concept, such as quality circles, groups for continuous improvement and operative meetings at factory floor level. Although nearly all the companies visited have experimented with such mechanisms, none has been capable of sustaining them for long. The only initiative to survive long term has been the application of project management principles at the management level. Other initiatives to improve the involvement of the workers in the organizational processes and to make better use of their knowledge of the work processes have not borne fruit.

A certain common trend was observed in the failure of the quality circles or 'groups for improvement'. These initiatives did bear fruit in the first phase: in their own opinion and also that of the managers, the workers showed interest in participating and produced ideas for improvement. In the medium term, however, all the groups failed because of a lack of feedback from the management; in other words, the failure of the groups was due to the passive attitude to communication by the management. If the management had been more proactive in commenting on the receipt of ideas, implementing suggestions or explaining why they were not being implemented, the groups could have been motivated to continue. This would have recognized employees' knowledge of the work processes. However, company management was not willing to accept this change in the capital structure of the companies, particularly with regard to its implications for the organizational capital. Explicit recognition of the validity of the employees' suggestions would have meant a change in their institutionalized roles in the companies. Managers would have become accountable to the workers for implementing their ideas for improvement, and a new kind of management based on communicative dialogue would have been introduced in place of routinized information flows.

Nevertheless, progress has been made in the sector towards other forms of organizing work and towards a 'new professionalism', not in the broad sense in which we have used this term, but rather based particularly on the following three criteria:

a) Technological change means that today, work in this branch of industry is less manual and more abstract than before, requiring retraining.
b) Technological change and the need to reduce the number of employees have led companies to introduce multi-skilling. Most companies apply this principle in a limited way.

c) Most companies have also opted for some measures to enrich work, especially through introducing quality systems into the production process. However, work enrichment does not extend much beyond this, for example to maintenance tasks or involvement of lower levels of the hierarchy in decision-making.

The organizational form of the companies in this industrial sector could be described as neo-Taylorist. When compared with pure Taylorist forms of work, the new forms of organizing work are based on workers' knowledge of the work process, but without recognizing it expressly and without using it as a reason for reorganizing the decision-making procedures to any major extent. In this way, business reality contradicts the business discourse observed in the sector, which advocates going beyond Taylorist forms of work. One reason is that the neo-Taylorist use of the workers' cultural capital by the companies has been a source of tension. Multi-skilling and job enrichment have made worker requalification a highly disputed matter. Existing wage categories have become obsolete and company managements have unilaterally introduced additional ways of recognizing competencies. In one case, for example, workers who agree to work in three different posts receive a bonus regardless of whether in the end they actually work in the three positions or not. In another company, the salary classification of the workers has been revised but has nevertheless caused discontent among both employees and the company committees, which demand collective negotiation on such matters. Generally, workers have perceived that the principles of multi-skilling and job enrichment as forms of work intensification have not been adequately rewarded financially. The next step would be to create symbolic recognition of the acquisition of a knowledge of overall working processes and the competences that go with this; this will mean reviewing the occupational classification in companies by formally recognizing this knowledge as has been attempted in Germany (see the study by Fischer and Rauner, Chapter 12). In fact, recognition of competence achieved through knowledge of the overall work process acquired through experience has become a central theme in collective negotiations.[6]

Empowerment: some theoretical remarks

The concept of work process knowledge encompasses a combination of work experience and theoretical learning. It is not limited to the individual workplace but embraces the whole work process, including product, labour organization, company and the latter's environment. If work process knowledge refers to the entirety of the structures of a process in the production of goods and services (including knowledge) then the concept can serve as a guide for improving work processes. The above examples of the difficulties of implementing new work organization and promoting the acquisition of work process knowledge requires a theoretical instrument that can be used to evaluate the possible effects of the implicit or explicit application of work process knowledge to labour relations. To do this, we turn to the macro-sociological concept of capital as developed by Bourdieu (1979). Organizational change must be analysed on two levels:

1 the structural process of a specific social change – that is, the organizational structure, the formal definitions of the roles and the formal rules of the game; and
2 the change in the forms of the 'habitus' – that is, the forms in the organization with respect to the performance of the roles.

The problem with all projects that attempt to initiate a process of planned change lies in the co-ordination of the transformations on these two levels.[7] Organizations are a set of complex multilateral and asymmetrical power relations. The power of a person depends as much on personal resources as on the organizational resources available to that person. Therefore, two power levels are distinguished: the structural level and the level of the specific action. Bourdieu distinguishes between four forms of capital: economic, cultural, social and symbolic. On the level of organizations, we would like to propose the addition of a further type of capital, which we will call organizational capital. This refers to the control of the key points in the organization. Within the idea of 'cultural capital', we stress cultural resources such as manual and technical abilities, but also other forms of knowledge. This is knowledge in the broadest sense of the word, since it goes beyond academic and school knowledge.

Bourdieu's 'social capital' refers to the network of social relationships into which individuals are integrated and to which they have access when they need the support and help of other people. Two kinds of social capital can be distinguished in organizations:

• the social relationships within the organization, referring to the large number of informal relationships maintained by a person. Here, we exclude formal relationships because they are included in the concept of organizational capital;
• the social relations that an individual maintains outside the organization and which have no formal relevance to the organization. We include external formal relationships within organizational capital.

The value of the specific social relationships depends on the general evaluation of the contacts by the organization, and the scope of the social network – in this sense, individuals might increase their social capital by taking care of their relationships. Through the positive recognition and evaluation of the social relationships by the organization, social capital might have a multiplying effect on the other kinds of capital (Bourdieu 1992).

The notion of 'organizational capital' refers to formal, structural power resources, such as the relationship with one's surroundings, control of the channels of communication and information and the use of organizational rules (Crozier and Friedberg 1979). By applying Bourdieu's capital theory to organizations, we reveal the complexity of the multiple resources available to the individual or collective actors to establish their position in the games of organizational power. An organization is then a set of different 'games' brought together, which are social constructions and conditional on people participating in them. Nevertheless, these power games are not zero-sum. In other words, they are not games with clear rules, where the gains and losses can be clearly calculated along the principle that what one gains the other loses. On the contrary, they are a series of games that are interconnected, where there are no obvious rules. Furthermore, the actors do not work in an objectively rational way, but pursue strategies of limited rationality, despite following micro-political strategies in their actions. It is also possible for everyone to win or to lose in these games, even though these are two extreme, improbable results.

The structures in the organizations are the starting point for each new game and mark the steps of its development. Different actors participate in the games on the basis of the capital available to them. It is not sufficient for an actor or a group of actors to have this capital; the important thing is rather that the other actors should recognize these elements as power resources. The existence of power resources and the possibility that they can be used does not mean that the actors who control them may use them in the game of organizational power, but rather that the availability of capital and its possible use must be perceived by others (Ortmann 1995).

In the light of this analysis, the strategic relationships of work process knowledge become clear. The acquisition of work process knowledge as an individual and collective learning process is equivalent to the empowerment of the employees within the social system of the company, which can promote the development of the company, if it is granted social recognition.

Outlook: a dual perspective on work process knowledge

According to the theoretical focus developed here, possession of organizational and work process knowledge is one of the most important resources in the process of internal negotiation. However, these processes are embedded in a specific social and cultural context, which we have described here in terms of the system of industrial relations and the strategies of management. As we see it, professional knowledge may be broken down into knowledge of the particulars of a job, knowledge of the work process and knowledge of the organizational structure. This could give more power to the workers involved, and should not imply that the management would lose all its powers in the negotiation process, although it would equalize the positions to a greater extent than previously. The organizational change from the implicit use of workers' knowledge of work processes to the recognition of this knowledge constitutes a transition from a traditional, narrow Taylorist organization to a new type. However, the two examples given in this chapter demonstrate the difficulties in building new organizational structures based on sharing knowledge of the work process, caused by the resulting changes in the power structure of companies and the resistance of certain social groups in the face of this change.

The problem of encouraging all employees to share a common understanding of the overall work process relates to the behaviour of the different social groupings within the organization. Naturally, all these groups are aware that organizational changes and a change to the management of human resources means a change in the power structure. However, they generally interpret this in zero-sum game terms and fail to perceive that the games do not add up to zero. If this attitude of a large sector of the company is not changed, resistance will always be found. On the other hand, the new distribution of cultural and organizational capital requires changes both in the habits of the managers and employees. Behind it all there is a change in the structure of roles in the organization and in related behaviour.

According to Kruse (1985):

> We are convinced that work process knowledge will become an important organizational requirement for effective control, optimization and maintenance. In this way, the individual availability of developed work process knowledge will become an essential prerequisite for taking up qualified employment in this sector.

This also applies to the effective introduction and exploitation of new technologies.

> Work Process Knowledge means an understanding of the whole work process in which the individual participates, in its product-related, technical, employment organizational, social and system-related dimensions.

As far as methodology is concerned, the point is to understand the present form of work organization as historically created and open to alternatives. However, change can only occur in the context of the articulation of interests, implying the need for an active involvement of workers in organizational change. This necessitates an analytical monitoring of the work process as it changes, ideally in the form of co-operation between the different groups of employees. The collective possession of work process knowledge is thus becoming an essential prerequisite for successful action by organizations facing the need to change. Such knowledge sharing implies a partnership between both sides of industry.

Notes

1 See Estatuto de los Trabajadores, Art. 64. and Krüger (1997).
2 Examples are the regular collective bargaining process in enterprises with their own collective agreements. In these enterprises the workers play an important role in the bargaining process and often the agreement approved by the trade unions or the major trade union must be approved through a referendum. A more concrete example is the bargaining process with respect to the introduction of new forms of work organization in the production centre of General Motors in Sargasso in the 1990s. Here management and the trade unions signed an agreement on a pilot project and the general application of the dispositions of the agreement upon completion of the pilot project and should the workers vote in favour of the agreement. But the majority of the workers voted against this agreement.
3 Compare Kruse (1994).
4 The following processes were chosen: service, sales and new product design.
5 Based on the initial indications of the organizational diagnosis and in parallel, a broad programme of professional training aimed at new professional competencies was drawn up. Later, this training was provided in different companies of the sector that had already begun or intended to begin a process of change in their organizations in a third phase. The effect of the training on the organization of work process cannot be discussed here, because we do not yet have the results.
6 This is, for example, one of the key elements in the discussion of the recently founded Spanish National Qualification Institute.
7 The dynamics of social evolution are closely related to the dialectic relationship between structure and action or social field and forms of habit respectively. The fact that these two forms are unable to coincide totally is the basis for the processes of social transformation occurring throughout the whole of society, social organization and social groups. However, we must distinguish processes of transformation that have been initiated consciously to achieve a certain social state.

References

1 Work process knowledge in technological and organizational development

Appelbaum, E. and Batt, R. (1994) *The New American Workplace: Transforming Work Systems in the United States*, Ithaca, NY: ILR Press/Cornell University Press.

Boreham, N.C. (1995) 'Error analysis and expert–novice differences in medical diagnosis', Chapter 7 in J-M. Hoc, E. Hollnagel and C. Cacciabue (eds) *Expertise and Technology*, Hove: Lawrence Erlbaum Associates, pp. 91–103.

Duncan, K.D. (1981) 'Training for fault diagnosis in industrial process plant', in J. Rasmussen and W.B. Rouse (eds) *Human Detection and Diagnosis of System Failures*, New York: Plenum.

European Communities (1997) *Green Paper: Partnership for a New Organization of Work*, Luxembourg: Office for Official Publications of the European Communities.

Fischer, G. and Nakakoji, K. (1997) 'Computational environments supporting creativity in the context of lifelong learning and design', *Knowledge Based Systems*, 10: 21–8.

Fischer, M. (1995) *Technikverständnis von Facharbeitern im Spannungsfeld von beruflicher Bildung und Arbeitserfahrung*. Bremen: Donat Verlag.

Fischer, M., Jungeblut, R. and Rommermann, E. (1995) *'Jede Maschine hat ihre eigene Marotten!' Instandhaltungsarbeit in der rechnergestützten Produktion und Möglichkeiten technischer Unterstützung*, Bremen: Donat Verlag.

Kern, H. and Schumann, M. (1984) *Das Ende der Arbeitsteilung? Rationalisierung in der industriellen Produktion*, München: Verlag C.H. Beck.

Kruse, W. (1986) 'On the necessity of labour process knowledge', in J. Schweitzer (ed.) *Training for a Human Future*, Basle: Weinheim, pp. 188–93.

Morris, N.M. and Rouse, W.B. (1985) 'Review and evaluation of empirical research in troubleshooting', *Human Factors*, 27: 503–30.

Nonaka, I. and Takeuchi, H. (1995) *The Knowledge Creating Company*, Oxford: Oxford University Press.

Patrick, J., Barwell, F., Toms, M. and Duncan, K.D. (1986) *Fault Finding Skills – an Appraisal of Training Methods*, Sheffield: Manpower Services Commission.

Polanyi, M. (1958) *Personal Knowledge*, London: Routledge and Kegan Paul.

Weick, K. (1995) *Sensemaking in Organizations*, London: Sage.

Zuboff, S. (1988) *In the Age of the Smart Machine: The Future of Work and Power*, New York: Basic Books, Inc.

2 Work process knowledge in a chemical company

Bordogna, L. (1989) 'Il caso del petrolchimico Montedison di Ferrara', in M. Regini and C. Sabel (eds) *Strategie di riaggiustamento industriale,* Bologna: Il Mulino.

Boreham, N. (1998) *Unpublished working paper* for the EU Whole Project.

Boreham, N.C. and Lammont, N. (2001) *Work Process Knowledge in Technological and Organizational Development.* Final Report of Project SOE1-CT97-1074 of the EU Targeted Socio-Economic Research Programme. Brussels: European Commission, Directorate General for Research. Available: <http://www.cordis.lu/improving/socio-economic/publications.htm>

Burns, T. (1963) 'Industry in a new age', *New Society,* 31 January 1963.

Carbognin, M. (1997) *Relazioni di lavoro, apprendimento e sistema sociale in CER-Montell,* unpublished internal report.

Catino, M. and Fasulo A.M. (1998) *Organization for Innovation. A Case Study in 'G. Natta' Montell Research Centre in Ferrara,* Milano: Angeli.

Conklin, J. (1996) *Designing organizational memory: Preserving Intellectual Assets in a Knowledge Economy.* Available: <http://www.cmsi.com>

Davenport, T.H., De Long, D.W. and Beers, M.C. (1998) 'Successful knowledge management projects', *Sloan Management Review,* 39 (2): 43–57.

Drucker, P.F. (1997) 'The future that has already happened', *Harvard Business Review,* 75 (4): 20–4.

Fasulo, A.M. (1990) *Analisi del funzionamento organizzativo del dipartimento Tep/CER-Himont-Ferrara,* unpublished report.

Foschi, G. (1995) *Assetto e funzionamento di una unità di ricerca tecnologica,* unpublished site internal document.

Galli, P. (1998) 'Introduction', in M. Catino and A.M. Fasulo (1998) *Organization for Innovation. A Case Study in 'G. Natta' Montell Research Centre in Ferrara,* Milano: Angeli.

Gandini, A., Foschi, G. and Flammini, R. (1999) *Apprendere lavorando. Programmi formativi e inserimento dei giovani nelle imprese,* Reggio Emilia: Diabasis.

Govoni, G. (1998) 'Some relevant aspects of the history, the organization and the CER people', in M. Catino and A.M. Fasulo (eds) *Organization for Innovation. A Case Study in 'G. Natta' Montell Research Centre in Ferrara,* Milano: Angeli.

Kontogiannis, T. (1999) 'Training effective human performance in the management of stressful emergencies', *Cognition Technology and Work,* 1 (1): 7–24.

Kruse, W. (1986) 'On the necessity of labour process knowledge', in J. Schweitzer (ed.) *Training for a Human Future,* Basle: Weinheim.

Nonaka, I. and Takeuchi, H. (1995) *The Knowledge-Creating Company,* Oxford: Oxford University Press.

O'Dell, C. and Grayson, C.J. (1998) 'If only we knew what we know: Identification and transfer of internal best practices', *California Management Review,* 40 (3): 254–74.

Reich, R.B. (1991) *The Work of Nations. Preparing Ourselves for 21st Century Capitalism,* New York: Vintage Books.

Simon, H.E. (1981) *The Sciences of the Artificial,* Massachussets: MIT Press.

Suchman, L. (1987) *Plans and Situated Actions: The problem of Human-Machine Communication,* Cambridge: Cambridge University Press.

Taylor, F. (1947) *Scientific Management,* New York: Harper & Row.

Weick, K.E. (1995) *Sensemaking in Organizations,* Beverly Hills: Sage.

3 The concept of the core task and the analysis of working practices

AIB (Accident Investigation Board) (2001) *Maritime Accidents and Incidents 1/2001 M*, Helsinki: Oy Edita Ab.

Antonovsky, A. (1988) *Unravelling the Mystery of Health: How People Manage Stress and Stay Well*, San Francisco: Jossey-Bass Publishers.

Antonovsky, A. (1993a) 'The structure and properties of the sense of coherence scale', *Social Science and Medicine*, 36 (6): 725–33.

Antonovsky, A. (1993b) 'Complexity, conflict, chaos, coherence, coercion and civility', *Social Science and Medicine*, 37 (8): 969–81.

Bereiter, C. and Scardamalia, M. (1993) *Surpassing Ourselves: An Inquiry into Nature and Implications of Expertise*, Chicago: Open Court.

Boreham, N.C., Mawer, G.E. and Foster, R.W. (1996) 'Medical diagnosis from circumstantial evidence', *Le Travail Humain*, 59: 69–85.

Bourdieu, P. (1990) *The Logic of Practice*, Cambridge: Polity Press.

Cannon-Bowers, J.A. and Bell, H.H. (1997) 'Training decision makers for complex environments: Implications of naturalistic decision making perspective', in C.E. Zsambok and G. Klein (eds) *Naturalistic Decision Making*, Mahwah, New Jersey: Lawrence Erlbaum Associates.

Cellier, J.M., Eyrolle, H. and Marine, C. (1997) 'Expertise in dynamic environments', *Ergonomics*, 40 (11), Special Issue.

Charmaz, K. (1995) 'Grounded theory', in J.A. Smith, R. Harré and L. Van Langehove (eds) *Rethinking Methods in Psychology*, London: Sage.

Chi, M., Glaser, R. and Farr, M.J. (eds) (1988) *The Nature of Expertise*, Hillsdale, NJ: Lawrence Erlbaum.

Dewey, J. (1901/1991) *Lectures on Ethics, 1900–1901*, ed. by D.F. Koch, Carbondale and Edwardsville: Southern Illinois University Press.

Dewey, J. (1929/1999) *The Quest for Certainty. A Study of the Relation of Knowledge and Action*, Finnish translation, Helsinki: Gaudeamus.

Dewey, J. (1938) *Experience and Education*, New York: Macmillan.

Engeström, Y. (1987) *Expansive Learning*, Jyväskylä: Orienta.

Engeström, Y. (1999) 'Activity theory and individual and social transformation', in Y. Engeström, R. Miettinen and R-L. Punamäki (eds.) *Perspectives in Activity Theory*, Cambridge: Cambridge University Press.

Eteläpelto, A. (1997) 'The changing definitions of expertise', in J. Kirjonen, P. Remes and A. Eteläpelto (eds) *Changing Expertise*, Jyväskylä: University of Jyväskylä Press (in Finnish).

Gibson, J.J. (1979) *The Ecological Approach to Visual Perception*, Boston: Houghton Mifflin.

Hacker, W. (1998) *Allgemeine Arbeitspsychologie. Psychische Regulation von Arbeitstätigkeiten*, Bern: Verlag Hans Huber.

Hackman, J.R. (1969) 'Toward understanding the role of task in behavioural research', *Acta Psychologica*, 31: 97–128.

Heiskanen, T. (1999) 'From information society to learning society', in A. Eteläpelto (ed.) *Learning and Expertise: Perspectives in Work and Education*, Juva: WSOY (in Finnish).

Hoffman, R. and Woods, D. (2000) 'Studying cognitive systems in context: Preface to the special section', *Human Factors*, 42 (1): 1–7.

Holmberg, J., Hukki, K., Norros, L., Pluckier, U. and Pay, P. (1999) 'An integrated approach to human reliability analysis – decision analytic dynamic reliability model', *Reliability Engineering and System Safety*, 65: 239–50

Hukki, K. and Norros, L. (1993) 'Diagnostic judgement in the control of disturbance situations in nuclear power plant operation', *Ergonomics*, 36 (11): 1317–28.

Hukki, K. and Norros, L. (1998) 'Subject-centred and systemic conceptualization as a tool of simulator training', *Le Travail Humain*, 4: 313–31.

Kirwan, B. and Ainsworth, L.K. (1992) *A Guide to Task Analysis*, London: Taylor & Francis.

Kivinen, O. and Ristelä, P. (2000) *Truth, Language and Practice. Pragmatist Perspectives to Action and Expertise*, Helsinki: Werner Superstore (in Finnish).

Klein, G.A. (1993) 'A recognition-primed decision (RDP) model of rapid decision making', in G.A. Klein, J. Oarsman, R. Calderwood and C.E. Zsambok (eds) *Decision Making in Action: Models and Methods*, Norwood, NJ: Able.

Klemola, U-M. and Norros, L. (1997) 'Analysis of the clinical behaviour of anaesthetists: recognition of uncertainty as basis for practice', *Medical Education*, 31: 449–56.

Klemola, U-M. and Norros, L. (2000) 'Logics of anaesthetic practice – interdisciplinary methodology for analysing decision making in an open, complex system', presented at the 5th Conference of Naturalistic Decision Making, Stockholm, May 2000.

Klemola, U-M. and Norros, L. (2001) 'Practice-based criteria for assessment of anaesthetists' habits of action. Outline for a reflexive turn in practice', *Medical Education*, 35: 455–64.

Laird, J.D. and Apostoleris, N.H. (1996) 'Emotional self-control and self-perception: feelings are the solution, not the problem', in R. Harré and W.G. Parrot (eds) *The Emotions. Social, Cultural and Biological Dimensions*, London: SAGE Publications.

Launis, K. and Engeström, Y. (1999) 'Expertise in the changing working activity', in A. Eteläpelto (ed.) *Learning and Expertise: Perspectives in Work and Education*, Juva: WSOY (in Finnish).

Lave, J. (1991) 'Situated learning in communities of practice', in L. Resnick, J. Levine and S. Teasley (eds) *Perspectives on Socially Shared Cognition*, Washington, DC: American Psychological Association.

Lave, J. and Wenger, E. (1991) *Situated Learning: Legitimate Peripheral Participation*, Cambridge: Cambridge University Press.

Lehtinen, E. and Palonen, T. (1997) 'Knowledge networking – A challenge for expertise', in J. Kirjonen, P. Remes and A. Eteläpelto (eds.) *Changing Expertise*, Jyväskylä: University of Jyväskylä Press (in Finnish).

Leontiev, A.N. (1973) *Probleme der Entwicklung des Psychischen*, Berlin: Volk und Wissen.

Leontiev, A.N. (1978) *Activity, Consciousness, and Personality*, Englewood Cliffs: Prentice Hall.

Leplat, J. (1991) 'Organization of activity in collective tasks', in J. Rasmussen, B. Brehmer, and J. Leplat (eds) *Distributed Decision Making. Cognitive Models for Cooperative Work*, Great Britain: John Wiley & Sons.

Luria, A.R. (1976) *Cognitive Development: Its Cultural and Social Foundations*, Cambridge, MA: Harvard University Press.

Megill, A. (ed.) (1997) *Rethinking Objectivity*, Durham: Duke University Press.

Merleau-Ponty, M. (1962) *Phenomenology of Perception* (translated from the French by C. Smith), London: Routledge.

Norros, L. (1995) 'An orientation-based approach to expertise', in J-M. Hoc, P.C. Cacciabue and E. Hollnagel (eds) *Expertise and Technology*, Hillsdale, NJ: Lawrence Erlbaum Associates.

Norros, L. (1996) 'System disturbances as a springboard for the development of operators' expertise', in Y. Engeström and D. Middleton (eds) *Cognition and Communication at Work*, Cambridge: Cambridge University Press, pp. 159–76.

Norros, L., Hukki, K., Haapio, A. and Hellevaara, M. (1998) *Decision Making on the Bridge in Piloting Situations*, VTT Publications 833, Espoo: Technical Research Centre of Finland (in Finnish).

Nuutinen, M. (2000) 'Working practice and safety culture in nuclear power plant operations', in T. Vanttola, E.K. Puska and A. Marttila (eds) *FINNUS. The Finnish Research Programme on Nuclear Power Plant Safety. Interim Report 1999 – August 2000*. VTT Research Notes 2057, Espoo: VTT.

Nuutinen, M. and Norros, L. (2001) 'Co-operation on the bridge in piloting situations. Analysis of 13 accidents on Finnish fairways', in R. Onken (ed.) *CSAPC'01. 8th Conference on Cognitive Science Approaches to Process Control. The Cognitive Work Process: Automation and Interaction*, Munich, 24–26 September 2001: 3–13.

Oatley, K. (1992) *The Best Laid Schemes. The Psychology of Emotions*, USA: Cambridge University Press.

Oatley, K. (1996) 'Emotions: Communications to the self and the others', in W.G. Parrot and R. Harré (eds) *The Emotions. Social, Cultural and Biological Dimensions*, London: SAGE Publications.

Pantzar, E. (1997) 'Knowledge Society – a learning society?', in K. Stachon (ed.) *Perspectives to the Information Society*, Tampere: Caudeamus Kirja/Oy Yliopistokustannus, Tammer-Paino Oy (in Finnish).

Parrot, W.G. and Harré, R. (1996) 'Introduction. Some complexities in the study of emotions', in W.G. Parrot and R. Harré (eds) *The Emotions. Social, Cultural and Biological Dimensions*, London: SAGE Publications.

Peirce, C.S. (1903/1998) 'The Harvard Lectures on Pragmatism', in *The Essential Peirce. Selected Philosophical Writings*, Volume 2, Bloomington: Indiana University Press.

Peirce, C.S. (1931–58) *Collected Papers of Charles Sanders Peirce*, Cambridge, MA: Harvard University Press, 1–6, ed. by C. Hartshorne and P. Weiss, cited in Kilpinen 2000, p. 70.

Perrow, C. (1984) *Normal Accidents: Living with High-risk Technologies*, New York: Basic Books.

Polanyi, M. (1958) *Personal Knowledge. Towards a Post-critical Philosophy*, Chicago: The University of Chicago Press.

Polanyi, M. (1983) *The Tacit Dimension*, USA: Peter Smith.

Rasmussen, J. (1986) *Information Processing and the Human–Machine Interaction: An Approach to Cognitive Engineering*, New York: North Holland.

Reiman, T. and Norros, L. (2002) 'Regulatory culture: Balancing the different demands of the regulatory practice in nuclear industry', in A.R. Hale, A. Hopkins and B. Kirwan (eds) *Changing Regulation – Controlling Hazards in Society*, Elsevier Science.

Rogalski, J. (1995) 'From real situations to training situations: Conservation of functionalities', in J-M. Hoc, P.C. Cacciabue and E. Hollnagel (eds) *Expertise and Technology*, Hillsdale, NJ: Lawrence Erlbaum Associates.

Schön D.A. (1983) *The Reflective Practitioner: How Professionals Think in Action*, New York: Basic Books.

Schön, D.A. (1988) 'From technical rationality to reflection-in-action', in J. Dowie and A. Elstein (eds) *Professional Judgment. A Reader in Clinical Decision Making*, New York: Cambridge University Press.

Theureau, J. (1996) 'Course of action analysis and ergonomics design', paper presented at the Conference on Work and Learning in Transition, San Diego, 22–23 January 1996.

Vicente, K.J. (1999) *Cognitive Work Analysis. Toward Safe, Productive, and Healthy Computer-Based Work*, Mahwah, NJ: Lawrence Erlbaum.

Vygotski, L.S. (1978) *Mind in Society. The Development of Higher Psychological Processes*, Cambridge: Harvard University Press.

Wenger, E. (1998) *Communities of Practice. Learning, Meaning, and Identity*, Cambridge: Cambridge University Press.

Zuboff, S. (1988) *In the Age of the Smart Machine. The Future of Work and Power*, New York: Basic Books.

4 The work process knowledge of chemical laboratory assistants

Aristotle (1982) *Aristoteles' Metaphysik*, Bücher I(A)-Vi(E), Hamburg: Felix Meiner.

Ciommer, B. (1996) *Gegenwart und Zukunft der Analytik, LABO Trend*, pp. 10ff.

Drescher, E. (1996) *Was Facharbeiter können müssen*. Bremen: Donat.

Engeström, Y. (1987) *Learning by Expanding. An Activity Theoretical Approach to Development Research*. Helsinki: Orienta Konsultit Oy.

Engeström, Y. and Cole, M. (1997) 'Situated cognition in search of an agenda', in D. Kirshner and J.A. Whitson (eds) *Situated Cognition. Social, Semiotic and Psychological Perspectives*, Mahwah, NJ, London: Lawrence Erlbaum, pp. 301–9.

Fischer, M. (1996) 'Überlegungen zu einem arbeitspädagogischen und -psychologische Erfahrungsbegriff'. *Zeitschrift für Berufs- und Wirtschaftspädagogik*, 3: 227–44. Stuttgart: Franz Steiner Verlag.

Fischer, M. (2000) *Von der Arbeitserfahrung zum Arbeitsprozeßwissen*, Opladen: Leske and Budrich.

Fischer, M. and Röben, P. (1997) 'Arbeitsprozeßwissen im chemischen Labor.' *Arbeit, Zeitschrift für Arbeitswissenschaft, Arbeitspsychologie und Arbeitsgestaltung*, 3 (6): 247–66.

Fischer M. and Röben, P. (2001) *Ways of Organizational Learning in the Chemical Industry and their Impact on Vocational Education and Training. A Literature Review*. Bremen: ITB.

Fischer, M. and Röben, P. (2002) *Cases of Organizational Learning in the Chemical Industry. An Empirical Study*. Bremen: ITB.

Fleig, J. and Schneider, R. (1995) *Erfahrung und Technik in der Produktion*, Berlin, Heidelberg: Springer.

Kruse, W. (1986). 'Von der Notwendigkeit des Arbeitsprozeß-Wissens', in J. Schweitzer (ed.) *Bildung für eine menschliche Zukunft*, Weinheim, Basel: Juventa-Verlag, pp. 188–93.

Laur-Ernst, U., Gutschmidt, F. and Lietzau, E. (1990) *Neue Fabrikstrukturen – veränderte Qualifikationen*. Ergebnisse eines Workshops zum Forschungsprojekt:

'Förderung von Systemdenken und Zusammenhangsverständnis – Lernen und Arbeiten in komplexen Fertigungsprozessen', Berlin: Bundesinstitut für Berufsbildung.

Mohler, W. (1970) *Der Laborant. Entstehung und Entwicklung eines Berufes in der Baseler chemischen Industrie.* Bern: Verlag Herbert Lang.

Röben, P. (1997) 'Zur Bedeutung des Arbeitsprozeßwissens bei der Mitgestaltung von Arbeit und Technik in Labor und Produktion', in P. Storz and F. Siebeck, *Computergestütztes erfahrungsgeleitetes Lernen und Gestalten*, Band 12 der Reihe Arbeit–Bildung–Beruf, Dresden: VMS, pp. 53–63.

Röben, P., Siebeck, F. and Storz, P. (1998) *Computergestütztes erfahrungsgeleitetes Lernen in der Chemiearbeit.* Inhaltlicher Abschlußbericht des Projektes CELCA, Bd. 14 der Reihe Arbeit–Bildung–Beruf, Dresden: wbw Verlag.

Rubinstein, S.L. (1973) *Sein und Bewußtsein.* Die Stellung des Psychischen im allgemeinen Zusammenhang der Erscheinungen in der materiellen Welt, s' Gravenhage.

Schmauderer, E. (1973) *Der Chemiker im Wandel der Zeit. Skizzen zur geschichtlichen Entwicklung des Berufsbildes.* Weinheim: VCH.

Schumann, M., Baethge-Kinsky, V., Kuhlmann, M., Kurz, C. and Neumann, U. (1994) *Trendreport Rationalisierung. Automobilindustrie, Werkzeugmaschinenbau, Chemische Industrie*, Berlin: Edition Sigma.

Strube, W. (1989) *Der historische Weg der Chemie*, Köln: Aulis-Verlag Deubner.

Wehner, T. (1993) 'Fehlervermeidung – eine riskante Forderung für Gesundheit, Sicherheit und Arbeit', in D. Milles (ed.) *Gesundheitsrisiken, Industriegesellschaft und soziale Sicherung in der Geschichte.* Schriftenreihe Gesundheit Arbeit Medizin Bd. 7, Bremerhaven: Wirtschaftsverlag NW.

5 Technological change and the construction of competence

Adler, P.S. (1992) *Technology and the Future of Work*, New York: OUP.

Böhle, F., Carus, U. and Schulze, H. (1994) 'Technical support for experience-based work: a new development perspective for CNC machine tools', *International Journal of Human Factors in Manufacturing*, 4(4): 391–408.

Clot, Y. (1999) *La fonction psychologique du travail. Le travail humain*, Paris: PUF.

Engeström, Y. (1991) 'Developmental work research: reconstructing expertise through expansive learning', in M.I. Nurminen and G.S.R. Weir (eds) *Human Jobs and Computer Interfaces*, Elsevier Science Publishers.

Fischer, M. and Stuber, F. (1998) 'Work process knowledge and the school to work transition', in E. Scherer (ed.) *Shop Floor Control – A System Perspective*, Berlin: Springer Verlag, pp. 367–80.

Jeantet, A. and Tiger, H. (1988) *Des manivelles au clavier*, SYROS Alternatives.

Kuuti, K. (1995) 'Activity theory as a potential framework for human–computer interaction research', in B. Nardi (ed.) *Context and Consciousness*, Cambridge, MA: MIT Press.

Leplat, J. (1997) 'Skills and tacit skills: a psychological perspective', *Applied Psychology: An International Review*, 39(2): 143–54.

Malsch, T. (1987) 'Die Informatisierung des betrieblichen Erfahrungswissens und der "Imperialismus der instrumentellen Vernunft". Kritische Bemerkungen zur neotayloristischen Instrumentalismuskritik und Interpretationsvorschlag aus arbeitssoziologischer Sicht', *Zeitschrift für Soziologie*, 16(2): 77–91.

Ozaki, M. (1992) *Technical Change and Labour Relations*, Geneva: International Labour Organization.

Rabardel, P. (1995) *Les hommes et les techniques, une approche cognitive des instruments contemporains*, Paris: Armand Colin.

Rabardel, P., Rak, I. and Verillon, P. (1988) 'Machines outils à commande numérique: approches didactiques', *Collection Rapports de Recherche*, no. 3, INRP, Paris.

Rogalski, J. (1995) 'Former à la coopération dans la gestion des sinistres: élaboration collective d'un dispositif d'actions. Le développement des compétences, analyse du travail et didactique professionnelle', *Education Permanente*, no. 123.

Samurçay, R. (1995) 'Conceptual models for training', in J.M. Hoc, P.C. Cacciabue and E. Hollnagel (eds) *Expertise and Technology: Cognition and Human–Computer Cooperation*, Hillsdale, NJ: Lawrence Erlbaum Associates, pp. 107–24.

Samurçay, R. and Rabardel, P. (1995) 'Work competencies: some reflections for a constructivist theoretical framework', in Proceedings of the 2nd Work Process Knowledge Meeting: Theoretical approaches of competencies at work, Courcelle sur Yvette France, 19–21 October 1995.

6 Work process knowledge and creativity in industrial design

Arnheim, R. (1969) *Visual Thinking*, Berkeley, CA: Berkeley University of California Press.

Banathy, B.H. (1996) *Designing Social Systems in a Changing World*, New York: Plenum Press.

Bateson, G. (1972) *Steps to an Ecology of Mind*, New York: Ballantine Books.

Beck, M. (1994) *The Concept of Dialogue*, unpublished manuscript.

Binder, T. (1996) 'Learning and knowing with artifacts: an interview with Donald A. Schön', *AI & Society*, 10(1): 51–7.

Boden, M. (1994) *The Creative Mind*, London: Abacus, Little, Brown and Company.

Brandt, E. (2001) *Event Driven Product Development*, Copenhagen: PhD dissertation. IPL, DTU.

Bucciarelli, L.L. (1994) *Designing Engineers*, Cambridge, MA: MIT Press.

Corbett, J.M., Rasmussen, L.B. and Rauner, F. (1991) *Crossing the Border*, London: Springer Verlag.

Cross, N. (1995) 'Observations of teamwork and social processes in design', *Design Studies*, 16: 143–70.

Csikszentmihalyi, M. (1988) 'Society, culture and person: a systems view of creativity', in R. Sternberg (ed.) *The Nature of Creativity*, Cambridge: Cambridge University Press.

Ferguson, E. (1977) 'The mind's eye: nonverbal thought in technology', *Science* 197: 827.

Ferguson, E. (1992) *Engineering and the Mind's Eye*, Cambridge, MA: MIT Press.

Gardner, H. (1984) *Frames of Mind: The Theory of Multiple Intelligence*, New York: Basic Books.

Hachman, R. (1986) 'The psychology of self-management in organizations', in M. Pallak (ed.) *Psychology and Work*, Washington, DC: American Psychological Association, pp. 89–136.

Henderson, K. (1991) 'Flexible sketches and inflexible data bases', *Science, Technology and Human Values*, 16 (4): 448–73.

Henderson, K. (1998) *On Line and on Paper*, Cambridge, MA: MIT Press.

Isaacs, W. (1993) 'Dialogue, collective thinking and organizational learning', *Organizational Dynamics*, Fall, 24–39.

Jones, C.J. (1980) *Design Methods*, New York: John Wiley.

Jones, C.J. (1984) *Essays in Design*, New York: John Wiley.

Katzenbach, J. and Smith, B. (1993) 'The discipline of teams', *Harvard Business Review* 71(2): 111–20.

Kosslyn, S.M. (1990) 'Mental imagery', in D.N. Osherson (ed.) *Visual Cognition and Action*, vol. 2, Cambridge, MA: The MIT Press.

Langley, P. and Jones, R. (1988) 'A computational model of scientific insight', in R.J. Sternberg (ed.) *The Nature of Creativity*, Cambridge: Cambridge University Press.

Latour, B. (1986) 'Visualization and cognition: thinking with eyes and hands', *Knowledge and Society: Studies in the Sociology of Culture Past and Present*, 6: 1–40.

Lawson, B. (1980, 1983) *How Designers Think*, London: The Architectural Press Ltd.

Levi, D. and Slem, C. (1995) 'Team work in research and development organizations: the characteristics of successful teams', *International Journal of Industrial Ergonomics*, 16: 29–42.

Manz, C. and Sims, J. (1987) 'Leading workers to lead themselves', *Administrative Science Quarterly*, 32: 106–28.

Piaget, J. (1981) 'Creativity', in J.M. Gallagher (ed.) *The Learning Theory of Piaget and Inhelder*, Monterey, CA: Brooks-Cole (original work published in 1972).

Poincaré, J.M. (1952) 'Mathematical creation', in B. Ghisilin (ed.) *The Creative Process*, Mentor Book, Penguin Books, Canada.

Polanyi, M. (1958) *Personal Knowledge*, London: Routledge & Kegan Paul.

Polanyi, M. (1967) *The Tacit Dimension*, London: Routledge & Kegan Paul.

Polanyi, M. and Prosch, H. (1975) *Meaning*, Chicago: The University of Chicago Press.

Rasmussen, L.B. (1985) *Industrial Designers* (in Danish). Unpublished.

Rasmussen, L.B., Eriksen, E.R. and Hansen, F. (1987a): 'Tacit knowledge versus system knowledge', in M. Rader, B. Wingert and U. Riehm (eds) *Social Science Research on CAD/CAM*, Heidelberg: Physica Verlag, pp. 66–86.

Rasmussen, L.B., Tottrup, P., Andersen, E., Andersen, K.M. and Hansen, F. (1987b) *Work Culture and CAD Requirements*. Deliverable 12, ESPRIT Project 1217, IS, Denmark. Unpublished

Rasmussen, L.B., Læssøe, J. and Tøttrup, P. (1989) *The Electronic Sketch Pad*, Copenhagen: Reproset.

Rasmussen, L.B. (1998/1999) Sample of interviews with industrial designers. Unpublished.

Sacks, O. (1993) 'To See and Not to See', *New Yorker* (May), pp. 59–73.

Safizadeh, M. (1991) 'The case of workgroups in manufacturing operations', *California Management Review*, 33(4): 61–82.

Schön, D.A. (1983) *The Reflective Practitioner*, New York: Basic Books.

Schön, D.A. (1987) *Educating the Reflective Practitioner*, San Francisco: Josey Bass.

Schön, D.A. and Rein, M. (1994) *Frame Reflection*, New York: Basic Books.

Shepard, R.N. and Cooper, B. (1982) *Mental Images and their Transformation*, Cambridge, MA: MIT Press.

Suchman, L. (1988) 'Representing practice in cognitive science', *Human Studies*, 11: 305.

Sundström, E. (1990) 'Work teams', *American Psychologist*, 45(2): 120–33.

Torrance, P. (1988) 'The nature of creativity as manifest in its testing', in R.J. Sternberg (ed.) *The Nature of Creativity*, Cambridge: Cambridge University Press.

Ullman, D.N. (1997) *The Mechanical Design Process*, McGraw-Hill.

Vincenti, W.G. (1990), *What Engineers Know and How They Know It*, Baltimore: Johns Hopkins University Press.

7 Creating work process knowledge with new technology in a financial services workplace

Alvesson, M. (1993) 'Organizations as rhetoric: knowledge intensive firms and the struggle with ambiguity', *Journal of Management Studies*, 30(6): 997–1015.

Appelbaum, E. and Alpin, P. (1992) 'Computer rationalisation and the transformation of work: lessons from the insurance industry', in S. Wood (ed.) *Transformation of Work*, London: Routledge.

Boland, R.J. and Tenakasi, V. (1995) 'Perspective making and perspective taking in communities of knowing', *Organization Science*, 6(4): 350–72.

Chaiklin, S. and Lave, J. (1988) *Cognition in Practice*, Cambridge: Cambridge University Press.

Conklin, E.J. (1992) 'Capturing organizational memory', in C. Coleman (ed.) *Groupware '92*, San Francisco: Morgan Kaufmann.

Dunphy, D. (1997) 'Organizational learning as the creation of corporate competencies: the use of reshaping competencies', *Journal of Management Development*, 16(4): 232–45.

Fischer, G. and Nakakoji, K. (1997) 'Computational environments supporting creativity in the context of lifelong learning and design', *Knowledge Based Systems*, 10(1): 21–8.

Fleck, J. (1997) 'Contingent knowledge and technology development', *Technology Analysis and Strategic Management*, 9(4): 383–97.

Garrigou, A. (1998) 'The role of "know-how" in maintenance activities and reliability in a high-risk process control plant', *Applied Ergonomics*, 29(2): 127–31.

Gibbons, M., Limoges, C., Nowitny, H., Swartzman, S., Scott, P. and Trow, P. (1994) *The New Production of Knowledge*, London: Sage.

Grant, E.B. (1997). 'Tacit knowledge: the life cycle and international manufacturing transfer', *Technology Analysis and Strategic Management*, 9(2): 149–61.

Haider, H. (1992) 'Implicit knowledge and learning: an artifact', *Zeitschrift für Experimentelle und Angewandte Psychologie*, 39(1): 68–100.

Halal, W.E. (1996) 'The rise of the knowledge entrepreneur', *The Futurist*, 30: 13–16.

Harper, R.H.R. and Hughes, J.A. (1993) 'What a f–ing system! Send 'em to the same place and then expect us to stop 'em hitting: making technology work in air traffic control', in G. Button (ed.) *Technology in Working Order: Studies of Work, Interaction, and Technology*, London: Routledge.

Henning, P.H. (1998) 'Ways of learning: an ethnographic study of the work and situated learning of a group of refrigeration service technicians', *Journal of Contemporary Ethnography*, 27(1): 85–136.

Hirschorn, L. (1984) *Beyond Mechanisation: Work and Technology in a Post-industrial Age*, Cambridge, MA: MIT Press.

Howells, J. (1995) 'Tacit knowledge, innovation and technology transfer', *Technology Analysis and Strategic Management*, 8(2): 91–106.

Ingold, T. (1992) 'Prospects for anthropology', *Man*, 27(4): 693–7.

Ingold, T. (1996) 'Culture, perception and cognition', in J.T. Haworth (ed.) *Psychological Research: Innovative Methods and Strategies*, London: Routledge.

Kramlinger, T. (1992) 'Training's role in a learning organization', *Training*, 29(7): 46–51.

Lam, A. (1997) 'Embedded firms, embedded knowledge: problems of collaboration and knowledge transfer in global cooperative ventures', *Organizational Studies*, 18(6): 973–97.

Lei, D.T. (1997) 'Competence-building, technology fusion and competitive advantage: the key roles of organizational learning and strategic alliances', *International Journal of Technology Management*, 14(2–4): 208–37.

Leontiev, A. (1976) *Le développement du psychisme*, Paris: Editions Sociales.

McNaughton, S. (1996) 'Ways of parenting and cultural identity', *Culture and Psychology*, 2(2): 173–201.

Maeve, M.K. (1994) 'The Carrier Bag theory of nursing practice', *Advances in Nursing Science*, 16(4): 9–22.

Meerabeau, L. (1992) 'Tacit nursing knowledge: an untapped resource or a methodological headache?' *Journal of Advanced Nursing*, 17(1): 108–12.

Nonaka, I. (1991) 'The knowledge-creating company', *Harvard Business Review*, Nov–Dec: 96–104.

Nonaka, I. (1996) 'A theory of organizational knowledge creation', *International Journal of Technology Management*, 11(7–8): 833–45.

Nonaka, I. and Takeuchi, H. (1995) *The Knowledge Creating Company*, New York: Oxford University Press.

Raelin, J.A. (1997) 'A model of work-based learning', *Organization Science*, 8(6): 563–78.

Read, W.H. (1996) 'Managing the knowledge-based organization: five principles every manager can use', *Technology Analysis and Strategic Management*, 8(3): 223–32.

Rose, H. (1991) 'The importance of tacit knowledge for operating CNC machines', *Zeitschrift für Wirtschaftliche Fertigung und Automatisierung*, 86(1): 45–8.

Senker, J. (1993) 'The contribution of tacit knowledge to innovation', *AI and Society*, 7(3): 204–24.

Suchman, L. (1993) 'Technologies of accountability: of lizards and aeroplanes', in G. Button (ed.) *Technology in Working Order*, London: Routledge.

Tenakasi, R.V. and Boland, R.J. (1996) 'Exploring knowledge diversity in knowledge intensive firms: a new role for information systems', *Journal of Organizational Change Management*, 9(1): 79.

Verillon, P. and Rabardel, P. (1995) 'Cognition and artifacts: a contribution to the study of thought in relation to instrumented activity', *European Journal of the Psychology of Education*, X: 77–101.

Vygotsky, L.S. (1930/1985) 'La méthode instrumentale en psychologie', in B. Schneuwly and J.P. Bronckart (eds) *Vygotsky aujourd'hui*, Neuchâtel: Delachaux et Niestlé.

Zuboff, S. (1988) *In the Age of the Smart Machine*, New York: Basic Books.

8 Dimensions of work process knowledge

Alaluf, M. (1986) *Le temps du labeur – formation, emploi et qualification en sociologie du travail*, Bruxelles: Ed. de l'Université de Bruxelles.

Ambrósio, T. and Alves, M. (2000) 'Criteria, tools and practices of evaluation of the relationship university–labour market', *Anais Educação e Desenvolvimento 2000*, Lisboa: ed. UIED/FCT/UNL.

Ambrósio, T. and Alves, M. (1994) 'Formação contínua de recursos humanos de nível superior', *Relatórios do Projecto Telos*, FCT/UNL, Lisboa.

Berger, P. and Luckman, T. (1991) *The Social Construction of Reality*, London: Penguin.

Boreham, N. (2002) 'Transforming vocational curricula with work process knowledge', in P. Kamarainen, G. Attwell and A. Brown (eds) *Transformation of Learning in Education and Training*, Luxembourg: Office for Official Publications of the European Communities.

Boreham, N.C. and Lammont, N. (2001) *Work Process Knowledge in Technological and Organizational Development*. Final Report of Project SOE1-CT97-1074 of the EU Targeted Socio-Economic Research Programme, Brussels: European Commission, Directorate General for Research. Available: <http://www.cordis.lu/improving/socio-economic/publications.htm>

Borzeix, A. (1995) 'La Parole en Sociologie du Travail', *Paroles au Travail*, Paris: L'Harmattan, pp. 225–245.

Dominicé, P. (1990) *L'histoire de vie comme processus de formation*, Paris: Ed. L'Harmattan.

Dominicé, P. (1991) 'La formation experientielle: un concept importé pour penser la formation', *La formation experientielle des adultes*, Paris: La Documentation Française.

Dubar, C. (1991) *La socialisation – construction des identités sociales et professionnelles*, Paris: Ed. Armand Colin.

Dubois, P. (1998) 'Évaluation et auto-évaluation des universités en Europe', *Relatórios do projecto Evalue*, Université de Nanterre, Paris.

Evans, K. (2000) *Learning and Work in the Risk Society: Lessons for the Labour Market of Europe from Eastern Germany*, UK: Macmillan Press.

Evans, K. and Hoffman, B. (2000) 'Situated learning. How far can the concepts be used in work re-entry programs?', paper presented at Faculdade de Ciências e Tecnologia, Universidade Nova de Lisboa, Lisboa

Finger, M. (1989) *Apprendre une issue – l'éducation des adultes à l'âge de la transformation de perspective*, Lausanne: Ed. L.E.P.

Gama, A. (1997). 'Participação dos actores na formação profissional contínua em contexto de trabalho; um estudo de caso numa empresa qualificante', Tese de Mestrado, FCT/UNL, Lisboa

Gelpi, E. (1989). 'Quelques propos politiques sur l'education experientielle', *Education Permanente*, No. 100/101, Paris.

Harrison, R. (1996) 'Personal skills and transfer – meanings, agendas, and possibilities', in Edwards, Hanson and Raggat (eds) *Boundaries of Adult Learning*, London: The Open University.

Josso, C. (1988) 'Da formação do sujeito . . . ao sujeito da formação', in *O método (auto)biográfico e a formação*, Lisboa: DRH, Min. Saúde.

Josso, C. (1989) 'Ces experiences au cours lesquelles se forment identités et sub- jectivités', *Education Permanente*, No 100/101, Paris.

Josso, C. (1991), 'L'experience formatrice: un concept en construction', in *La formation experientielle des adultes*, Paris: La Documentation Française.

Kovács, I. (1992) 'Novas tecnologias, organização e competitividade', in *Sistemas flexíveis de produção e reorganização do trabalho*, Lisboa: CESO I&D /Pedip/DGI.

Lammont, N. (2000) Literature review on work process knowledge and techno- logical and organizational development. Available: <http://www.man.ac.uk/ education/euwhole/home.htm>

Lave, J. and Wenger, E. (1991) *Situated Learning: Legitimate Peripheral Participation*, Cambridge: Cambridge University Press.

Lazar, A. (1998) *Langages et Techonologie: Connaissances et Reconnaissance des Lan- gages Professionnels*, Paris: INRP.

Le Bouedec, G. (1988) *Les défis de la formation continue*, Paris: Ed. L'Harmattan.

Madelin, P. and Thierry, D. (1992) 'Organisations qualifiantes: quelles definitions et quelle méthodes d'evaluation?' *Education Permanente*, No. 112, Paris.

Mallet, L. (1995) 'Organização qualificante, coordenação e incentivo', in *Formação Profissional*, No. 5, CEDEFOP.

Meneses, M.T. (1996) 'Formação expereincial e desenvolvimento de competên- cias', Tese de Mestrado, FCT/UNL, Lisboa.

Oliveira, T. (1998) 'Language, work and training', paper presented at the WHOLE Workshop in Siena.

Onstenk, G. (1995). 'Aprendizagem no local de trabalho no âmbito da reforma organizativa na indústria transformadora', *Formação Profissional*, No. 5, CEDEFOP.

Pain, A. (1991) 'Education informelle: les mots . . . et la chose (réponses à un prac- ticien)', in *La Formation Experientielle des Adultes*, Paris: La Documentation Française.

Pineau, G. (1989) 'La formation experientielle en auto, eco et co-formation', *Edu- cation Permanente*, No. 100/101, Paris.

Pineau, G. (1991a) 'La reconnaissance des acquis comme passage – frontière entre les mondes des individues et celui des organisations', in *Reconnaitre les acquis – démarches d'exploration personnalisée*, Paris: La Mesonnance.

Pineau, G. (1991b) 'Formation experientielle et théorie tripolaire de la forma- tion', in *La Formation experientielle des adultes*, Paris: La Documentation Française.

Pires, A. (1995) 'Desenvolvimento pessoal e profissional: um estudo dos contextos e processos de formação das novas competências profissionais', Tese de Mestrado, FCT/UNL, Lisboa.

Pires, A. (1998) 'Competencies, work and training processes: looking for a dynamic coherence', paper presented at the WHOLE Workshop in Leuven.

Rolo, C. (1996) 'Formação em contexto de trabalho – dinâmicas formativas das professoras de uma escola do primeiro ciclo do ensino básico', Tese de Mestrado, FCT/UNL, Lisboa.

Sainsaulieu, R. (1996) 'L'identité et les relations de travail', *Education Permanente*, No. 128, Paris.

Wenger, E. (1998) *Communities of Practice: Learning, Meaning and Identity*, Cam- bridge: Cambridge University Press.

Zarifian, P. (1986) 'Les approches de plus récentes de la qualification', *L'introu- vable relation formation-emploi*, Paris: La Documentation Française.

Zarifian, P. (1992) 'Acquisition et reconnaissance de compétences dans une organisation qualifiante', *Education Permanente*, No. 112, Paris.

Zarifian, P. (1995) 'Organização Qualificante e modelos de competência: que razões? Que aprendizagens?', in *Formação Profissional*, No. 5, CEDEFOP.

9 Work experience as an element of work process knowledge

Adolph, G. (1983) 'Leistet die Technische Bildung im Berufsbildungssystem einen Beitrag zur intellektuellen Entwicklung der auszubildenden Facharbeiter?', in Universität Bremen (ed.) *Arbeit und Technik. Analyse von Entwicklungen der Technik und Chancen in der Gestaltung von Arbeit.* Tagungsband zum Bremer Symposium Arbeit und Technik, Bremen: University, pp. 456–65.

Adolph, G. (1984) *Fachtheorie verstehen*, Wetzlar: Jungarbeiterinitiative an der Werner-von-Siemens-Schule.

Aebli, H. (1980/1981) *Denken: Das Ordnen des Tuns*. Vol. I, Kognitive Aspekte der Handlungstheorie. Vol. II, Denkprozesse, Stuttgart: Klett-Cotta Verlag.

Berry, D.C. and Broadbent, D.E. (1984) 'On the relationship between task performance and associated verbalizable knowledge', *The Quarterly Journal of Experimental Psychology*, 36 A: 209–31.

Berry, D.C. and Broadbent, D.E. (1987) 'The combination of explicit and implicit learning processes in task control', *Psychological Research*, 49: 7–15.

Binder, T. (1995) *Designing for Workplace Learning: AI & Society*, London: Springer.

Böhle, F. and Milkau, B. (1988) *Vom Handrad zum Bildschirm: Eine Untersuchung zur sinnlichen Erfahrung im Arbeitsprozeß*, Frankfurt a. M., New York: Campus Verlag.

Böhle, F. and Rose, H. (1992) *Technik und Erfahrung: Arbeit in hochautomatisierten Systemen*, Frankfurt a. M., New York: Campus Verlag.

Böhle, F. (1995) 'Qualifizierung für erfahrungsgeleitetes Arbeiten – neue Anforderungen an die berufliche Bildung', in G. Dybowski, H. Pütz and F. Rauner (eds) *Berufsbildung und Organizationsentwicklung: Perspektiven, Modelle, Grundlagen*, Bremen: Donat Verlag, pp. 122–33.

Boreham, N.C. (1994a) 'Error analysis and expert–novice differences in medical diagnosis', in J.-M. Hoc, E. Hollnagel and C. Cacciabue (eds) *Expertise and Technology*, Hove: Lawrence Erlbaum Associates.

Boreham, N.C. (1994b) 'The dangerous practice of thinking', *Medical Education*, 28: 172–9.

Brater, M. (1984) *Künstlerische Übungen in der Berufsausbildung*, in Projektgruppe Handlungslernen (ed.). *Handlungslernen*. Wetzlar: Jungarbeiterinitiative an der Werner-von-Siemens-Schule, pp. 62ff.

Brose, H.-G. (1983) *Die Erfahrung der Arbeit*, Opladen: Westdeutscher Verlag.

Dahmer, H.-J. (1994) *Zum Verhältnis von Erfahrungswissen und Planungswissen bei industriellen Arbeitstätigkeiten*, in T. Krogoll (ed.) *Betriebliche Weiterbildung und Erfahrungswissen von Facharbeitern*, Stuttgart: IRB Verlag, pp. 129–46.

Dehnbostel, P. and Peters, S. (eds) (1991) *Dezentrales und erfahrungsorientiertes Lernen im Betrieb*, Alsbach/Bergstraße: Leuchtturm-Verlag.

Dehnbostel, P., Holz, H. and Novak, H. (eds) (1992) *Lernen für die Zukunft durch verstärktes Lernen am Arbeitsplatz – Dezentrale Aus- und Weiterbildungskonzepte in der Praxis*, Berlin: BIBB, Berichte zur beruflichen Bildung, No. 149.

Dewey, J. (1934) *Art as Experience. The Later Works*, Vol. 10, Carbondale and Edwardsville, Ill.

Dieckmann, B. (1994) *Der Erfahrungsbegriff in der Pädagogik*, Weinheim: Deutscher Studien Verlag.

Dreyfus, H.L. (1972) *What Computers Can't Do: The Limits of Artificial Intelligence*, New York: Harper & Row.

Dreyfus, H.L. and Dreyfus, S.E. (1986) *Mind over Machine*, New York: The Free Press.

Eicker, F. (1983) *Experimentierendes Lernen: Ein Beitrag zur Theorie beruflicher Bildung und des Elektrotechnik-Unterrichts*, Bad Salzdetfurth.

Engler, U. (1992) *Kritik der Erfahrung: Die Bedeutung der ästhetischen Erfahrung in der Philosophie John Deweys*, Würzburg: Königshausen and Neumann.

Fischer, M. (1995) *Technikverständnis von Facharbeitern im Spannungsfeld von beruflicher Bildung und Arbeitserfahrung*, Bremen: Donat Verlag.

Fischer, M. (2000) *Von der Arbeitserfahrung zum Arbeitsprozeßwissen*, Opladen: Leske & Budrich.

Fischer, M., Jungeblut, R. and Römmermann, E. (1995). *'Jede Maschine hat ihre eigenen Marotten!' Instandhaltungsarbeit in der rechnergestützten Produktion und Möglichkeiten technischer Unterstützung*, Bremen: Donat Verlag.

Fischer, M. and Lehrl, W. (1991) *Industrieroboter: Entwicklung und Anwendung im Kontext von Politik, Arbeit, Technik und Bildung*, Bremen: Donat Verlag.

Fleig, J. and Schneider, R. (1975) *Erfahrung und Technik in der Produktion*, Berlin: Springer.

Gerds, P. (1989) *Symbolisierungsfähigkeit und technische Bildung. Die Eliminierung präsentativer Symbolik aus der technischen Bildung – ein Beitrag zur Diskussion um das Bildungsziel 'Befähigung zur Technikgestaltung'*, Bremen: University.

Güßbacher, H. (1988) *Hegels Psychologie der Intelligenz*, Würzburg: Königshausen & Neumann.

Hacker, W. (1992) *Expertenkönnen: Erkennen und Vermitteln*, Göttingen, Stuttgart: Verlag für angewandte Psychologie.

Hegel, G.W.F. (1807/1970) *Phänomenologie des Geistes*, Frankfurt a.M., Berlin, Wien: Ullstein.

Hegel, G.W.F. (1830/1970) *Enzyklopädie der philosophischen Wissenschaften*, Die Philosophie des Geistes. Theorie Werkausgabe, Vol. 10. Frankfurt a.M.: Suhrkamp.

Holzkamp, K. (1993) *Lernen: Subjektwissenschaftliche Grundlegung*, Frankfurt a.M., New York: Campus Verlag.

Jones, L. (1994) *NVQs, competency and the acquisition of work process knowledge: a theoretical critique. Work Process Knowledge. Seminar Papers*, University of Manchester, 15–17 December 1994: 5–9.

Kade, J. and Geißler, Kh. (1980) *Erfahrung und Erziehung zur Subjektivität*. Forschungsbericht 80.05, Fachbereich Pädagogik, Neubiberg: Hochschule der Bundeswehr.

Korndörfer, V. (1985) 'Qualifikationsanforderungen und Qualifizierung beim Einsatz von Industrierobotern', Kh. Sonntag (ed.) *Neue Produktionstechniken und qualifizierte Arbeit*, Köln: Wirtschaftsverlag Bachem, pp. 117ff.

Lave, J. (1988) *Cognition in Practice: Mind, Mathematics and Culture in Everyday Life*, Cambridge: Cambridge University Press.

Lave, J. and Wenger, E. (1991) *Situated Learning: Legitimate Peripheral Participation*, Cambridge: Cambridge University Press.

Malsch, T. (1984) 'Erfahrungswissen versus Planungswissen: Facharbeiterkompetenz und informationstechnologische Kontrolle am Beispiel der betrieblichen Instandhaltung', in U. Jürgens and F. Naschold (eds) *Arbeitspolitik: Materialien zum Zusammenhang von politischer Macht Kontrolle und betrieblicher Organisation der Arbeit*, Opladen: Westdeutscher Verlag.

Malsch, T. (1987) 'Die Informatisierung des betrieblichen Erfahrungswissens und der "Imperialismus der instrumentellen Vernunft". Kritische Bemerkungen zur neotayloristischen Instrumentalismuskritik und ein Interpretationsvorschlag aus arbeitssoziologischer Sicht', *Zeitschrift für Soziologie*, Jg. 16, Heft 2, April 1987, pp. 77–91.

Martin, H. (ed.) (1995) *CEA – Computergestützte erfahrungsgeleitete Arbeit*, Berlin et al.: Springer.

Negt, O. and Kluge, A. (1972) *Öffentlichkeit und Erfahrung: Zur Organisationsanalyse von bürgerlicher und proletarischer Öffentlichkeit*, Frankfurt a.M.: Suhrkamp.

Negt, O. (1978) 'Marxismus und Arbeiterbildung – Kritische Anmerkung zu meinen Kritikern', in A. Brock, H.D. Müller and O. Negt (eds) *Arbeiterbildung: Soziologische Phantasie und exemplarisches Lernen in Theorie, Kritik und Praxis*, Reinbek: Rowohlt, pp. 43–86.

Peters, S. (1991) 'Erfahrungslernen – Ein Modebegriff für die Verknüpfung von neuen Methoden und Zielen der beruflichen Weiterbildung?', in P. Dehnbostel and S. Peters (eds) *Dezentrales und erfahrungsorientiertes Lernen im Betrieb*, Alsbach/Bergstraße: Leuchtturm-Verlag, pp. 21–34.

Piaget, J. (1973) *Einführung in die genetische Erkenntnistheorie*, Frankfurt a.M.

Polanyi, M. (1966) *The Tacit Dimension*, New York.

Rauner, F. (1985) 'Experimentierendes Lernen in der technischen Bildung', in K. Steffens (ed.) *Experimentelle Statik an Fachhochschulen: Didaktik, Technik, Organisation, Anwendung*, Alsbach/Bergstraße: Leuchtturm-Verlag, pp. 15–28.

Rauner, F. and Zeymer, H. (1991) *Auto und Beruf: Technischer Wandel und Berufsbildung im Kfz-Gewerbe*, Bremen: Donat Verlag.

Reber, A.S. and Lewis, S. (1977) 'Implicit learning: An analysis of the form and structure of a body of tacit knowledge', *Cognition*, 5: 333–61.

Reber, A.S. (1989). 'Implicit learning and tacit knowledge', *Journal of Experimental Psychology (General)*, 118: 219–35.

Rubinstein, S.L. (1973) *Sein und Bewußtsein: Die Stellung des Psychischen im allgemeinen Zusammenhang der Erscheinungen in der materiellen Welt*, s' Gravenhage.

Samurçay, R. (1994) *Knowledge developed in/for work situation in dynamic environment management*, First Work Process Knowledge Seminar, University of Manchester, 15–17 December 1994.

Shilling, C. (1988) 'The School Vocational Programme: "Factories and Industry". A deficit project for the transition of youth from school to labour market', A. Pollard, J. Purvis and G. Walford (eds) *Education, Training and the New Vocationalism*, Milton Keynes: Open University Press.

Siebeck, F. (1994) 'Arbeitserfahrungen und Erfahrungslernen – was ist das?', in K. Drechsel, P. Storz and G. Wiesner (eds) *Gestaltungsperspektiven der Chemiearbeit in Produktion und Labor*. Reihe Arbeit – Bildung – Beruf, Vol. 6. Hamburg, Dresden: VMS Verlag, pp. 100–24.

Simon, D. (1980) *Lernen im Arbeitsprozeß*, Frankfurt a.M., New York: Campus Verlag.

Volpert, W. (1988) *Zauberlehrlinge: Die gefährliche Liebe zum Computer*, München: DTV.

Waibel, M. and Wehner, T. (1994) *Über den Dialog zwischen Wissen und Erfahrung in der betrieblichen Lebenswelt. Teil I: Kognitive Umstrukturierung der planerischen Vorgaben zur Bewältigung des Fertigungsalltags. Harburger Beiträge zur Psychologie und Soziologie der Arbeit*, Hamburg-Harburg: Technical University.

10 Training for collective competence in rare and unpredictable situations

Amalberti, R. (1996) *La conduite des systèmes à risques*, Paris: PUF.

Antolin-Glenn, P. (1977) *Analyse de l'activité de l'instructeur*. Technical Report, Saint Denis: CNRS-Université Paris.

Baerentsen, K.B. (1996) 'Episodic knowledge in system control', in B. Homqvist, P.B. Andersen, H. Klein and R. Posner (eds) *Signs of Work. Semiosis and Information Processing in Organizations*, Berlin: Walter de Gruyter.

Bainbridge, L. (1988) 'Types of representation', in L.P. Goodstein, H.B. Andersen and S.E. Olsen (eds) *Tasks, Errors and Mental Models*, London: Taylor and Francis.

Brannick, M.T., Salas, E. and Prince, C. (eds) (1997) *Team Performance Assessment and Measurement. Theory, Methods, and Applications*, Mahwah, NJ: LEA.

Dubey, J. (1997) 'Faire "comme si" n'est pas faire', in P. Béguin and A. Weill-Fassina (eds) *La simulation en ergonomie: connaître, agir et interagir*, Toulouse: Octarès.

Endsley, M.R. (1995) 'Toward a theory of situation awareness in dynamic systems', *Human Factors*, 37: 32–64.

Flin, R.H. and Slaven, G.M. (1995) 'Identifying the right stuff: Selecting and training on-scene emergency commanders', *Journal of Contingencies and Crisis Management*, 3: 113–23.

Hoc, J.-M. (1993) 'Some dimensions of a cognitive typology of process control situations', *Ergonomics*, 36: 1445–55.

Jansens, L., Grotenhuis, H., Michiels, H. and Verhaegen, P. (1989) 'Social organizational determinants in nuclear power plants: Operators training in the management of unforeseen events', *Journal of Occupational Accidents*, 1: 121–9.

Ochanine, D.A. (1992) 'The operative image of controlled object in "man-automatic machine" systems', in J. Leplat (ed.) *L'analyse du travail en psychologie ergonomique*, Toulouse: Octarès (first published in *Actes du XVIIIe Congrès International de Psychologie, Moscou, 27ème symposium*, 1966, pp. 48–56).

Plat, M. and Amalberti, R. (2000) 'Crew training to automation surprises', in N. Sarter and R. Amalberti (eds) *Cognitive Engineering in the Aviation Domain*, Hillsdale, NJ: LEA.

Plat, M. and Rogalski, J. (1999) 'Human/Human and Human/Systems interactions in highly automated cockpits; instructors' interventions during full size simulator sessions in qualification training', in J.-M. Hoc, P. Millot, E. Hollnagel and C. Cacciabue (eds) *CSAPC'99: Human–Machine Reliability and Co-operation*, Valenciennes: Valenciennes University.

Rogalski, J. (1991) 'Distributed decision making in emergency management: Using a method as a framework for analyzing cooperative work and as a decision aid', in J. Rasmussen, B. Brehmer and J. Leplat (eds) *Distributed Decision Making. Cognitive Models for Cooperative Work*, Chichester: Wiley.

Rogalski, J. (1994) 'Formation aux activités collectives', *Le Travail Humain*, 54: 367–86.

Rogalski, J. (1995) 'Former à la coopération dans la gestion de sinistres. Elaboration collective d'un dispositif d'actions', *Education Permanente*, 47–64.

Rogalski, J. (1996) 'Co-operation processes in dynamic environment management: Evolution through training experienced pilots in flying a highly automated aircraft', *Acta Psychologica*, 91: 273–95.

Rogalski, J. and Antolin-Glenn, P. (1997) 'Training in open dynamic environment management: The case of operational management in public safety', *SMC'97. IEEE International Conference on Systems, Man and Cybernetics*, 2: 1867–72, Orlando, FL: IEEE.

Rogalski, J. and Samurçay, R. (1994) 'Modélisation d'un savoir de référence et transposition didactique dans la formation de professionnels de haut niveau', in J. Arsac, Y. Chevallard, J.-L. Martinand and A. Tiberghien (eds) *La transposition didactique à l'épreuve*, Grenoble: La Pensée Sauvage.

Rouse, W.B., Cannon-Bowers, J.A. and Salas, E. (1992) 'The role of mental models in team performance in complex systems', *IEEE Transactions on Systems, Man and Cybernetics*, 22: 1296–308.

Samurçay, R. and Rogalski, J. (1998) 'Exploitation didactique des situations de simulation', *Le Travail Humain*, 61: 333–59.

Sarter, N. and Woods, D.D. (1995) 'How in the world did we ever get into that mode? Mode error and awareness in supervisory control', *Human Factors*, 37: 5–19.

Sarter, N. and Woods, D.D. (1997) 'Team playing with a powerful and independent agent: operational experiences and automation surprises on the Airbus A-320', *Human Factors*, 39: 553–69.

de Terssac, G. and Chabaud, C. (1990) 'Référentiel commun et fiabilité', in J. Leplat and G. de Terssac (eds) *Les facteurs humains de la fiabilité*, Marseille: Octarès.

Volpe, C. (1996) 'The impact of cross-training on team functioning. An empirical investigation', *Human Factors*, 38: 87–100.

Weick, K.E. (1993) 'The collapse of sensemaking: The Mann Gulch Disaster', *Administrative Science Quarterly*, 38: 628–52.

11 The contribution of work process knowledge to competence in electrical maintenance

Battmann, W. and Klumb, P. (1993) 'Behavioural economics and compliance with safety regulations', *Safety Science*, 16: 35–46.

Béguin, P. and Rabardel, P. (2000) 'Design for instrument-mediated activity', *Scandinavian Journal of Information Systems*, 12: 173–90.

Boreham, N. and Samurçay, R. (1998) 'Models for the analysis of work competence: a critical review', *2nd WHOLE workshop on Work Process Knowledge*, 2–4 December, Siena, Italy.

Cru, D. (1995) *Règles de métier, langue de métier: dimension symbolique au travail et démarche participative de prévention. Le cas du bâtiment et des travaux publics*, Mémoire, École pratique des hautes études, Paris.

De la Garza, C. and Weill-Fassina, A. (2000) 'Régulations horizontales et verticales du risque', in T.H. Benchekroun and A. Weill-Fassina (eds) *Le travail collectif. Perspectives actuelles en ergonomie*, Toulouse: Octarès Editions.

Education Permanente (1995) Special issue: Le développement des compétences, 123.

Faverge, J.-M. (1967) *Psychosociologie des accidents du travail*, Paris: Presses Universitaires de France.

Fischer, M. (1998) 'Understanding professional competence: questions raised by the Work Process Knowledge Approach', *3rd WHOLE workshop on Work Process Knowledge*, 2–4 December, Siena, Italy.

Gaudard, C. and Weill-Fassina, A. (1999) 'L'évolution des compétences au cours de la vie professionnelle: une approche ergonomique', *Formation Emploi*, 67: 47–62.

Hale, A.R. (1984) 'Is safety training worthwhile?', *Journal of Occupational Accidents*, 6: 17–33.

Human Factors (1995) Special Issue: Situation Awareness, 37: 1.

Lefort, B. (1982) 'L'emploi des outils au cours de tâches d'entretien et la loi de ZIPF-Mendelbrot', *Le Travail Humain*, 45, 2: 307–16.

Mayen, P. (1999) 'Des situations potentielles de développement', *Education permanente*, 139: 65–86.

Mayen, P. and Savoyant, A. (1999) 'Application de procédures et compétences', *Formation et Emploi*, 67: 77–92.

Mhamdi, A. (1998) *Les activités de réflexion collective assistées par vidéo: un outil pour la prévention*, Doctorat d'ergonomie, Conservatoire national des Arts et Métiers, Paris.

Nardi B.A. (1996) 'Studying context: a comparison of activity theory, situated action models and distributed cognition', in B. Nardi (ed.) *Context and Consciousness*, Cambridge, MA: MIT Press.

Norros, L. (1998) 'Accident and incident analysis as a tool for the elicitation of work process knowledge', *3rd WHOLE workshop on Work Process Knowledge*, 2–4 December, Siena, Italy.

Pastré, P., Plénacoste, P. and Samurçay, R. (1998) *Analyse didactique de l'utilisation des simulateurs*, deuxième rapport d'étape, EDF-Université Paris 8, Février 1998, Saint-Denis.

Rabardel, P. (1995) *Les hommes et les technologies. Approche cognitive des instruments contemporains*, Paris: Armand Colin.

Rabardel, P. and Samurçay, R. (1995) 'Compétences au travail: réflexions pour un cadre théorique constructiviste', *2nd workshop on Work Process Knowledge: Theoretical approaches to competencies at work*, 19–21 October, Courcelle sur Yvette, France.

Rabardel, P. and Six, B. (1995) 'Outiller les acteurs de la formation pour développer des compétences au travail', *Education permanente*, 123: 33–46.

Reason, J. (1998) *Managing the Risk of Organizational Accidents*, Aldershot: Ashgate.

Rogalski, J. and Samurçay, R. (1994) 'Modélisation d'un savoir de référence et transposition didactique dans la formation de professionnels de haut niveau', in G. Arsac, Y. Chevallar, J.-L. Martinand and A. Tiberghein (eds) *La transposition didactique à l'épreuve*, Grenoble: La pensée sauvage.

Rousseau, C. and Monteau, M. (1991) *La fonction de prévention chez l'opérateur: mise en évidence de conduites sécuritaires au cours d'une activité de chantier*, Notes scientifiques et techniques 88, Institut national de recherche et de sécurité, Paris.

Samurçay, R. and Pastré, P. (1995) 'La conceptualisation des situations de travail dans la formation des compétences', *Education permanente*, 123: 13–31.

Samurçay, R. and Rogalski, J. (1998) 'Exploitation didactique des situations de simulation', *Le Travail Humain*, 61, 4: 333–59.

Thébaud-Mony, A., Cru, D., Frigul, N. and Clappier, P. (1995) *La construction sociale de l'accident du travail chez les jeunes*, Rapport de recherche, CPC, Ministère de l'Education Nationale, Paris.

Wagenaar, W.A. (1998) 'People make accidents but organizations cause them', in A.M. Feyer and A. Williamson (eds) *Risk, Prevention and Intervention*, London: Taylor & Francis.

12 The implications of work process knowledge for vocational education and training

Bannwitz, A. and Rauner, F. (eds) (1993) *Wissenschaft und Beruf. Berufliche Fachrichtungen im Studium von Berufspädagogen des gewerblich-technischen Bereiches*, Bremen: Donat Verlag.

Boreham, N.C. (1995) *Making sense of events in the workplace*. Papers of the Second Work Process Knowledge Meeting: Theoretical approaches of competences at work. Courcelle sur Yvette 1995.

Drescher, E. (1996) *Was Facharbeiter können müssen. Elektroinstandhaltung in der vernetzten Produktion*, Bremen: Donat Verlag.

Dreyfus, H.L. (1979) *What Computers Can't Do – the Limits of Artificial Intelligence*, New York: Harper & Row.

Dreyfus, H.L. and Dreyfus, S.E. (1986) *Mind over Machine: The Power of Human Intuition and Expertise in the Era of the Computer*, Oxford: Basil Blackwell.

Ehn, P. (1985) *Work Oriented Design*, Stockholm.

Fischer, M. (2000) *Von der Arbeitserfahrung zum Arbeitsprozeßwissen*. Habilitation, University of Bremen 1998. Opladen: Leske and Budrich.

Fischer, M. and Stuber, F. (1998) 'Work process knowledge and the school-to-Work-transition', in E. Scherer (ed.) *Shop Floor Scheduling and Control – A Systems Perspective*, Berlin: Springer, pp. 367–80.

Fischer, M., Römmermann, E. and Benckert, H. (1996) 'The design of technical artifacts with regard to work experience. The development of an experience-based documentation system for maintenance workers', *AI & Society*, 10: 39–50.

Fischer, M., Jungeblut, R. and Römmermann, E. (1995) *Jede Maschine hat ihre eigenen Marotten!' Instandhaltungsarbeit in der rechnergestützten Produktion und Möglichkeiten technischer Unterstützung*, Bremen: Donat Verlag.

Fischer, M. (1995) *Technikverständnis von Facharbeitern im Spannungsfeld von beruflicher Bildung und Arbeitserfahrung. Untersucht anhand einer Erprobung rechnergestützter Arbeitsplanungs- und -steuerungssysteme*, Bremen: Donat Verlag.

Georg, W. (1996) 'Lernen im Prozeß der Arbeit', in H. Dedering (ed.) *Handbuch zur arbeitsorientierten Bildung*, München and Wien: Oldenbourg Verlag, pp. 637–59.

Heinz, W.R. and Witzel, A. (1995) 'Das Verantwortungsdilemma in der beruflichen Sozialisation', in E.H. Hoff and L. Lappe (eds) *Verantwortung im Arbeitsleben*, Heidelberg: Asanger Verlag, pp. 99–113.

Kruse, W. (1985) 'Ausbildungsqualität, Arbeitsprozeß-Wissen und soziotechnische Grundbildung', *Gewerkschaftliche Bildungspolitik*, 5: 150–2.

Kruse, W. (1986) 'Von der Notwendigkeit des Arbeitsprozeß-Wissens', in J. Schweitzer (ed.) *Bildung für eine menschliche Zukunft*, Weinheim and Basel: Juventa-Verlag, pp. 188–93.

Mandl, H., Gruber, H. and Renkl, A. (1993) 'Neue Lernkonzepte für die Hochschule', *Das Hochschulwesen*, 41: 126–30.

Moritz, E., Rauner, F. and Spöttl, G. (1997) *Austauschen statt reparieren. Der 'Erfolg' des japanischen Kfz-Service*, Bremen: Donat Verlag.

Pahl, J.-P. and Rauner, F. (eds) (1998) *Betrifft: Berufsfeldwissenschaften. Beiträge zur Forschung und Lehre in den gewerblich-technischen Fachrichtungen*, Bremen: Donat Verlag.

Pätzold, G. (1997) 'Rechnergestützte Facharbeit und Kritik am berufsschulischen

Lehren und Lernen', in M. Fischer (ed.) *Rechnergestützte Facharbeit und berufliche Bildung*, Bremen: Institut Technik and Bildung der Universität (ITB-Arbeitspapier Nr. 18), pp. 219–35.

Polanyi, M. (1966) *The Tacit Dimension*, New York.

Rauner, F. and Spöttl, G. (1996) *The Automobile, Service and Occupation in Europe*, Bremen: Donat Verlag.

Rauner, F. and Spöttl, G. (2002) *Der Automobilmechatroniker – vom Neuling zum Experten*, Bielefeld: Bertelsmann.

Rauner, F. and Zeymer, H. (1991) *Auto und Beruf. Technischer Wandel und Berufsbildung im Kfz-Gewerbe*, Bremen: Donat Verlag.

Renkl, A., Gruber, H., Mandl, H. and Hinkofer, L. (1994) 'Hilft Wissen bei der Identifikation und Steuerung eines komplexen ökonomischen Systems?' *Unterrichtswissenschaft*, 22: 195–202.

Renkl, A. (1996) 'Träges Wissen. Wenn Erlerntes nicht genutzt wird', *Psychologische Rundschau*, 47: 78–92.

Schön, D.A. (1983) *The Reflective Practitioner: How Professionals Think in Action*, New York: Basic Books.

Spöttl, G. (1997) 'Entwicklungstendenzen von Arbeit und Ausbildung im internationalen Kfz-Handwerk', in M. Fischer (ed.) *Rechnergestützte Facharbeit und berufliche Bildung*, Bremen: Institut Technik and Bildung der Universität (ITB-Arbeitspapier Nr. 18), pp. 27–50.

Spöttl, G. and Gerds, P. (1999) *Car Mechatronic*. A European occupational profile – Manual for trainers and teachers (draft). Produced as part of the European Commission LEONARDO DA VINCI pilot project 'Car Mechatronic'. Bremen: ITB and Flensburg: BIAT.

Spöttl, G., Rauner, F. and Moritz, E. (1997) *Vom Kfz-Handwerk zum Qualitätsservice. Der US-amerikanische Kfz-Sektor nach der Trendwende*, Bremen: Donat Verlag.

Witzel, A. and Kühn, Th. (1999) *Berufsbiographische Gestaltungsmodi*. Eine Typologie der Orientierungen und Handlungen beim Übergang in das Erwerbsleben. Arbeitspapier Nr. 61, Bremen: Sonderforschungsbereich 186 der Universität.

13 Professionalization and work process knowledge in the UK's National Health Service

Abbott, A. (1988) *The System of Professions: An Essay in the Expert Division of Labour*, Chicago: Chicago University Press.

Armstrong, P. (1993) 'Professional knowledge and social mobility', *Work, Employment and Society*, 7: 1–21.

Ashcroft, J. (1992) 'Rising to the challenge', *Nursing Times*, 88(38): 30.

Atkin, K. (1993) *Nurses Count: a National Census of Practice Nurses*. York: Social Policy Research Unit.

Atkin, K. and Lunt, N. (1996) 'Negotiating the role of the practice nurse in general practice', *Journal of Advanced Nursing*, 24(3): 498–505

Barr, H., Hammick, M., Koppel, I. and Reeves, S. (1999) 'Evaluating interprofessional education: two systematic reviews for health and social care', *British Educational Research Journal*, 25: 533–44.

Boreham, N.C., Shea, C.E. and Mackway-Jones, K. (2000) 'Clinical risk and collective competence in the hospital emergency department in the UK,' *Social Science and Medicine*, 51: 83–91.

Briggs, A. (1972) *Report of the Committee on Nursing*, London: HMSO/DHSS.

Collins, R. (1990) 'Changing conceptions in the sociology of the professions', in R. Torstandahl and M. Burrage (eds) *The Formation of Professions: Knowledge, State and Strategy*, London: Sage.

Department of Health and Social Security (1977) *The Extending Role of the Clinical Nurse: Legal Implications and Training Requirements*, London: DHSS.

Department of Health (1992) *Withdrawal of Guidance on the Extended Role of the Nurse EL (92) 38*, London: Department of Health.

Department of Health (1994) *The Challenge for Nursing and Midwifery in the 21st Century: The Heathrow Debate*, London: HMSO.

Dowling, S., Martin, R. and Skidmore, P. (1996) 'Nurses taking on junior doctors' work: a confusion of accountability', *BMJ*, 312: 1211–14.

General Medical Council (1995) *Duties of a Doctor: Guidance from the General Medical Council*, London: GMC.

Handysides, S. (1994) 'New roles for general practitioners', *BMJ*, 308: 513–16.

Hopkins, S. (1996) 'Junior doctor's hours and the expanding role of the nurse', *Nursing Times*, 92(14): 35–6.

Jewell, D. and Turton, P. (1994) 'What's happening to practice nursing?' *BMJ*, 308: 735–6.

Kingmire, J. (1989) 'The law and the nurse', *Nursing Standard*, 4(12): 20–2.

Larson, M.S. (1990) 'In the matter of experts and professionals, or how impossible it is to leave nothing unsaid', in R. Torstandahl and M. Burrage (eds) *The Formation of Professions: Knowledge, State and Strategy*, London: Sage.

Leathard, A. (1994) (ed.) *Going Inter-Professional*, London: Routledge.

Marsh, G.N. (1991) *Efficient Care in General Practice*, Oxford: Oxford University Press.

Miller, C. (1999) 'Shared learning for pre-qualification health and social care students: have the universities missed the point?' Paper presented to the Annual Conference of the British Educational Research Association, University of Sussex, September 1999.

Pirrie, A. (1999) 'Rocky mountains and tired Indians: on territories and tribes. Reflections on multidisciplinary education in the health professions', *British Educational Research Journal*, 25: 113–26.

Robinson, K. (1993) 'Attitudes towards practice nurses – survey of a sample of general practitioners in England and Wales', *British Journal of Medical Practice*, 43: 25–9.

Salvage, J. (1989) 'Shifting boundaries', *Nursing Times*, 85(10): 24.

Sbaih, L. (1995) 'To do or not to do: use of the Scope of Professional Practice in accident and emergency work', *Accident and Emergency Nursing*, 3(1): 7–13.

Secretaries of State for Health, Social Security, Wales and Scotland (1989) *Caring for People, Cmnd 849*, London: HMSO.

Shepherd, J. (1993) 'Nurses are changing, not extending their roles', *British Journal of Nursing*, 2: 447.

Standing Medical and Nursing and Midwifery Advisory Committee (1996) *In the Patient's Interest. Multi-professional Working across Organizational Boundaries*, London: HMSO.

UKCC (United Kingdom Central Council for Nursing, Midwifery and Health Visiting) (1992) *The Scope of Professional Practice*, London: UKCC.

UKCC (1994) *The Council's Standards for Education and Practice following Registration*.

Programmes of Education Leading to Qualification of Specialist Practitioner. London: UKCC.

Wilson-Barnett, J. and Beech, S. (1994) 'Evaluating the clinical nurse specialist. A review', *International Journal of Nursing Studies*, 31(6): 561–71.

14 A delayed transformation? Changes in the division of labour and their implications for learning opportunities

Berggren, C. (1992) *The Volvo Experience. Alternatives to Lean Production*, London: Macmillan.

Dankbaar, B. (1988) 'New production concepts, management strategies and the quality of work', *Work, Employment and Society*, 2(1): 25–50.

de Sitter, L.U. (1994) *Synergetisch Produceren. Human Resources Mobilisation in de Productie*, Assen: Van Gorcum.

de Sitter, L., Den Hartog, J. and Dankbaar, B. (1997) 'From complex organizations with simple jobs to simple organizations with complex jobs', *Human Relations*, 50(5): 497–534.

de Sitter, L.U., Vermeulen, A.A.M., van Amelsvoort, P., van Geffen, L., van Troost, P. and Verschuur, F.O. (Groep Sociotechniek) (1986) *Het flexibele bedrijf. Integrale aanpak van flexibiliteit, beheersbaarheid, kwaliteit van de arbeid en produktie-autonomie*, Deventer: Kluwer Bedrijfswetenschappen.

Gyllenhammer, P. (1977) *People at Work*, Reading: Addison-Wesley.

Huys, R., Sels, L. and Van Hootegem, G. (1995) *The Delayed Transformation: Technical and Socio-organizational Restructurations in the Automobile, Chemical and Machine Tool Industry*, Leuven: K.U. Leuven, Dept. Arbeids- en Organisatiesociologie, AB/2001-4.

Huys, R., Sels, L., Van Hootegem, G., Bundervoet, J. and Henderickx, E. (1999) 'Toward less division of labour? New production concepts in the automotive, chemical, clothing and machine tool industries', *Human Relations*, 52(1): 67–94.

Jürgens, U., Malsch, T. and Dohse, K. (1993) *Breaking from Taylorism: Changing Forms of Work in the Automobile Industry*, Cambridge: Cambridge University Press.

Karasek, R. (1979) 'Job demands, job decision latitude and mental strain: implications for job redesign', *Administrative Science Quarterly*, 24.

Katz, H. and Sabel, C. (1985) 'Industrial relations and industrial adjustment in the car industry', *Industrial Relations*, 24(3): 295–315.

Kern, H. and Schumann, M. (1984) *Das Ende der Arbeitsteilung? Rationalisierung in der industriellen Produktion*, München: Verlag C.H. Beck.

Lutz, B. (1988) 'Wie neu sind die "neuen Produktionskonzepte"?', in T. Malsch and R. Seltz (eds) *Die neuen Produktionskonzepte auf dem Prüfstand. Beiträge zur Entwicklung der Industriearbeit*, Berlin: Edition Sigma, pp. 195–208.

Schumann, M., Baethge-Kinsky, V. and Kuhlmann, M. (1994) *Trendreport Rationalisierung. Automobilindustrie, Werkzeugmaschinenbau, Chemische Industrie*, Berlin: Edition Sigma.

Shingo, S. (1981) *The Toyota Production System*, Tokyo: Japan Management Association.

van Amelsvoort, P. (1989) 'Een model voor de moderne besturingsstructuur volgens de sociotechnische industrie', *Gedrag en Organisatie*, 2, 4–5, 253–67.

Visser, J. (1991) 'Trends in trade union membership', in *OECD Employment Outlook*

1991, Paris: Organization for Economic Development and Cooperation, pp. 97–134.

WEBA-Project team (1990) *Outlines of the WEBA-instrument: a conditional approach for the assessment of the quality of work*, Leiden: NIPG.

WEBA-Projectgroep (1995) *De WEBA-methode*, Ministerie SZW/TNO/NIA.

15 Work process knowledge and industrial and labour relations

Alcalde, N. and Blasco, S. (1994) *El Cambio de Actitudes. Origen de la Nueva Cultural Profesional*, Zaragoza (manuscript).

Bourdieu, P. (1992) *Die verborgene Mechanismen der Macht*, Hamburg.

Bourdieu, P. (1979) *La distinction. Critique sociale de judgement*, Paris.

Castells, M. (1997) *La Sociedad red: la era de la información: economía, sociedad y cultura*, Madrid.

Crozier, M. and Friedberg, E. (1979) *Macht und Organization. Die Zwänge kollektiven Handelns*, Königstein: Taunus.

European Communities (1997) *Green Paper: Partnership for a New Organization of Work*, Luxembourg: Office for Official Publications of the European Communities.

European Foundation for the Improvement of Living and Working Conditions (eds) (1997) *New Forms of Work Organization. Can Europe Realise its Potential?* Dublin.

Folk, R., Krüger, K. and Caprile, M. (1998) *Nueva Profesionalidad en la Siderúrgia*, Barcelona: CIREM.

Fontana, D. (1990) *Social Skills at Work*, London: Routledge & Kegan Paul.

Harrison, P. (1996) 'Personal Skills and Transfer – meanings, agendas and possibilities', in R. Edwards (ed.) *Boundaries of Adult Learning*, Milton Keynes: Open University Press.

Heidenreich, M. (1990) *Bildungsexpansion und betriebliche Informatisierungsprozesse. Ein Drei-Länder-Vergleich.* Fakultät für Soziologie. Universität Bielefeld. Forschungsschwerpunkt Zukunft der Arbeit. Arbeitsberichte und Forschungsmaterialien. Nr. 50. Bielefeld. August.

Krüger, K. (1997) *Kontinuitäten im Wandel gewerkschaftlicher Kommunikationsstrukturen und -muster*, Hans-Böckler Stiftung Graue Reihe – Neue Folge 125, Düsseldorf.

Kruse, W. (1994) 'Eléments de participation directe dans le système de relations industrielles en Espagne', in O. Seul (ed.) *Participation par Délégation et Participation directe des Salaries dans l'Entreprise*, Paris.

MacBer (1987) 'Organisations qualifiantes: quelle définition et quelles méthodes d'évaluation?', *Education permanente*, 112.

Nyhan, B. (1989) *Desenvolvera capacidade de aprendizagem das messoas: perspectivas europeias sobre a competencias de auto-formação e mudança technologica*, Brussels: Eurotecnet.

Ortmann, G. (1995) *Formen der Produktion. Organization und Rekursivität.*, Opladen.

Pries, L. (1991) 'Industrial change in modern societies such as "risk societies"', in *Sociología del Trabajo*, 12.

Priore, M.J. and Sabel, C.F. (1984) *The Second Industrial Divide*, New York.

Schumann, M. (1997) 'Frißt die Shareholder-Value-Ökonomie die moderne Arbeit?', *Frankfurter Rundschau*, 18.11.1997.

Index